Shadow over the Land

1730 – 1807

D. G. ALDERTON

Copyright © 2022 D. G. Alderton
All rights reserved
First Edition

Fulton Books, Inc.
Meadville, PA

Published by Fulton Books 2022

ISBN 978-1-63710-894-9 (paperback)
ISBN 978-1-63710-895-6 (digital)

Printed in the United States of America

INTRODUCTION

In the summer of 2002, a companion and I were traveling on Highway 95 in Idaho, heading north. We found ourselves passing through a location by the name of White Bird. We stopped at a gift shop there that was along the roadside. It was where we became informed of the origin of the name that was given to that place. White Bird was a Nez Perce chief who led a battle against the US Army at that same location in 1877. It was the first of a series of fights, skirmishes, and sorties that began there and ended in eastern Montana, near the Canadian border. It ended with the surrender of most of the Nez Perce, who had fled Idaho for their very existence. Chief Joseph negotiated the terms of their surrender, which were never honored. Chief White Bird, however, did not surrender, and with a small group of followers, he and those with him managed to fight their way into Canada, taking refuge in the camp of the exiled Sitting Bull. White Bird lived out his remaining time thereabouts, which was an area traditionally known to be Blackfeet Country, an area that is also revisited in this tale.

It was said by the chief trader for the Hudson Bay Company of the era, who operated in these northwestern territories, that White Bird was the closest thing to a Hannibal that the Indians had ever produced. This man was well-informed of all the exploits that took place concerning the Nez Perce during this tragic conflict. He gave him the mantle of their main tactician for these embattled fugitives from their homelands. There is more to tell concerning White Bird's notable life. Perhaps the opportunity will present itself, to convey more, owing to a response generated through this story.

My initial encounter with this place was the first of numerous others that combined with certain events, which at times felt to be a destiny of sorts. The most bizarre to me was a friend returning from a trip to Scotland some years later with a book for me full of firsthand accounts of the activities of this territory during most of the 1800s. It also contained a lot of firsthand accounts of the Nez Perce. One of the persons in this book actually interviewed Chief White Bird while in Sitting Bull's camp.

This story, however, is a novel that begins more than a generation before the time of the birth of White Bird. Precontact, so to speak, as far as any outside influence is concerned. Yet some of the characters are implied to be his ancestors. I made an attempt to refer to the tribes by the names they used in referring to themselves before others selected their names for them. I also tried to stay away from some contemporary terms that are widely used today, solely for the purpose of trying to capture the atmosphere of that place of an earlier time. I also tried to use native names when available. This story begins not long after these people, who referred to themselves as the Nimipu, acquired the horse. They have also been attributed to being the originators of the Appaloosa breed. This tale is a horse story as well.

In Kamiah, Idaho, near the Clearwater River, is a place that the Nimipu believe to be the location where Coyote slew the monster, sprinkled its blood there, and brought about the origin of the Nimipu people. The monster's heart remains there today in the form of what appears to be a large stone set in the center of a clear field. I came upon it in my travels through their country. I found it impressive in a satisfying way. I traveled the Lolo Pass, the course that the Lewis and Clark discovery expedition took to arrive at the location where the Kooskia band of the Nimipu made their home. Those famed Nez Perce assisted Lewis and Clark and no doubt had a big part in their succeeding in their endeavor. I've traveled to where Chief Joseph called home, the area of the Wallowa Mountains in Oregon, a very fine place. In the Palouse River country, with its magnificent waterfall, not far before it meets up with the Snake River of which Lewis and Clark traveled on their journey to the Pacific Ocean. I was born and raised in Washington state. I have had an interest in the Yakima tribe ever since I visited the old Washington State Historical Museum and saw an old black-and-white photograph of an encampment of the Yakima, looking like they could have been Sioux. They were surrounded with dapple ponies and hide teepees, with some wearing feather headdresses. When I came to understand that the Nez Perce of the Palouse band called Washington home also, it stirred me with interest. I hope this related story of our history as a people, we the people, will make a difference in some way for the better and stir some interest in others as well.

Shadow Land

GLOSSARY

Absaroke—Crow
Beartooth Mountains—Sawtooth, Idaho
Big Water—Pacific Ocean
Chief Mountain—Glacier Park, Montana
Cold Wind Grandfather—North
Crescent Moons falls—Lower Falls, Lewis River, Washington
fish with bones on the outside—Giant sturgeon
Haven of the Tribes—Indian Heaven, Gifford Pinchot Forest, Washington
Knife Edge mountains—Tetons, Wyoming
Kenistenoag—Cree
Kooskia band—Clearwater River area, Idaho
Kooskia River—Clearwater, Idaho
Land of the Thorn Plants—South
Lower Red Fish River—Salmon, Idaho
Mother River—Columbia, Washington and Oregon
Narrow River—Yakima, Washington
Nimipu—Nez Perce
Nimipu Pass—Nez Perce Pass, Idaho
of the Rising Sun—East
of the Setting Sun—West
old buffalo hunt pass—Lolo Pass, Idaho
Pahpo—Mt. Adams, Washington
Palus band—Palouse River area, Washington
Palus River—Palouse, Washington and Idaho
Peoples Falls—Palouse Falls, Washington

Place of Big Medicine—Glacier, Montana
Place of the Smoking Water—Yellowstone, Wyoming
Red Fish Mountain—Salmon River Mountains, Idaho
red meat fish—Buffalo fish, salmon
sacred place of the Nimipu origin—Kamiah, Idaho
Salish—Flathead
Salish lake—Flathead Lake, Montana
Siksika—Blackfeet
Small Mountains—Blue Mountains, Washington
Tahoma—Mt. Rainier, Washington
Upper Red Fish river—Salmon, Idaho
Upper Lower Red Fish bands—Salmon River area, Idaho
Wallowa band—Wallowa River area, Oregon
Waptailmin—Yakima
Winding River—Snake, Idaho, Oregon, and Washington

CHAPTER 1

THE ABDUCTION OF RAIN

Cloud Shadow looked on at the Siksika maiden as she crouched by the clear running mountain stream while drawing water for her camp. He looked for signs of any others around, and when he was convinced that she was alone, he began to move in her direction as quickly and quietly as he was able. His heart raced, not just for the danger that was near but also for the very act he was about to undertake. He was stealing the daughter of the war chief Gray Wolf.

When he saw her stand and begin to move in his direction, he stayed motionless in his concealment behind some dense foliage and waited for what he would determine to be the right moment to seize her. Then he stepped past his place of concealment and reached out, placing his hand over her mouth and then pulling her back till she lost her footing. He then forced a ball of deer hide into her mouth and wrestled her hands behind her and bound them. Then he fought her kicking legs and bound her ankles as well.

The next step was to draw an arrow from his quiver and stab it into the ground.

He then hoisted the young woman onto his shoulder and hurried away to his Appaloosa stallion and gelding that he had hobbled just out of sight.

When Shadow had set out on his journey to kill Gray Wolf, he hadn't planned on abducting Rain. He didn't even know of her existence. Even now, he still wasn't sure if she was his woman or his daughter. He did, however, feel strongly that she was one or the other.

When he came onto Gray Wolf's camp and observed the movement there, he saw her leave from Gray Wolf's tipi lodge. He then began to formulate a plan.

When Rain failed to return to camp with the water, Gray Wolf went searching for his only child.

After a relatively short time, he came across an arrow stuck in the ground and a water container laying nearby. He stared at the arrow for a moment before pulling it closer to his eyes. Then he spat on it and snarled the words "Shadow Hand." Then he snapped the arrow in two.

Immediately, Gray Wolf hurried back to the camp area to mount a search and pursuit of his hated enemy and abductor of his daughter.

It was one thing to attempt to abduct the war chief's daughter, but it was another thing altogether to get away with it.

Shadow immediately decided that he would not try to take her to any camps of his allies. Instead, he planned to take her into seclusion till the danger subsided.

As Shadow rounded a nearby hill, he found that he and his captive, who was secured to his pack pony, had run directly into a herd of Siksika ponies. Once they had reached the center of the herd, he made a sharp turn up the hill and over the top and away.

He knew of a cave some distance away that he had found in his wanderings that they would make for.

Once there, he would ponder the next course of events.

He looked for any cover along the way, behind hills and clusters of trees and shrubs, ravines that were deep enough, as well as groups of large stones.

Late time was approaching, and soon it would be dark.

Gray Wolf had left camp with a small but lethal band of fighters shortly after Shadow had departed. Right after he had cleared the top of the hill, Gray Wolf and his small band of braves came up to the herd as well.

The trail that Shadow had left was obvious but now was altogether indistinguishable and utterly lost to the eye.

Gray Wolf sent out his men to scour the area for signs.

It took some discouraging amount of time before one of his men yelled out that he had picked up their trail again.

Before Gray Wolf followed after him down the hill, he scanned the vista for a short moment. As it happened, Shadow was traversing through a ravine that covered their appearance for the much-needed time being. Things had worked out for his escape thus far.

Gray Wolf followed the tracks that had been left but was feeling angrily frustrated that Shadow managed to slip out of the area so covertly.

Shadow was glad when he reached the stream he had been pointing after, which led toward the cave and also to conceal their tracks.

Before he turned into the stream, he had created evidence of his heading in the opposite direction, with hopes that it would earn him some time.

After following the stream for a while, it became dark. He stopped to give the ponies a needed rest and to check on his captive. He was sure that she was miserably unhappy.

Shadow was a long way from home but was a veteran traveler and had been in these parts some years before with his friends Little Bear and Many Arrows. They had explored the area as much as they could during that time, always leery that Siksika could come upon them at any moment. The Siksika, it seemed, were never open to intruders into their domain.

During a time of adventuring, Shadow and his companions came upon this cave, where they stayed for a time, while they continued to familiarize themselves with the surrounding country.

Shadow slid the woman off the back of the pony, where she had been bound like a bundle of hides. She could barely stand for all she had been through. Her hands and feet were still bound, and Shadow didn't like the idea of releasing her bonds at that time. It wasn't that he was altogether unsympathetic, but experience had taught him not to be overly trusting.

She urinated as she stood before him. He thought that the time to clean herself would have to wait, and for the most part, she seemed all right.

He helped her to lay down then wrapped a leather strap around a small tree. Then he tied it to the strap on her hands and ankles. He then hobbled the ponies and lay down for some rest.

As the dawn began to break, he untied the leather strap and lifted the young woman to her feet, then once again onto the geldings back and then secured her there. They then proceeded up the stream toward the base of the nearby mountains before them.

He could see that the location of the cave was not far now.

The stream passed near the cave, but the opening wasn't visible from the stream. There was a stand of brush and small trees between the cave mouth and the stream as he remembered it. He didn't turn directly toward the cave but proceeded ahead, another stone's throw before backtracking toward the cave's location.

The entrance of the cave was wide and tall so the ponies could enter and be sheltered also.

Shadow left the woman bound while he used a long leather cord along with the strength of his stallion to pull a large piece of fallen tree back to the cave opening. He then worked to drag it to the very back of the cavern. Then he pulled his captive off the gelding once again, helping her to gain her footing. He knew she must be very thirsty, for he hadn't removed the ball of deer hide from her mouth since he had placed it there.

He secured her there again to the piece of tree he had brought in and then carefully removed the ball from her mouth as to avoid possibly being bitten. It took her awhile to adjust her mouth to being useable again, and in the meanwhile, her eyes tore him to pieces in the most hateful manner possible.

Shadow went to the stream and filled an animal bladder container full of water and brought it back with him. He let her drink her fill as he tipped it into her mouth. Then he fed her pemmican off the end of a stick, still being cautious of being bitten.

Not long after she had eaten, she signed that she needed to make water and waste. Shadow thought about it for a short moment, and then he unbound a leg then retied the strap to the length of tree, freeing her to spread her legs. He then placed a piece of hide down on the ground beneath her then signed to her to go. She had to spend a moment taking in the reality that it was this way and nothing else.

After she had finished, he took the hide to the stream and washed it there. He then brought it back and replaced it in the same place for any further use.

He then signed to her that he would assist her if she didn't resist. Again, she hesitated and then consented.

Afterward, he noticed she wasn't looking at him so hatefully now but more with curiosity.

Shadow left the confines of the cave and looked out across the horizon of this place he had come to. He began to contemplate all he had gotten himself into and what it was going to take to hold this woman captive. It wearied him to think on, but it also challenged and intrigued him as well.

He was a mature, brave hunter and warrior. He was Nimipu, and he feared little.

CHAPTER 2

MEMORIES TO BE CONSIDERED

Shadow began to reflect on how he had come to be where he was and what had led him to this situation. He began to recall the story he had been told by his father and mother of his coming into this world.

It was a clear sky as Black Eagle stood and surveyed the shallow valley before him. It was the clearest he remembered with the snows not long passed. The leaves were beginning to appear on the trees again with the warmer weather returning. He awaited the birth of his first child. His woman, Fawn, squatted in labor within a nearby lodge while his sister, She's Tall, waited on her every need.

As Black Eagle thought on the coming young one, a shadow began to develop on the hill just off his strong shoulder. He watched it as it came into view, absorbing his attention. Just at that moment, his sister approached him with the news: "You have a son."

Black Eagle turned to look behind him to see a cloud moving between himself and the sun, casting a shadow over the hills.

He spoke to She's Tall, saying, "He shall be called Cloud Shadow, for the Great Spirit has put this on my heart."

The Nimipu camp rejoiced with Black Eagle and Fawn. Black Eagle was a highly respected medicine man known to be very wise. His woman was also looked up to as a leader among the women.

So when Cloud Shadow was born, everyone in the village expected great things from him in time.

As a child, he was very inquisitive and daring. He loved to play hard with his peers. His parents could hardly get him to stop and eat.

On one occasion, when his mother called him to stop and eat, his father asked him, "What have you learned in these times, my son?"

"Well, my father, I enjoy looking on and considering all that the Great Spirit has given us as it works in perfect unity to provide all that is needed. The sun for our warmth, the moon for light in the darktime, the snow on the mountains to give us water below, the animals to feed us, and the beauty of it all to make our hearts glad."

Needless to say, Black Eagle and Fawn and all who it was retold to were impressed with this boy's reply, for he was only the fingers of both hands in winters.

Cloud Shadow loved his father and mother and younger brother and sister very much and enjoyed their company. But even as a boy, he longed for adventure to faraway places. But in the meantime, he ventured to places not so far away.

He and the other boys liked to go to the river to swim and explore.

Life was peaceful for the most part for their camp and the surrounding area. Sometimes, there were skirmishes with their not-too-distant neighbors, the Shoshone. But neither liked to be the aggressor just to stir up trouble for one another. Although they made preparation for battle with diligence, they much preferred the defensive stance. It better suited their nature, but riled, they were more than capable of becoming formidable foes.

Most of their fighting took place when they ventured toward the rising sun and across the mountains into the hunting grounds of the temperamental Siksika and Lakota and sometimes the Absaroke. The Utes could be troublesome if they were made contact with, which wasn't often. They also had to travel a long distance to reach the country where the Nimipu sought to do their hunting of the buffalo.

Many tales of bloody conflicts in that place did the boys hear tell of.

For now though, it was peaceful enough, so Shadow and his closest friend, Little Bear, spent their days developing the skills of spying and stalking, always trying to improve on their cunning and stealth.

They also loved to be around the ponies to learn all they could in training and riding them. They also trained with the bow and arrow to try to gain the mastery over them and become proficient archers. To harness the power of the deadly missile with accuracy at high speed as to bring down the intended target, whether man or beast. To learn to draw the bow and let fly the arrow while riding at a full gallop as the pony makes its adjustments to the constant changing conditions of the terrain. It would take countless sessions of practice.

Life was boundless in the freshness and splendor of the wild country they called theirs.

Shadow loved to spend time with his father and the other men of the band as they worked with the ponies. They were a band of close-knit family members and fellow tribesmen who chose to stay close and share in the efforts, as well as the struggles and celebrations, being of those who lived along the Palus and Winding River.

They hadn't given names to every hill, valley, mountain, or waterway, but they definitely laid claim to a large and wondrous region filled with rivers, forests, and mountains, along with vast plains and great scenic canyons.

As a band, they had become very great collectors of horse flesh, which was becoming a superior stock, thought so by any who had the privilege to spend time with them.

If a mare didn't meet their standard, they would trade her away to another band or tribe. If a stallion fell short of their expectations, he would be gelded.

Black Eagle had acquired several spotted ponies from a tribe beyond the mountains and in the direction of where the thorn plants grow. He went on a quest because of a vision he had—that they had a medicine that would be what his people needed to strengthen their herds.

As they interbred the many spotted ponies with their own solid-colored stock, Shadow remembered the day his father told him he wanted to show him something. As they neared the riverbank where the ponies liked to graze and drink, Shadow saw a very young foal standing by its mother.

"This is something I have not seen," he said.

"I think it is a first, my son," his father replied.

There before them was neither a solid foal nor a many spotted one but a solid with a many spotted rump.

As the time went by, the band was able to repeat the process with the breeding pair on several more occasions and then recreate it through interbreeding these new ones with one another.

Black Eagle told Shadow, "I believe this is from the Great Spirit. These are A-Palus, born of the river."

When Shadow became a couple winters older, Black Eagle told him, "As you spend time among the ponies, watch to see the one that is to be for you. Then tell me, and we will separate it from the herd so you can begin to become joined in purpose."

An early time not long after his father had spoken to him of the matter, he awoke before first light with a desire to go to the river to be with the ponies. As he approached the herd with the rising of the sun, there, apart from the herd, a lone Appaloosa stallion was prancing about and kicking up his heels. Then it stood on its hind legs, thrashing at the air with its forelegs and hooves, throwing its head to and fro, while his mane and tail seemed to dance with the wind. At the same time, the sun bursting orange just fully crested the horizon, silhouetting his entire outline.

Cloud Shadow was completely taken with the whole experience and became immediately devoted to the animal.

Later, as he told Little Bear the story, he heard himself say, "He will be called Sun Dancer, for the Great Spirit has put this on my heart."

Black Eagle was well pleased as he heard tell of what had happened between his son and the Appaloosa, and he had the stallion brought to the camp.

From that day forward, Shadow and Sun Dancer were nearly always together. Some days, he would leave him with a mare in heat, for his offspring were much prized throughout the tribe. He would also keep some of the young for himself.

When he was again another winter older, his father took him on a trip to visit the heart of the monster. They journeyed to the Kamiah valley along the Kooskia River, several sleeps travel away from the Palus camp. Black Eagle had been telling him the story of how the Nimipu had come to be a people and why they lived where they did. That they were the inhabitants of the territory because it had been designated unto them by the Life Giver, whom they called Coyote.

As they came to the place that was the center of their culture, there, not far from the Kooskia River, stood the heart of the monster. It was quite large and somewhat brownish red in color. It appeared as stone sitting alone in the meadow.

Black Eagle had explained that before there were the Nimipu, Coyote had fought the monster here and slew him. He then took the blood from the monster and sprinkled it about, and from it sprang the best of all the tribes, the Nimipu.

While Shadow stood before the heart, he began to feel a very strong urging come over him and believed that he was being impressed to stand up straighter, because he was Nimipu. Then a feeling of great pride flooded over him, a pride that would carry him all his days, because he believed it was so.

Chapter 3

A Change of Circumstances

Several sleeps had passed since Shadow had abducted Rain. When he awoke, he sensed that there was something going on outside the cave. His ponies were skittish. As he stepped out to have a look, he was pummeled from behind and then lost consciousness.

Gray Wolf was no fool. He was able, through the process of elimination, to locate the hiding place. Although it would have been better if he would have located it sooner, for now, his daughter had willingly become known intimately by Shadowhand.

Shadow regained consciousness off and on during their return to the Siksika camp. He tried to fit the pieces of his situation together. He began to recall his time with Rain and how she had revealed her name to him. They had found, after he unbound her hands, that they could converse quite well together in sign talk.

He saw to it that she never was without whatever she needed, and she seemed to be appreciative of it. She was brave also and showed little fear.

They found they could entertain one another in communication. Not long after their conversing began, he released her from any confines as he began to feel more like a companion to her than her captor. Things seemed to be going well enough between them when he made an advancement on her and while she stared into his eyes. She readily complied. Maybe there was something about being away from home that caused her to drop her inhibitions.

The next early time, he was captured and bound and on his way to a fate that held no good promises.

Shadow again began to reflect. He recalled when he was the fingers of both hands and the toes of one's foot in winters. He decided it was his time to go on the vision quest for his life.

His mother's family was from the Wallowa Valley area belonging to the Wallowa band of the Nimipu. It was a trip that was several sleeps away from the place of his father's people. He had heard tell of the beautiful lake that sat at the base of the mountains there. He felt compelled to go there in search of his spirit guide and all that could be found there.

In the back of his consciousness, he thought he could hear Rain arguing about something that might have a thing to do with the fact that when her father finally located her, she was walking about as she pleased, altogether unfettered by all appearances.

Whatever feelings Rain had for Shadow, she could only but guess at the hatred her father possessed for him.

Gray Wolf and his warriors were practiced at the art of retribution and torture.

Shadow retreated into his mind again, seeing himself across the Wallowa River while he peered up into those snowcapped mountains before him. He would camp there and prepare himself with prayer, meditation, and cleansing. The first thing he set about doing was to build himself a sweat lodge, as was the custom of his people.

Shadow always considered himself in accord with the Life Giver, and so prayer, he felt, was a natural and spontaneous thing for him. He had confidence that he was being heard and his words were being considered and weighed by the one who knew and saw all.

After his cleansing, he left to climb into the nearby Wallowa Mountains. He left Sun Dancer penned in a makeshift pen with provisions, feeling confident as well to the fact that he was in the midst of his people's lands, trusting to the safety of his possessions. As far as wild beasts attacking were concerned, he was certain he could easily jump the flimsy poles that surrounded his pony, if need be.

Following the animal trails and vales, he climbed ever upward until he was near the tree line, where he stopped. There, next to the place he had come to, was an exquisite and not all so small of a waterfall, fed by the immediate snowpack that sat directly above it. It was a grassy location surrounded by a varied abundance of flowers shaded in many colors of blue, red, orange, yellow, purple, and white, causing a deep appreciation for Earth Mother.

With the sound of the plunging falls and subtle flow of the creek, along with the fine warm caress of the sun, the sweet aroma of the plant life, and mountain freshness, he truly felt the exhilaration of his place in the Life Giver's world.

He had been abstaining from food as part of his cleansing to help himself become more spiritually aware.

As the lighttime began to fade into darkness, he settled in to wait for the light to return. He left again with the sunrise to ascend higher still. He climbed until he felt he couldn't get any higher. He stopped and lay down to stare out at the heavens and began to pray for guidance. His mind drifted through many places, and he fell into a dream of bounding from cliff top to cliff top. He believed he could see into all the horizons of the earth, not understanding what it all meant, except to keep on seeking what he could find that was needed for his time in this life.

Suddenly, he felt compelled to open his eyes, and when he did, he found himself looking into another set of eyes. He had to try to formulate just what he was seeing. Slowly, his mind began to understand that it was a large mature mountain goat with jet black eyes and terrible dagger-tipped black horns. It was agile, strong, and very wise. He received the comprehension that this was the natural visual representative of his spirit guide and was to be with him throughout his journey in this world.

Then the big white billy leaped away and was gone, right when a very dark eagle flew past, calling out as he moved in the direction that Shadow had come. A profound confidence came over him as he made his way back down to the river, where his life awaited him.

When Shadow had been taken back to the Siksika camp, it was approaching darktime. They staked him to the ground near Gray Wolf's lodge. As he laid there listening to the sounds of the revelry taking place in the center of the encampment, he felt the least confident he ever remembered having felt in his life thus far.

He spent a tense and unnerving time in the darkness about him, watching in the blackness, sometimes thinking he could see movement. All the while, he was certain that his captors would come soon to take him to his end. Then something startled him, and there was the flash of a blade coming at him. It never touched him but cut the hide strap at his wrist, then another strap, then another until he was loose. He could make out Rain before him. She helped him to his feet and led him through the brush to his stallion and gelding that were there waiting for him. She then grabbed Shadow around the neck and placed her cheek up against his, and she was gone.

Shadow leaped upon the back of his Appaloosa stallion with the gelding in tow, and away they ran. He gave thanks for providence from the master of all things in heaven and earth.

Once again, after finding that his captive had escaped, Gray Wolf and a band of followers left out in pursuit of Shadowhand.

Shadow traveled hard and fast, bound for his own country. He had a lot on his mind, and Rain was one of the subjects of thought that occupied him. He sincerely hoped to meet with her again someday, somewhere, somehow.

He also, once again, began to reflect to his younger, more carefree times.

CHAPTER 4

WINTERING WITH THE WALLOWA

When Shadow had gotten back to the river where Sun Dancer awaited him, he had come to the decision to visit his mother's people of the Wallowa band. When he arrived, he was received with the warmth of family from his uncle Big Cat, his mother's brother.

His uncle, on hearing Shadow's telling of his experience, was glad for him, as he thought that the son was going to share the same path as his father, one of a close walk with the Life Giver. Big Cat was very familiar with the powerful medicine of Black Eagle. They had traveled many trails together.

A vision that powerful was something to be admired by all who heard tell of it. It was rare to hear of such things of wonder. At least it was, up till now. With Shadow, it would become a lifestyle.

Shadow stayed with his uncle for a while before he was informed by him that they were going to begin preparations to move to their winter camp. "We go to this place because it protects us so well from the cold wind. I would like for you to come with us and see it for yourself, of what I tell you," Big Cat explained.

"I would be honored to help with the moving of your camp and to winter with you there as well, my uncle," Shadow responded, appearing very glad at what he had been told.

When the time had come and all the gear and provisions and stock were made ready, they left for the canyon that was to become their home during the coming cold time.

The canyon the Wallowa band wintered in was a massive thing. It was so deep that from the top, it was impossible to distinguish anything along the bottom with any clarity.

The first order of business when they arrived was to build longhouses from lodgepoles and cedar bark. They managed to build them quite large, large enough to house many families in a single longhouse.

It made for close living conditions, but they passed the time with much storytelling. Of course, there was always constant wood gathering for the women and children as well as hunting and trapping for the men.

Shadow soon began to earn the respect of the other men through hard work and his prowess as a hunter with strength, cunning, and accuracy with the bow and arrow.

He didn't fail to catch the attention of the young women of the band either. There were opportunities for him in that way, but he felt it could lead to embarrassment for others or himself, so he worked hard at avoiding it.

The confidence with which he carried himself and his horsemanship and fine stallion didn't go unnoticed, all adding to a distinguished personality coming into fruition.

As the cold began to recede, he let his uncle know as well as others he had befriended that he would be leaving soon.

Big Cat surprised Shadow by informing him that he would be coming along with him when he left. "It has been long enough since I have seen my sister and your father. I will go to your camp as well, my nephew." Also, Big Cat had lost his woman and child sometime back in an attack by a Siksika war party in buffalo country. He never felt the need to take another wife. All Nimipu were free to go wheresoever they pleased and very much enjoyed the custom. Shadow knew his mother would be happy to see her brother again, as well as himself. It would be a fine reunion.

When he and his uncle arrived at the Palus band camp, it was a joyous time. Shadow's mother and father were relieved to see that he was all right. He had stayed gone much longer than was expected, although once the cold time began to set in, they suspected that he would hold up till it passed.

When the story came out, as told by Shadow and his uncle together, they could see that he not only was all right but was flourishing.

Big Cat was no stranger to the Palus camp. He and Black Eagle were close companions of many winters in time.

As the elders conversed on the standing of stores, they came to the decision that there was a real need to make another hunting expedition to buffalo country.

Shadow had looked forward to the day as long as he could remember to be able to go on the lengthy buffalo trail hunt. Finally, with his successful vision quest behind him and an obvious growth in stature, both physically and in character, he was offered to be in the hunt with the other hunters that would be going along.

To get to buffalo country, they would have to travel across the high mountainous trail that was set between Nimipu lands and the plains of the land of the rising sun. There were many enemies of the Nimipu in that place.

It became a time of much excitement and anticipation throughout the band. They needed the buffalo to sustain them, but the danger was hard to ignore.

It wasn't just the men who had to ponder the danger, but the women were possibly affected by the idea of it even more so. Shadow's mother didn't want him to go, feeling that he was still too young, as it often was between a mother and her son. After all, the preparations were made, and the party was leaving. Shadow was among them.

Shadow thought on the stories passed down from the ancient ones, that there once were buffalo in their country but had disappeared because of drought and fire and disease. There was a time, it was told, that the ancestors would stampede them off high cliffs to fall to their death. Now the Great Spirit had provided them with ponies so they could travel the long distances it took to reach them.

It would be a long and arduous trip. They would be gone for many sleeps, but for Shadow, the prospect of the adventure was thrilling beyond anything he had experienced thus far.

The snow had melted considerably in the not-too-distant mountains, since the warming time had started to take place. The trail they would take to their destination would lead them to elevations that quite possibly were still covered with snow. Although, where they were at that time was full of the scents of new leaves and other thriving plant growth on the soft warm breezes that flowed all about them. Shadow could not help but feel that it was good to be alive, and he was appreciative of Earth Mother's goodness.

He could tell that Sun Dancer was feeling the same way as he rode him along on this fine day. He was powerful, limitless, and free.

His thoughts went back to their departure from the Palus encampment and how, as they were leaving, the young women seemed to notice him as well as the other young men. The time of being a boy had passed with the seasons.

There was one young woman in particular that he was especially attracted to, and he found himself thinking of her often. He believed her to be called Running Wild.

If he could kill enough buffalo, he would have plenty of hides to have his own tipi lodge to provide shelter for himself and a wife. Then they could build a good life for themselves. He then reminded himself to stop dreaming and start focusing on the trail ahead.

The hunting party had brought plenty of additional ponies to have fresh mounts and to be able to pack all they needed or wanted on their return.

There was a time when the whole camp would make the trip, with the exception of a few that would stay behind to watch over things while the band was away. The large party would stay for long periods, maybe a couple of winters, but it hadn't been so in the time that Shadow could recall. There was too much danger there. Now only half of the able men would go, so if by chance they never returned.

The elders spoke of a couple of routes that could be taken to the buffalo hunting grounds. On this trip, they had passed along the Kooskia River and the place of the heart of the monster at Kamiah, to the Lochsa River, and were basically moving along parallel to it as it flowed out of the mountains, fed by many tributary creeks, streams, and brooks.

They had bathed in the Lochsa River that morning, and Shadow could definitely tell that it was a lot closer to the snow compared to bathing in the Palus or the Winding River, much closer to their home.

Since the time that Shadow had the vision of acquiring a mountain goat as his guardian spirit guide, he desired to spend his time at places of higher elevations. To climb again made him feel good in a fulfilling way.

As the hunters continued to ascend, the country began to take on a different appearance. It went from open grassy hills with sparse foliage and rocky crags to heavily forested mountainous terrain. It was always nearby to the beautiful, sometimes talking, sometimes singing flowing waters. It sometimes moved fast, other times slowly in deep wide stretches, cluttered with large granite boulders and fallen trees.

There was the ever lighttime presence of lots of flying, fluttering birds of so many types, singing their favorite songs as they sought the different insects that were buzzing and humming along, all in perfect harmony. It was to be enjoyed while basking in the freshness and fragrance of every breath he took.

Shadow told himself he wanted to come back to this place, to search the many tributary waterways and vales, just to be part of such a great place and for it to be a part of him, being in his memory stored.

They made camp early, having had a long travel day. While they relaxed around the blazing fire, Shadow and the other young men listened to the older and more experienced voices tell of past trips to the buffalo country. They talked of other tribes they had encountered. Some were wary of strangers; others were hospitable and desired lasting friendship. Then there were those who were outright hostile.

Sometimes the Nimipu would flee the area. Sometimes that wasn't possible. Shadow's father and uncle had fought many skirmishes with different bands and tribes. Some were minor, but others were very bitter, with pain, suffering, and death on both sides. There were several battles that came up in their stories repeatedly, but a couple that had a common thread came to the forefront when it came to this particular topic.

They once again retold the tale of their initial encounter with these Siksika, who became their chief nemesis.

CHAPTER 5

THE MAKING OF A BLOOD FEUD

It was back before Shadow could remember. It had been a severe and hungry winter previously, and it was the last time the entire band had gone to the buffalo country together. They had camped along a creek at the edge of the forest, just before it opened to a plain, where they came onto a substantial herd of buffalo, more than their small band could kill in a lifetime. Right away, the hunters took down enough for their immediate needs. Then Black Eagle and Big Cat, along with a small group of other hunters, took a scouting trip to check out the lay of the land around about them. They wanted to be able to put together the best strategy to take the most animals for their efforts.

After they had traveled till the sun was high above them and had begun to climb a hill for the overall view below, they were startled by loud shouting and shrill cries as a group of riders began to descend on them. When they turned to flee, they saw another small band galloping at them from the direction that they had just come.

It was a fight for their lives. In an instant, hunters became warriors. They had already let arrows fly in the directions of their attackers. There were also arrows landing among them as ponies reared and lunged.

Big Cat saw an elegant young warrior taking aim with his bow and arrow, straight at Black Eagle. Trying to beat his release, Big Cat cast his arrow at the young man. His arrow hit him in his side, but not before the warrior's arrow had grazed Black Eagle's face, taking off the lower part of his strong side ear. Black Eagle then went straight at the young man with his war club in hand and drove it into his face with a deadly crushing blow.

At that same moment, all could hear a scream of anguish and defiance come from a member of the opposing band. They looked to the source of the scream. There they saw the face of an older fierce-looking warrior who bore a strong resemblance to the young man who had just been slain by Black Eagle.

The older warrior released an arrow at Black Eagle just as he rolled his upper body to avoid being hit.

There was confusion and a lull that took place concerning the tragic and untimely death of that particular young man. The Nimipu took advantage of it as they began to retreat toward their camp. It appeared that they had gotten out of the fray without any of their party being killed, but they had suffered some injuries as well as being put on a high state of alert over a very real and present danger.

The older Siksika warrior was Three Bulls, a chieftain of the band who had just witnessed the killing of his youngest son by these intruding outsiders.

As Cloud Shadow listened to the story, he looked upon the scar that ran along his father's face, as well as the ear with the missing piece. He had heard the story before, but it never failed to capture his attention.

Big Cat went on to tell how they had stayed in the area after having moved the camp to another location considerably farther from the point of the fight. They stayed and hunted from that place, managing to kill a substantial number of buffalo from there.

After remaining there for some time, there was an attack on their camp.

It came just after first light, and the camp was just beginning to stir. Fawn was in the process of plaiting Black Eagle's hair when the air was pierced with the cries of angry warriors set on revenge. They came racing into the camp on horseback, unleashing arrows at any moving target, women and children not excluded.

As the Nimipu returned the fight as quickly as they were able, Black Eagle grabbed his war club and ran out from their tipi lodge and into the attack. Three Bulls came into close proximity, and his eyes focused on Black Eagle. The war club struck him in the shoulder. It had been thrown with much force. Then after he was struck, Three Bulls's pony reared, tossing him high in the air.

When he came down, Black Eagle was on him with his white quartz blade already in hand. And with a single action, he sliced his throat, causing a long moment of excruciating death. Black Eagle saw the life pass from him.

One of the Siksika warriors called Red Crow, Three Bulls's oldest son and father of one called Gray Wolf, gave out a call that stopped the attack. He then dismounted without a weapon and strode over to his father's lifeless body and muscled it up onto his father's pony. He strode back to his own mount and hopped on its back in an effortless motion. He then pointed at Black Eagle, indicated a slashing of his throat, and then rode away with his father's dead corpse in tow.

The Nimipu suffered a number of deaths as a result of the attack. Among the dead were Big Cat's young wife and infant male child. After he had placed them to burial, he had not mentioned their names again. It was too painful for him to speak of. Shadow had heard it told by his father and mother and was careful not to bring it up himself.

The following lighttime after that attack, there was a breaking of camp. Once all the gear and provisions, which included many loaded pack ponies carrying much dried meat and hides, were all readied, they left that terrible and wonderful place.

On their return trip, for the first few lighttimes, they knew that they were being followed. There were several more attacks on some who had been caught away from the main party.

After these forays by their incited enemies, the Nimipu came across another band of hunters. On their initial contact, the strangers indicated that they had peaceful intentions and wanted to powwow and pass the pipe.

Their leader introduced himself as Long Hair, and indeed his hair was extraordinarily long, as it reached the ground as he stood, and he was a tall man. An Absaroke chieftain.

As they conversed through sign talk, Black Eagle told of their harrowing encounter with the Siksika.

Long Hair made it known that they, too, were enemies of the Siksika and that they would cover their backs as they left the area.

When they concluded their time together, there was a real and genuine alliance formed, of which both sides were glad for and spoke of their hopes of meeting again.

The rest of the return trip was without further aggressions against them.

CHAPTER 6

The Feud Continues

So now Cloud Shadow was on a journey to the land of glory and great peril. He thought back on all he had been told and had overheard concerning this place that played at the imagination but was soon to become all so real to his own life's experiences.

Shadow was glad that Little Bear was able to come along on the hunt as well. As they conversed, Little Bear asked him if he was worried about the danger of this hunt.

Shadow replied, "Sometimes I think of things that cause me to worry, but mostly I look forward to the possibilities of the dangers. I want to run with the buffalo and take them down with the power of my pony and bow and to defend our right to hunt them also."

"I'm glad to hear you say those words. It makes me happy to be with you, to be able to do this together. Our time has come. We will do well," Little Bear responded. Shadow felt pride and strong friendship toward Little Bear and for his words. It was their time now.

He and Little Bear had been taught well and practiced much. They had become skilled horsemen and archers, as well as skilled in hand-to-hand combat with blades and clubs. Life was full of expectations as well as dangers. So it was with them as it had been before them. A man must do whatever it takes to make it work out, although it's good to have help when you need it.

The time came when it was made know to them that soon they would be coming into buffalo country. They had traveled through some area that was still covered with snow, but it had been passable. It was always an important issue to be done with hunting in this place before the cold time began to set back in. They didn't want to spend the winter here if they didn't have to.

They finally came out of the pass and into open country. They continued farther into the plains, and after several sleeps, they came upon a vast herd of buffalo. It was so large that it appeared to reach until the sky touched the earth. Shadow was astounded with a sight that defied his imagination.

The time for just talking about it was fast coming to an end. Now it was the time of doing. Black Eagle led them in close. Then they began to run along the perimeter of the herd. Each hunter chose a target and let fly an arrow.

With the quickly changing movement of the panicked prey, each hunter had to react to the situation as soon as it presented itself. Sun Dancer took Shadow right to the close proximity needed to drive the deadly arrow, then another and another. Dust, debris, sweat, stench, panic, chaos, laughter, joy, exuberance—all this almost quicker than they could be recognized.

Eventually, the hunters ceased their assault on the herd and withdrew to take a tally on what had been accomplished.

They had done well. There were many buffalo strewn across the area.

They looked on the job that lay ahead. The men all wished the women were along right then, because there was much skinning and butchering to be done. They knew that they had better get on with the task before them.

They skinned and butchered until the sun went down. They ate raw liver and heart and tongue while they worked.

When they awoke at dawn, they started again. Some of the men set up drying racks. By the end of the next lighttime, they had finished the primary butchering. They staked out hides and continued to flay and strip the meat. They made fires just to roast ribs over. They were exhausted but filled with satisfaction with their accomplishment.

The following early time, they began to establish their camp. They wouldn't be able to leave the area until they were able to properly dry the meat and hides they had come for. Now they would pitch camp and defend their stake on the ground where they stood.

The first defense they had to address was the very large force of wolves throughout the entire area. Even though they had killed a lot of buffalo, the main body of bison had remained in the area still. It included the packs of wolves that continually followed the herd wheresoever they went.

Eventually, the main herd moved off, and the wolves then moved off with them, but it was a trying time for what seemed like a tormented lifetime until then to keep them from over running the campsite.

Their nature as bloodthirsty killers was on full display. The older hunters showed the younger ones how to repel them with sharpened poles, which at dark time had to include some flaming torches also.

The Nimipu hunting party was basking in the abundance of their existence at that point in time, having repelled the wolves and thus far secured their bounty.

They were hunters, gatherers by their very nature, in the prime of success. There was much celebration with laughter and singing and dancing. All were happy. All that is except Gray Wolf and his hunting party, who had happened to come across these Nimipu in the middle of their celebration.

Gray Wolf spent a bit of time observing the camp. While he looked upon the markings on the ponies, he was able to formulate the fact that these were Nimipu, which in itself caused him to conclude that they were definitely going to attack them. He also wondered if these possibly could be some of the same group that were responsible for the deaths of his grandfather and uncle all those winters ago.

With the accidental death of his own father, Red Crow, being thrown from his pony into a buffalo stampede sometime back, he felt that any revenge for the family had been left to him.

As was their manner, they would strike at dawn. The unwary Nimipu would be caught off guard after much celebration. They were adept at many things but still susceptible to the wiles of the crafty.

Gray Wolf's fighters were slightly less in numbers than the Nimipu party, but with surprise on their side, they had ample ability to bring death and suffering with the attack on the camp that early time.

As they came on foot with loud war whoops and cries, they pounced on the Nimipu with fury. It was a confusing and adrenaline-pumping moment that brought Shadow and their camp awake. Their weapons were near, as they should be. Shadow quickly had his club in one hand and his blade in the other and headbutted the warrior coming through the opening of the tipi. The headbutted Siksika flew backward and landed with a thud as the air was pushed from his lungs. He then took a hard and fatal blow to the temple from Shadow, who then took a quick moment to take in the scope of the situation about him.

The battle was in full contact. May the best man win. There was no place for holding back. It was kill or be killed. Gray Wolf quickly understood something he should have already known. These Nimipu were skilled fighters, and they were in for all they could handle and more. He gave the call to pull out. At this, his warriors turned and ran for their ponies, which were being held in a nearby ravine.

As soon as Shadow saw their retreat, he ran and jumped on Sun Dancer's back and quickly pursued the fleeing enemy. At this, Gray Wolf turned toward Shadow's advancement. And as Shadow leaned to strike at him with his club, an arrow from a Siksika bow passed through Sun Dancer's neck, severing his main artery.

Shadow flew off as the Appaloosa collapsed. The dying stallion landed between Cloud Shadow and Gray Wolf, causing Gray Wolf to step back. This gave Shadow time to gain his balance and bearing. Gray Wolf was trying to move toward him to strike him down, but he couldn't maneuver a course around or over Sun Dancer's dead carcass. Just at that moment, Black Eagle yelled, "Shadow, watch for your chance!"

Gray Wolf caught the name then turned to see Black Eagle. He noticed the scarred face with the missing piece of ear. Right at that moment, Shadow leaped over the dead pony then sliced down Gray Wolf's thigh with his blade. Gray Wolf screamed with pain and rage.

Then, with all his effort, he was able to hit Shadow with a glancing blow of his club.

Then what seemed from merely thin air, a pony with a rider rushed in and locked arms with Gray Wolf, swinging him onto the back of the pony as several arrows passed ever so close to ending their lives. They galloped away from the Nimipu camp.

Shadow's first reaction was to lay down on top of Sun Dancer, with an outpouring of grief and sadness and a deep sense of loss like he had never known before then.

The next overwhelming feeling he had was hatred for those responsible.

Shadow then jumped to his feet and ran toward the nearest pony available. Big Cat and Black Eagle were already ahead of him, stopping him from leaving. Big Cat told him, "Plan your revenge. Do not go in haste."

A look came over Shadow's face that could be read by any who saw it. There would be a high price to be paid.

Gray Wolf had already paid a price. He was in a bad way. The blade had cut deeply into his thigh muscle. He also felt intense hatred for this one called Shadow, to become the one he would refer to as Shadowhand. He would destroy his medicine if he ever got the chance. He also couldn't help but think about the one with the missing section of his ear. He had been told for many winters about the battles with the Nimipu that cost the lives of his family members, always with the mention of the fact that the one responsible for their deaths had part of an ear taken off by a Siksika arrow. Someday, he determined, he must have his revenge.

CHAPTER 7

FRIENDS AND ALLIES

Once again, Black Eagle felt it was time to leave because of attacks from hostile Siksika. It was time to break camp and move out for home, away from these plains of plenty that always seemed to provide more than expected.

Not long after breaking camp, while on their return trip, they again came across an Absaroke hunting party. Big Cat conversed with them in sign talk. He inquired about the chieftain Long Hair. They answered that he still lived but no longer went out on the hunting trail. The Nimipu and the Absaroke camped near one another, and in the early time, they invited any who would care to come along with them on their return to their village, being several sleeps away.

Black Eagle knew that they needed to get their bounty back to the Palus village and could not deter from that. Shadow informed Black Eagle that he and Little Bear were going to take them up on their offer and go to their encampment with them. He said, "I feel a powerful urging to go with them. That it was meant to be that we crossed trails and that it is my place to try and create alliances where and when I can."

Black Eagle was concerned that it could be a wrong decision to go at this time but wouldn't consider trying to forbid it. He had too much respect for Shadow's judgment.

They all gave their friendly departing gestures and then went their separate ways.

It was an interesting trip to Shadow as they traveled to the Absaroke encampment. His guides made him understand that this place wasn't their primary village but a camp that they inhabited periodically, along with many other locations that allowed time for the place that they preferred to spend their time to become refreshed before they returned to it again. Shadow garnered just what they meant. The Nimipu did something similar by shifting from area to area yet still within the general proximity of what they called home.

Shadow also enjoyed being in a country that was altogether new to him. After all, he was an adventurer at heart.

When they arrived at the village, there was much excitement. The first thing that struck Shadow was the whiteness of the clothing and hide tipis. It was a sight that really made an impression. He had had it explained to him when he had inquired about it to the hunters that they traveled with, noticing the skins they wore for clothing had that quality. They informed him that it was a unique procedure that had been with their people for so long as anyone could speak of. They developed a lye from ash and used it to bleach the hides.

Coming into the camp, it almost seemed to glow. Everything was so white. Shadow and Little Bear were very impressed with it all.

Within a short time, they were brought before Long Hair's lodge. Long Hair and some of his family were gathered there to see and hear of what was taking place. It was obvious that something out of the ordinary was occurring. Long Hair had not met Shadow or Little Bear before, but he was a knowledgeable man and educated in many things, and to recognize the traits of the Nimipu was certainly one of them.

Long Hair was very receptive to his visitors and bid them to come off their ponies and to partake of any hospitality he could impart to them.

They dismounted and made their way to his lodge. And upon entering, they were shown to make themselves comfortable among the many fine pelts that were strewn about.

Shortly thereafter, a handsome pipe was brought out, and then a smoking ritual took place and continued for some time. After which, they got to know some things about one another. That also continued for a bit of time. It wasn't long before it was known that Shadow was Black Eagle's son, whom Long Hair remembered well.

Long Hair told Shadow that he was very pleased that Black Eagle's son had come to visit him. "I esteemed your father highly from our only encounter," Long Hair signed as he spoke.

There was some movement at the entrance of the lodge. In walked a young man who was introduced as Long Hair's son, Many Arrows. Many Arrows was a replica of his father. He was tall with very long hair but with an overbearing look of superiority about him that couldn't be helped.

As time passed, there was an ease of atmosphere that prevailed over the meeting between the cultures. At a seemingly appropriate time, Shadow brought up the attack that the Siksika made on their hunting party recently and the battle that followed. Shadow went on to sign on the loss of his beloved pony and his desire for revenge.

The Absaroke in turn had many things to relate concerning their hatred of the Siksika. They concluded with the telling of how their nemesis had been trying to drive them away from this country for as long as any could remember.

Little Bear and Shadow stayed among the Absaroke for many sleeps. They passed the cold time there, lodging with Many Arrows. Shadow formed a close bond with the Absaroke brave. While together, they hunted and sign talked concerning many things, as well as picking up some of the other's languages.

Many Arrows was a proficient hunter with the bow and arrow. He told of how he had acquired his name at a young age. He had the skill to place more arrows in flight at a time before the first arrow cast hit the ground than anyone else had seen before him. Shadow challenged him at it and was quite competitive but could not match his speed.

As the cold time began to come to an end, Shadow began to talk with Many Arrows about coming with Little Bear and himself to seek out adventure and exploration.

Many Arrows let him know he liked the idea. "I will be happy to go with my good friends to travel together, to see and find what we will." He signed as he spoke.

Not long after their agreement of purpose, they left to take in the wonder of it all.

After some sleeps of travel, they came across a fine cave near a creek that was ideal for a shelter for themselves and the ponies. It sat at the base of some mountains where the creek flowed from. They stayed over for a couple sleeps just enjoying the place. After some time, Shadow asked of Many Arrows if he knew of the whereabouts of the camp of the Siksika that he had described as the attackers upon their hunting party when they had first met.

Many Arrows replied, "I believe I know the place you seek. It is the camp of the one called Gray Wolf." He then went on to tell how the description of this one was the same as Shadow had described him.

They departed from the comfort of the cave, moving in the direction of the rising sun. When they had gotten to the place in question, cautiously approaching, there was no sign of those being sought after.

"I believe if one was to come here during the hot time, they would be found to inhabit this place," Many Arrows informed his friends.

Shadow took what had been shown him and stored it away for further reference. Before he left, he reached over his strong side shoulder and removed a personally marked arrow from his quiver and quickly cast it into the base of a nearby tree. "That will give him something to think about until the time we meet again," Shadow declared.

The companions then moved back in the direction of the setting sun as they ventured about, taking their time exploring and hunting for whatever they could find.

They returned to the cave they had found and stayed at that location for a time, doing a bit of trapping for fine fur pelts. Life was good, and they were enjoying the camaraderie they were experiencing. Again, they decided to leave their cave dwelling, and then they moved toward the land of the setting sun.

They had put in a long period of travel when they decided to make camp. Little Bear dismounted with a pressing need to make water. Shadow and Many Arrows were still astride their ponies, looking about the immediate area for a place that they could make camp and be sheltered from prying eyes.

Little Bear was standing at the edge of an elevated and heavily foliaged area leading into a forest. As he stood there relieving himself, he had an overpowering feeling that he was being watched and felt uncomfortable to the point of stopping short of finishing what he had started. Suddenly, in an instant, a huge dark form was beside him, with a roaring and then a crushing, and then he knew nothing.

As Shadow and Many Arrows watched in horror, a very large grizzly bear had sprung out of dense cover and dealt a tremendous sweeping blow across Little Bear's head and neck and was quickly over him, biting and tearing his flesh.

Without hesitation, Shadow and Many Arrows began unleashing arrows into the blood lusting carnivore. The first arrow hit the grizzly in the shoulder, which brought it to its full height as he turned toward the assault. In a short time, he had received a host of wounds. Finally, it took one arrow directly through the mouth, with the tip of the arrow protruding out the back of the neck. He dropped to the ground, dead.

Shadow jumped to the ground and ran to Little Bear. He knelt beside his torn body and believed Little Bear was still alive, but then his life passed on at the next moment. Shadow began to sing the death song, and Many Arrows joined in, as he knew it.

Shadow was experiencing his second great sense of loss. He had thoughts about how the Life Giver provided so many beautiful and wondrous things, but on the other hand, there was the side that was hard and sometimes cruel. It was beyond his understanding, and so he decided there and then to accept it as out of his control and that all he could do is move on.

Many Arrows suggested putting his body in a tree for his time of sojourning to the other side.

First, they tightly wrapped him in his buffalo robe. Then they worked together to place his corpse partway up a tree with hopes that he would be secure from the winds and the predators. They then departed from that place and made a camp not long after.

The next early time, after they had awakened and were preparing to leave, they took notice that they were closed in about them by a large party of mounted braves. Shadow, right away, signed that they were friends that came in peace.

One of the riders approached them and also signed of peaceful intentions. He then dismounted and came nearer. "We are Salish and have been following your trail," he signed while he spoke.

Shadow responded, "We are Nimipu and Absaroke, looking for friends and allies."

As the discourse continued, the brave explained, "I am Spotted Feather, and we are not looking to harm you. We came across your trail and found the dead yellow bear, as well as the body of your companion. Then we wanted to see those who had killed the bear. You are welcome in our country and are invited to stay with us in our camp to see if we can be friends."

Shadow answered, "Our hearts are laid low over the loss of our companion, but we will come with you to your camp. I am called Cloud Shadow, and this is Many Arrows, and we are always at peace with those who are friendly toward us."

Not so long a trip from where they had made camp the previous time, they arrived at the Salish village, amid loud voices and barking curs and the smell of food cooking and much laughter. It gave Shadow a feeling of gladness just from the general atmosphere of the camp. He felt at peace.

After several sleeps had passed there at the Salish village, and there had been plenty of time familiarizing themselves together, Spotted Feather had become very drawn to Shadow and Many Arrows.

At mealtime, there was served some brook fish. After they had eaten, Shadow, without giving it any serious thought, signed as he spoke, "Where I live, we have fish that have red meat like buffalo."

There happened to be a small group of people around them there, and each person stopped what they were doing and showed a look of surprise at what they believed had just been conveyed by their guest. Even Many Arrows was seen to smirk and shake his head in disbelief.

Spotted Feather responded, "That I would like to see."

"I would very much like to show you this thing and many others that you have never seen. I invite you and Many Arrows to come with me to my lands and be my guests there. I would be honored to have you, my good friends," Cloud Shadow stated, very much hoping they would accept.

CHAPTER 8

HOMEWARD BOUND

The following early time, when they were leaving, different ones were calling out, "Be careful that the buffalo fish doesn't stampede you, Spotted Feather." It was followed by much laughter. Shadow and Many Arrows weren't certain of what they were saying, but they waved at all the happy faces as they moved along to the outskirts of the village.

Within a couple sleeps, they were beginning to move onto the trail between the mountains that would take them through the mountain range to the Nimipu lands.

Shadow didn't want to hurry, for he loved this trail. They weren't too late in the cycle of weather changes that would eventually bring the snows that would make the trip impossible.

Each dusk they would watch the sun track over their heads, showing the direction of travel, as if beckoning, "Come hither, my sons of the trail."

At each lighttime, they explored and hunted, enjoying their time together and learning one another's languages, at least in part. When they signed a thing, they then in turn would speak it in their tongue. As this went on, they began to pick it up. Their time together was full, with their bodies and minds challenged and busy.

After sometime on the trail, they could feel a definite change in the weather. The leaves continued to fall from the trees, and each awake time it got colder and colder. One early time, as they stirred in their robes, it became apparent that it was snowing on them. It wasn't expected. It was early for snow.

The snow presented its problems but also its beauty and freshness. They tried not to concern themselves over the snow and focused on their camaraderie.

Shadow was happy to be heading home, as well as being in the company of new friends. He couldn't help but reflect on the passing of Little Bear as he made his way back to their home. His friend of many winters and his beloved pony, never to be together in this life again.

His attention was drawn back to the moment when he heard a voice say, "Fish as big as trees. I think this is maybe too much for us to believe." The voice belonged to Spotted Feather. Shadow had been telling them of many things of wonder.

They didn't want to start doubting Shadow, for they had come to trust him quite explicitly, but some of these things that he had told them of were beginning to trifle with their sense of reality. There was the buffalo fish, the heart of the monster, and a river he called the Mother River that was so deep and wide in places. If not for the moving water, you would think it was a lake. And then the fish with the bones on the outside that sometimes got to be as big as a tree.

Toward the end of the lighttime, the snow began to fall heavier, and the wind began to pick up strength. They all agreed to stop and seek shelter. Each rider also had a pack animal, so they were well stocked with provisions. They found a very large boulder that was positioned in a way that blocked the wind from blowing on them.

They hobbled their ponies and unloaded their burdens. Then they created a lean-to structure with an opening to allow the smoke from their fire a place to vent from.

They laid out their robes and then built a fire. Once the fire got to a sufficient place of usability, they set about roasting venison from a previous kill.

It all came to provide a natural sense of contentment. To have a fine camp in these poor weather conditions.

They hadn't eaten for some time and were weary from the trail. So the food went down with much satisfaction and added to their ability to pass into a very comfortable sleep. They would only stir to place some more fuel on the fire when needed.

When they awoke in the first light, the wind had dropped off considerably, but it continued to snow. It snowed for several more light and darktimes. They weren't particularly concerned about it because they knew that the time of continuous snow was not yet and that it would end soon enough.

During the lighttime, they would walk out from camp to stretch and exercise their limbs and take in the atmosphere. The pristine environment, with the snow glistening on the trees, was a cleanliness that surpassed most other conditions.

These brave and strong young men between them had an education in survival that could not be rivaled. They were feeling glad to be alive in that place, at that time.

As they stood observing their surroundings, Shadow pointed off in a direction. They watched a panther slip noiselessly through the trees. They all gave a grunt of appreciation, for they knew it was something one rarely was able to witness.

"This has been a good time we have had together at this place," remarked Spotted Feather, as he then stuck out his tongue, trying to catch a snowflake on the end of it.

Shadow said, "My friends, let us continue on our journey, for the weather is improving." As they stood watching, the clouds began to roll away, and a ray of sun came shining through.

"It will be good to get back on the trail again," responded Spotted Feather.

Many Arrows replied, "Let us be on our way, that we may see Shadow's land."

The following early time, they once again broke camp to begin their trek toward the land of the setting sun. By the time the sun had gotten up high in the sky, the snow was all but gone.

The weather remained agreeable for the most part as they continued through the mountainous country.

As they went along, the features of the landscape began to change from forested mountains to grassy, granite boulder covered hills.

The different tributary waterways had all merged into a single river, the Lochsa.

After some more travel, they came to Kamiah, the place of the battle between Coyote and the monster. Before they came to the spot where the petrified heart stood alone as a reminder to the victory won there, Shadow began to relate the story behind it to his companions.

As they approached the meadow, the new visitors began to experience some feelings of anticipation taking place. At a point, they came in view of the peculiar site. The most peculiar thing about it was that it did not seem to belong there. There was nothing else around it that it had any resemblance to. It could be considered heart shaped to a degree, and one might wonder what the shape of a monster's heart might be anyway. There was a general consensus that there was a certain aura about the place.

Many Arrows stated, "Let us begone from this place. I do not think that I am meant to be here."

"I think we should leave as well," responded Spotted Feather.

Shadow looked at the uncomfortable appearance of his friends and replied, "It is well what you say. We will stay with a band of my people not far from here."

They had to ford the river a couple of times to get to where the Kooskia band made their camp. When they arrived, there was a lot of activity around, and no one seemed to take notice of them as they rode along. At a point, someone did take notice to the difference in appearance of outsiders. Then it became widely known that there were visitors in their midst.

Shadow inquired to the whereabouts of Yellow Jacket.

Yellow Jacket was a cousin to Shadow who, on occasion, paid a visit to the Palus band.

Spotted Feather and Many Arrows looked about and saw a sight that was new to them. Not only were there tipi lodges but also longhouse structures as well, which they were not familiar with. Shadow's land was a curious place.

Yellow Jacket was summoned, being told he had callers, and they weren't of the sort that he was used to seeing. Within a short time, Yellow Jacket came striding in their direction, followed by a throng of young ones and others that weren't so young. All wanted to hear how and why it was that they had come among them.

Immediately, Yellow Jacket recognized Cloud Shadow but was puzzled over who his companions were.

Shadow dismounted, and they gave respectful salutations to one another. "It has been awhile, my cousin, since we have been together," Cloud Shadow spoke. "I have come from the buffalo country and have brought friends, that they could know how we do and that our people could know them as well."

"Welcome to our village. A friend to Cloud Shadow is a friend of this village." Yellow Jacket greeted these new visitors while gesturing with wide open arms.

Spotted Feather and Many Arrows didn't get all that was said, but they got the welcome part clear enough.

There was an atmosphere of friendship and excitement all around. Before long, they were all seated around a central fire and being served a meal of quamash root and fish. When the fish was presented, Spotted Feather and Many Arrows looked at each other, and both uttered, "Buffalo fish," for they both could plainly see that the meat was red. Shadow just smiled to himself.

CHAPTER 9

A HOMECOMING

While they remained with the people of the Kooskia band, there were a lot of festivities.

The men were showing off their fine ponies as well as had races. The women were cooking plenty of their favorite dishes while the children laughed and played.

At times, flocks of fowl filled the air while leaping fish fed on flying insects, ruffling the lazy waters. The whole setting contributed to a feeling of tranquility.

Shadow told of the troubles that the hunting party had while in buffalo country, along with the death of Little Bear. All who listened to his tale were very much intrigued.

Eventually, the time came to leave and move on for home. Shadow conveyed to his companions the distance they still needed to travel to come to the place that he was yet wanting to reach. It was the place where they would meet his immediate family, the lands of the Palus band.

As they traveled, they passed by the fishing Nimipu. They stopped to watch as the fishermen's hazel baskets caught the fish, whose failed attempt at leaping a rapid caused them to fall backward and land into the waiting entrapment.

After some time had passed, the fishermen would descend to the basket with club in hand and end the lives of the struggling fish before gathering them.

In other locations, there were stark naked men with long spears standing on foam-drenched cliffs. Just before the fish would make its leap, it would be pierced and dragged ashore.

It all made for a grand sight to behold. "This truly is a fine country where a man can catch the buffalo fish like they are doing," Spotted Feather commented.

"Yes, I am very glad to be able to come and see these things for myself," added Many Arrows as he peered out at the river.

"We are very thankful for this bountiful country the Life Giver has given us," Cloud Shadow responded to their compliments.

Their journey took several more sleeps before they drew near to the place of the Palus band's encampment.

While they were yet some distance off, they were treated with a view of vast grasslands, inhabited with immense herds of ponies. Shadow was very familiar with the sight, but it still did not fail to exhilarate him.

Spotted Feather and Many Arrows were awestruck. Eventually, Many Arrows exclaimed, "You did not speak of this!"

Cloud Shadow replied, "I had forgotten what a sight it can be."

Before long, a small group of riders came toward them. When the riders had gotten within a short distance of them, one of the riders was heard to cry out, "Cloud Shadow has returned!"

Not much time later, they were entering the village to a great stir and hearty reception.

One of the first to meet them was Black Eagle, with a loud exclamation of "My son, how fine to see you again!"

It seemed the whole encampment had gathered and was rejoicing. Many Arrows and Spotted Feather were very moved by the outpouring of emotions, as was Shadow, upon seeing the people's reactions.

After they had dismounted, Shadow quickly addressed Little Bear's family concerning his sad and tragic death. When these things had been told, it spread rapidly through the camp, followed by outbursts of grief by many.

For the respect that was due their guests, Shadow turned his attention back to Many Arrows and Spotted Feather. He then introduced his friends. Then Black Eagle said, "How good to meet the son of Long Hair. We are honored to have you for our guest and pleased to have you here with us." He then focused on Spotted Feather, saying, "We are also pleased to have a member of the Salish tribe among us, of whom I have a high regard. Welcome to our home. Come rest and refresh yourselves."

Black Eagle and Shadow's younger brother, Talon, expectedly wanted to know everything concerning Shadow's exploits since he had gone off on his mission of goodwill and friendship toward the Absaroke and apparently the Salish as well.

Shadow indulged them with a detailed story that had their attention throughout. In the end, it was surmised that the event of Little Bear's death was some type of big medicine that might be better understood in time.

Black Eagle, as always, was very proud of his son Shadow, and he was looked up to by his younger brother, Talon. The young women were also interested in all that was said concerning him. He was already beginning to take on a certain mystique within the band.

After all the homecoming festivities had died down, Shadow took his friends along to have a look at his stock of ponies. He was much delighted to find that his personal herd had increased substantially while he had been gone an entire cycle of the seasons. He found, to his great delight, that he now possessed the number of fingers on a hand in Appaloosa stallions, as well as plenty of Appaloosa mares. There was also a certain stallion among his herd he believed to be almost identical to his sire, Sun Dancer, whom he immediately took into his personal care.

He also presented Many Arrows and Spotted Feather with Appaloosa stallions. He said, "I would like to give my excellent friends the gift of an excellent pony, and may they serve you well."

They were both very moved and grateful at his show of kindness toward them.

They spent the following lighttime breaking their ponies into allowing themselves to be ridden. It took a lot of doing, given the fact that they were highly spirited animals. Everyone enjoyed the show, and in the end, it turned out well. No one was seriously injured, although the satisfying result did not come without pain and bloodshed.

Shadow and his friends, as well as many of the other men of the Palus band, toured about the area over the time following Shadow's return.

"This is great pony country that your people have, as we can clearly see how they flourish," Many Arrows expounded.

"I have been looking to see this Mother River of which you speak. It must be around here somewhere to be seen?" Spotted Feather inquired.

Black Eagle understood the look of suspense he saw in his countenance. "We shall gather for a journey to the great river as soon as the cold time has passed. It is a sight you must see while you are among us."

Spotted Feather grunted an approval, followed by a nod in recognition of what he had seen and heard in Black Eagle's response.

The following lighttime, the weather began to get cold, and everyone stayed near to camp. As the time progressed, it got colder and colder, and then it snowed and it snowed some more, until there was a significant amount in depth.

It had quickly become time to go into the cold weather mode and to get along as best as they could, which turned out to be quite well.

There had been an abundance to store away, and there was plenty for everyone.

It was a time of appreciation for what the Life Giver had provided for them. They felt a sense of fulfillment in their existence. If there was more to life, they could not imagine what it could be. The circle of life would meet their needs as long as they had the persistence and patience. It was commonly known.

So the cold time went on being filled in with the daily chores and preparations. As much storytelling as could be fit in was also the typical occurrence.

It gave Spotted Feather and Many Arrows opportunities to show their abilities of captivating their audience's full attention. They both did well enough at it to get requests for further opportunities as well.

One evening, when Many Arrows was telling of past cold times in the camp of the Absaroke and was relating a story about hunting on snowshoes, Shadow had to interrupt him, because he didn't understand these snowshoes. Others also went on to enforce the ignorance of this reference.

Before the evening was all said and done, Many Arrows had managed to finish his story, but not before he had given a complete explanation of what snowshoes were and how they were constructed.

Many Arrows never did get around to making a pair of snowshoes because the snow never did get unmanageable. They were able to get about sufficiently without such things.

So the cold time went on, with all looking forward to the warming time.

As it was with this area of the world, the warming time slowly began to make its appearance. All of creation in the region was poised to receive it. The people and plants and animals all waited for the change that was needed. All were aware as it began to develop. Not just by the warmth on the face, from the peering sun rays that would break through, but the transformations that went on all about, due solely to the just right placement of the sun. The grass and flowers seemed to show an immediate response to the change, and then it was not only felt and seen but also was literally smelled all about them.

Thanks to the Life Giver once again, as the plants and animals and people all offered up their praise.

As the change of weather progressed toward a warming, there naturally began to occur more activity everywhere and by every living thing.

When Black Eagle decided that the time had come to call for a hunting party to strike out in the direction of the Mother River, he was having a hard time locating Shadow to inform him of his decision. Eventually, he was found in the company of a young woman called Running Wild and was rather evasive on how he had been spending his time.

Once Shadow had been told of his father's idea for the hunt, he went about telling others to prepare. This news came as a breath of life-giving air to many, and none more so than Many Arrows and Spotted Feather.

CHAPTER 10

A STRANGE TALE

A large party left the village with anxiousness and much excitement. It included Spotted Feather and Many Arrows. All during the cold time, the stories of the Mother River had been added too, to the point of it being larger than their imaginations could hold.

Just riding out in a new direction on a fine day, on their fine ponies, made their hearts glad beyond just a mere description.

The young stallions that the companions rode weren't mortal enemies, but they weren't the best of friends either, and none liked being behind the other. There was a built-in competition between them, and they kept trying to outpace each other. There also had to be a degree of separation between, in an attempt to prevent them from kicking and biting one another. Being excellent horsemen, they were able to work with the situation well enough. But after a while, they knew that they were going to have to let their steeds have it out in a test of speed.

At a point, they stopped holding them back and as soon as one of them broke, they all bolted in pursuit of the lead.

They ran all out for a long distance over the endless rolling hills, until the ponies began to tire. It was give-and-take a lot of the way, but they all had to agree that Dancer Too, as Shadow had named his pony, had the edge over his cousins.

Many Arrows had named his pony Sparrowhawk, after his particular band of Absaroke. Spotted Feather had named his pony Storm, saying that it just came naturally to him after feeling the power that it always exhibited.

They spent their travels racing to and fro throughout the light-time, having great fun. The others joined in when they cared to. It added to the pleasure of the journey. They also had plenty of extra fresh mounts, if at any time they felt that their preferred mount needed the time to recuperate.

While they traveled, Black Eagle began to speak of their neighbors, the Waptailmin. He emphasized that even though they weren't a real large tribe, although larger than their band of Nimipu, they were a very fine, brave, and dignified people, and he always tried to respect their right of territory.

He said these things to inform Spotted Feather and Many Arrows, of which his own people were well aware. "I don't believe we will have any problems while visiting their homelands, but just to make you aware that we are not the only people traveling this area," Black Eagle concluded as they progressed toward nearing their destination.

The following lighttime, they received their first sighting of the Mother River. Her wide sweeping image was always a sight to behold. Many Arrows and Spotted Feather stopped and stared for a time, not speaking, just partaking in the impressive panorama before them.

Spotted Feather spoke first. "So there are fish as big as trees in there, with their bones on the outside?"

Black Eagle looked over at Shadow, whom he noticed was chuckling to himself.

"Well, there are very large fish in that river with their bones on the outside," replied Black Eagle.

"Not as big as some trees," responded Shadow. They all decided to leave it at that, although Spotted Feather couldn't conceal his look of possibly being the focus point of a practical joke.

Black Eagle made the decision. "We'll camp here and travel down to the river at early time."

When they awoke, it was fine weather, cloudless and as warm as they had experienced since the cold time thus far.

Shadow, Spotted Feather, Many Arrows, and several other braves left for the river. Black Eagle stayed in camp, not ready to go anywhere at that time.

Cloud Shadow and his companions approached the Mother River at the point where the Waptailmin's Narrow River and the Winding River were going to merge into the Mother River. When they arrived at a certain location along the river's edge, they noticed movement. Then as they focused on what had caught their attention, they came to realize that they were peering at a group of bathers made up of women and children. At the same time, the observers understood what it was they were seeing. The bathers realized they were being looked upon by strangers. Then there were cries and screams as the frightened bathers made a hasty withdrawal from the location they had previously occupied.

At first, Shadow felt uncomfortable, like he had done something wrong. But he soon got over it, knowing that they had just happened upon them with no intent of spying.

Shadow responded to the incident by saying, "Let us return to our camp. I think we have had enough to look at already this early time." There was some laughter and some startled looks from a few as they turned and headed back to the place of the rest of their party.

It wasn't long after their return to camp, and Shadow related of what had happened to Black Eagle. There appeared on the near horizon a large host of mounted warriors. There became a major unrest within the Nimipu camp at the sight of them.

"Waptailmin," stated Black Eagle. Then turning to Shadow, he calmly spoke, "You and I will ride out to meet them."

Then he and Shadow mounted and proceeded in the direction of the opposing force. When they got up close to the Waptailmin, it was obvious that they were in a state of agitation. With their painted faces and angry countenances, they confronted the pair of representatives of the Nimipu hunting party.

Near the center of the opposing line of warriors, there was one who gave off the appearance of the head of this force assembled to confront them. He was a very impressive figure indeed as he sat upon a beautiful black and white pinto pony.

He himself was a large man and gave off an aura of great strength in body and mind. He had fine features beneath a full eagle feather headdress and breast shield made of bone, holding a long lance under his strong arm, tipped at a downward angle.

As Black Eagle and Shadow approached, they signed for peace. The intimidating figure gave a nod in recognition of the gesture. Black Eagle continued to sign that they meant no trespass and were looking to find some sustenance after a long cold time. Again, there was a slight nod of affirmation.

Then this leading figure began to speak as he signed, "I am Red Dreamer. I am strong medicine. I lead this party to see who it is that has entered our lands and frightened our women and children away from the river. I see that you are not a threat and believe you come in peace. The warriors will leave, and I will stay to know more of you." After this, he gave a signal, and the party turned away toward their village.

Then Black Eagle signed as he spoke. "I am Black Eagle, and this is my son Cloud Shadow, and we welcome to know more of you as well. Come." He ended with a gesture toward their small camp.

Red Dreamer seemed very interested in their camp, carefully observing everything about him. When he was introduced to Many Arrows and Spotted Feather, he seemed amazed to find them in his country. Having been to buffalo country himself, he was well aware of who they were a part of. Although, for such a powerful figure, he gave off a splendid disposition. He seemed to enjoy meeting everyone, and everyone was enjoying him in return.

Soon, Black Eagle, Shadow, and Red Dreamer got off by themselves and began to confer concerning many things.

After they had covered the preliminaries, Red Dreamer began to relate some of his spiritual experiences, of which he went on to make known he was renowned for, and he had obtained his name and position of one who has great medicine.

Then Dreamer went on, signing as he spoke, telling of how his people have always looked to the Great Spirit, who could be found to inhabit the great mountain, pointing off toward what was the prominent mountain in the land of the setting sun, as he spoke the word "Tahoma."

He continued with the story, saying that sometime back, he had made a journey to the mountain to seek more understanding for his people. While there on the mountain, after a time of prayer and fasting, he was overcome by a dream trance wherein he received many visions. Of these visions, there was one that he felt would be of great interest to all the native peoples of the area.

By this time, he had their unflinching attention. He went on to tell of the coming of a white-skinned people who would take away their way of life and all that they had, forever.

Once Red Dreamer had made his point, which he did very well, there was a silence that followed after. It was more than anyone dared to imagine.

"How can these things be so?" Shadow signed as he spoke. Dreamer just held a stoic pose that indicated that he believed he was just the messenger.

After these serious considerations, Dreamer signed that he would like for any in the party that would want to join his people for an extended hunt into the not-too-distant mountain forests for deer and elk and bear, to feel welcome to come along, and his people would aid them in any way they could.

It was soon agreed that they would very much like to take Dreamer up on the offer. Preparations were made to leave the following early time. Black Eagle and several others of the party stayed behind to care for the ponies, which included the favored young Appaloosa stallions.

They parted early, not long after first light, to swim the ponies they had chosen for the trip across the merging rivers.

CHAPTER 11

Vision Confirmation

Once the party had crossed over to the other side to find themselves in Waptailmin country, they were met there by Dreamer.

Not long after leaving in the direction of their village, they noticed a commotion taking place by the river's edge. Red Dreamer led them closer to bear witness to an amazing sight. They watched several men and ponies attempt to pull a fish from the river. It appeared to be as big as a tree. After a prolonged struggle, they succeeded. It was a huge ugly fish with its bones on the outside that was as long as several ponies in line from nose to tail.

Shadow would have gloated to Many Arrows and Spotted Feather if he wouldn't have been so taken by the sight himself. Dreamer made mention that it was the biggest he had ever seen. After some time of gawking, Spotted Feather managed to say, "Is it good to eat?"

After which Shadow replied, "The best, you'll find out."

Eventually, they managed to pull themselves away from the intriguing circumstance that had just played itself out before them. Spotted Feather and Many Arrows once again reflected on the events that they had been subjected to since their coming to Shadow's land.

When they came to the village, they made their way to Dreamer's tipi lodge, where there were gathered a select group of hunters and elders to greet them. After a period of visiting, a meal was served.

Dreamer made it known that the meat was that of the giant fish. They all partook, and it was relished by all.

Spotted Feather felt compelled to say, "Very, very good." And then he quickly resumed his devouring of the delicacy.

The following lighttime, they left on their hunt. As they continued their travel, Dreamer conveyed to them that they would be going to a place where the first of many meadows existed, each a little more of an elevation than the other as they continued up the mountain trail.

The weather was clear, fresh, and comfortable.

Dreamer went on to let them know that this was a place of abundance and that it was right that they should have what they could bring down. Also, he enjoyed their company, being the upright people he found them to be. "There is plenty for all, as it was intended to be," he went on to explain.

The invited guests all gave their appreciation for the hospitality and conveyed their pleasure in the company of their fine hosts.

After a couple sleeps of travel, they had made their way high up into the forests and came to the first meadow Dreamer had spoken of. Dreamer then informed them that they still had a short distance to go before they would come to the meadow he had determined for their camp.

When they arrived at the location for their camp, looking up, there wasn't much to be seen because of the tall evergreen trees, but looking down, there was a magnificent vista of grassy rolling hills as far as the eye could see. Also, there was the great Mother River, making her way through her lands.

All the hunters started making camp, which included an adequate amount of lean-to structures for keeping the dew off them while they slept.

They had a pleasant evening in camp as they continued their getting to know one another, developing deeper friendships.

Dreamer took particular interest in Shadow's telling of the encounter with the Siksika the previous warm time, as did the others who had not heard of it.

Many Arrows had a considerable bit of telling to add to the Siksika story, his people having been in mortal conflict with them since time immemorial.

In the end, all had to agree of the danger that existed wherever the Siksika reigned.

Shadow ended the discussion on the subject by signing as he spoke. "I do not like the idea of attacking others, but I do plan to see Gray Wolf again, if he lives, and exact a price for his hateful ways. There was something in his eyes when he stated it. No one doubted him.

Dreamer changed the subject back to the hunt. He told of how he believed the elk would inhabit the meadow they had passed as they made their way up the trail. He felt certain they would feed there in the very early time, and he laid out a strategy accordingly. He would send a person ahead to see when the elk entered the meadow then get back word to the rest of the hunting party. Once they knew of the presence of the herd, they would approach the meadow in a wide berth at the meadow's perimeter. Then when he cast his arrow, they would all join in to take down as many as they were able.

At early time, they made their way to the proximity of the desired location before there was any trace of the needed light that they were waiting on. The scout had already been sent ahead and was in place to observe the meadow for the initial appearance of the awaited prey.

There was that eager anticipation upon those whose skill would soon be called on. Able archers all, they needed only the hopeful situation to present itself for them to enact the desired outcome.

After some time, the scout returned, giving them the good news that there was a substantial herd grazing in the meadow.

They then went about carrying out the plan that had been formulated. All went well, and soon they were in place.

The elk were occupied with their feeding, heads down, unconcerned with their surroundings, feeling confident and at ease with nothing but themselves stirring.

Red Dreamer's was the first arrow. It found its mark with a hail of arrows following. Within a short time, there laid strewn about nearly half the elk that had been present, either dead or dying.

The hunters were very happy with their efforts that had paid off so well. They spent the day butchering and bundling the meat into the hides.

The bounty was packed up onto ponies and immediately sent on a trip back to the village, with sufficient left for the remaining hunters.

They had a hearty feast later, with a celebration of thanks to the Life Giver, for they were all believers.

The following early time, they split up into pairs and set out to hunt black bear. They were fully aware of how nourishing bear meat was, and the fat was always a most welcome treat to be used for many things.

Spotted Feather and Many Arrows went together, and Shadow and Dreamer teamed up, as the remaining hunters did the same.

They all understood that as they scoured the area, if they came within proximity of the bear, the bear would climb a tree where the hunters could then easily bring it down.

While Dreamer and Shadow were hunting, Shadow began to inquire of him concerning spiritual things, remembering what had been conveyed by him on the day of their first encounter. Dreamer obliged him on various things to do with visions, spirit guides, and wisdom with knowledge that comes with understanding concerning difficult matters. He went on to tell how he believed all these things were accessible to him at the foot of Tahoma.

Shadow decided that he wanted to make the trip to the mountain and let it be known to Dreamer, who told him he was happy to know it and would be glad to be his guide there.

During the course of the hunt, there had been several bears taken, along with a few deer that had been caught unawares. The usual butchering took place, and then all the hunters went back down the trail toward home, except Shadow and Dreamer. Spotted Feather and Many Arrows let Shadow know that they would wait for his return.

Shadow and Dreamer kept minimal provisions and set off for higher ground. The Nimipu did not typically come to this area, and Shadow had not heard tell of this place in his memory. It had certainly become an area to be traveled on foot not long after they began the climb. The higher they went, the more enchanted and entranced Shadow became with this mountain paradise, the meadows and alpine lakes and sparkling streams, and the many varied colorful flowers and snowcapped peaks. Dreamer also seemed to thrive in this element. He glowed with a countenance of health and well-being.

They stopped toward the end of the lighttime and took rest. The air was colder, and they kept a large fire going throughout the darktime. Before they fell asleep, they heard the snarling growl of a panther in the not-too-distant darkness. To most persons alone in the forest, this could be an unsettling experience, but to these brave souls, it only added to the atmosphere of the place.

The following early time, they managed to trap a few brook fish and skewered and roasted them over the fire for their meal. They then set off for their final leg of the trek to Tahoma. As they began to approach the mountain of this wondrous place, they agreed to separate and to meet back at the location where they now stood. They both knew that they would be able to commune better if they were apart from one another.

As Shadow drew closer to the mountain, he took notice of some separate crags that he felt would be a good area to hold up at for his purpose. Once he had gotten to the desired position, he unhurriedly began to pray for more understanding on the many things that he wondered of in this life. With his commanding view of Tahoma, he tried to stand as straight and tall as he could while offering up praise and adoration to the Life Giver. To Shadow, the mountain was symbolic of the greatness of the Creator.

After opening his heart and mind to this place and time, he caught some movement from the corner of his eye. He turned to see what it could be, and his eyes revealed to him a family of mountain goats, consisting of a female and a couple of kids. As his natural instincts as a hunter first took hold, he thought of trying to take down one before they moved out of distance. Within moments, he began to think on the great goat of his quest in the Wallowa Mountains, not so many winters past. He thought about how he had received the strong impression that he was his spirit guide, which Shadow took to heart in a very serious manner. As he watched the goats move about in their next to impossible location, he once again became overwhelmed with a feeling of uplifting encouragement. He also had a most convincing feeling of providence at work in his life, and that it was certain that he was meant to be here at this time. "Thank you, Great Spirit, for touching my life in this way," Shadow spoke out loud.

The goats made their way out of Shadow's view, and not long after, he began to make his way along the perilous route back that would lead him to the meeting place with Dreamer.

When they were reunited, it was a happy reunion. Both had been given some personal attention in a profound way. Not long after heading back, they held over for another sleep before leaving again. They knew that Spotted Feather and Many Arrows had been waiting for them farther down the trail and did not want to keep them overly long.

Not long after their travels, they encountered the waiting pair of companions. Again, there was the feeling of joy and gladness in their joining, finding that all was well, as they hoped it would be.

Shadow made it known that he felt it important that they should be getting home as soon as they were able. He was also having longing thoughts for the one called Running Wild. Many Arrows and Spotted Feather also expressed the need to return to their homelands, of which they had been discussing while waiting for Shadow's return.

CHAPTER 12

The Coming and the Going

When they had gotten back to the Waptailmin village, they remained there for a couple sleeps, just for the rest.

Shadow then informed Dreamer that they would be leaving at first light.

When the time came for them to depart, there was a ceremony of sorts, with Shadow putting a lot of emphasis on conveying his strong friendship toward the Waptailmin people and with Red Dreamer in particular. He asked him to feel free to visit the Palus band's village as often as he cared to. Dreamer conveyed the same back to Shadow with genuine sincerity. Again, Shadow had had the good fortune to be able to establish another group of friends and allies for himself and his people.

When Shadow arrived, there was a flurry of excitement once again. Black Eagle and Fawn and his new love, Running Wild, greeted him with affection. His younger sister, Brook, and brother, Talon, also showed their joy at seeing him again as well.

While in the process of getting caught up with all that had gone on in their absence, Shadow was informed that the Waptailmin had been very generous in giving the Nimipu a significant share of the bounty that had been taken, which Black Eagle had transported back with him.

The following lighttime, Spotted Feather and Many Arrows said their goodbyes, with much affection on all sides. Invitations of reunions were exchanged, with Shadow saying, "We are brothers in our hearts, and we will meet again."

At this, they departed, riding their young Appaloosa stallions, with their other ponies trailing behind. There was an escort with farewells for a while along the way.

After his companions had departed, Shadow turned most of his focus to Running Wild. She had been given her name as a child as she had been somewhat incorrigible then, never allowing others to place her to task or anything else that she didn't have a mind to do. Although that was all behind her now, as she had become a well-respected member of the band, being very helpful in any way that was needed.

She was no longer a child but undoubtedly a woman, and an attractive one as well, with a sweet disposition. Not that she was tamed in every sense but matured and self-controlled. She had the winning combination that finally won over any self-restraint that Shadow might have been trying to hang onto.

When the hunting party had returned from the previous trip to buffalo country, they had brought back many hides, and Fawn began to prepare some for a tipi lodge for Shadow and his woman. Running Wild had been recruited to assist her, and it was becoming an anticipated event for its completion.

In the meanwhile, Shadow and Running Wild would have to steal away to be alone together. They were happy, and it all was the way they hoped for themselves. Life was good in this land of plenty, the place the Great Spirit had provided for them.

At that particular time, there was a large party returning from a foraging for huckleberries in the Small mountains. It was a rather long trip to make, so they took full advantage by taking a lot of women and children and containers and ponies. Everyone welcomed the bounty of berries. They enjoyed them fresh as well as dried. They mixed them into some of the pemmican that was produced as a rule each season before the cold time set in. It was one of the rare sweet treats for them in their lives and was looked forward to with relish.

The women were also busy with their skills in producing clothing and footwear, of which there was no end. All the hides had to be tanned so as to be turned into workable leather.

The men spent their time making bows and arrows, along with always striving to improve the quality of both. They did the same with flint and quartz stone blades that were needed for knives and hatchets, as well as some longer handled axes. They also made war clubs for combat when needed. They could not afford to be slack in this aspect.

All these things Shadow strived to be proficient at, as did the other men as well. Then of course, there were the ponies. Always, the ponies needed to be looked after. They kept the desired stallions separated so they wouldn't injure each other. They matched up breeding pairs and gelded those they didn't care to have breeding with their mares, and there was a continual breaking of those who came of age. They felt it was prudent to be able to ride any of the ponies if needed.

To Shadow, life was full but not overwhelming, simple but not boring. He also was glad for Running Wild. She had become such a joy that he did not know could be. He had developed a genuine interest in the opposite sex naturally, but it wasn't until he had come to experience his woman that he found a pleasure that made for many fulfilling times together. Also, the tipi lodge had been completed, which provided ample time for making love.

It was still the hot time, and Shadow's uncle, Big Cat, had come to visit. There were many festivities as the people took full advantage of the season. Big Cat expressed his disappointment at hearing of the departure of their previous guests, Many Arrows and Spotted Feather. He was someone who was familiar with their tribes and appreciative of them.

Soon it was the time of the red meat fish again, as they began to fill the rivers to be taken at will by the Nimipu with their fishing skills. It was always another busy time, catching them and filleting the meat to dry for preservation for the coming cold time.

It always seemed that being so busy brought the cold time on more quickly, but at least they were ready for it.

Not long after Big Cat had departed to the Wallowa band, the cold time began to set in once again in earnest. Shadow and Running Wild enjoyed keeping one another warm in their new large and spacious lodge. All the time Shadow knew, but never said, that come the warm time, he would be leaving again for Siksika country. He had unfinished business there that needed tending to.

When that time did eventually come around, Shadow found it difficult to tell Running Wild. He knew that she would take it hard. She seemed so happy, but he was not one to be put off from something once he had made up his mind. Finally, one lighttime when they were alone, he said, "I've determined to be going to buffalo country soon."

There was a pause before she questioned, "Why?"

He responded, "To hunt."

"We have just been joined together, and now you will be leaving?" Running Wild asked in a sad voice.

"I did not plan that we would be joined together. It just happened, but I did plan to be going back to buffalo country when the weather changed." He had been dreading telling her. Now the time was here, and it was as difficult as he supposed it to be. "I will be back by the coming of the next cold time. Now that we are joined together, I am glad. This is important to me. You'll just have to trust my way," he said.

"No, I do not have to," she replied. "But I will, because you are that important to me."

Shadow supplied himself with the food and provisions he would need and left on his Appaloosa stallion, Dancer Too, and an Appaloosa gelding especially chosen from his herd. He went off with mixed feelings about what laid ahead and what he was leaving behind, but he knew he needed to focus and channel his senses, and so that was what he did.

He had discussed his plans with Black Eagle and his uncle Big Cat while he was with them. In the end, they just advised him to use the wisdom the Great Spirit had given him and wished him success and a safe return. Also, he could see the concern on their faces at the extreme danger he would be up against.

This time, he decided to take the old Nimipu trail, continuing past Kamiah, the sacred site of the heart of the monster, then go on much farther still, gradually turning toward the land of the rising sun. He planned to come up beneath where he believed he would find Long Hair's encampment. It was a place Many Arrows called Absaroka. It was a long journey, but he was a traveler, as much as anyone would venture to be. He and his ponies traveled over and through many different types of terrain as well as water. It was all fine country though as far as Shadow was concerned. It was abundant in beauty and animal life. He never lacked for fresh meat.

There were weather issues he had to deal with—strong winds, driving rains, snow flurries, and hail. But he also had those calm and sweet lighttimes, along with clear starry darktimes with heavenly moonshine. No matter what the element he was in, it was his element, being one with the heavens and the earth.

He took many opportunities to bathe along the way in so many streams, rivers, and lakes. He shared the waterways with the animals, fish, and fowl.

Once, he was almost thrown in among a cluster of rattlesnakes that Dancer had reared away from. He and the ponies and the snakes were all startled at the encounter.

Shadow began to ponder the idea of a snake with a noisemaker on the end of its tail. He was definitely glad for the noisemakers, but it did seem strange to him. This wondrous place his Earth Mother certainly was.

At times, while he traveled, he would reflect to his time with Running Wild and their lodge, where they spent many times together under the robes, making love. How pleasant the remembering, as he pressed on with the trek.

Many sleeps came and went, many camps he had in his memories, and many sights he did see. Life was full.

As he traveled along, he thought about something Many Arrows had told him. This place Absaroka was located near an area that had many pools of different colors that bubbled and smoked, and hot water that spewed from the ground. He felt that he would really like to see that place.

Chapter 13

Old Friends and New Places

Finally, there came the time that Shadow believed he was coming near to where he would find the Absaroke village. He began to look for signs. Then one early time, as he peered into the horizon, he saw many streams of smoke drifting upward. He knew it was from a large village. He sought a vantage point where he could get a good look without being seen. When he had acquired the vantage point he sought for, he looked upon a splendid sight of many very white tipis, exquisitely decorated, set in a fine location of lush grass with a meandering stream. It was so peaceful and sublime.

Shadow knew at once it was the Absaroke village. No one else had tipis that looked like that. He did not worry to proceed into the encampment. He moved on down toward the village. And not long after he had allowed himself to be seen, a group of riders came toward him. A fine-looking group they were, with beautiful ponies ridden by excellent representatives of their tribe, the Absaroke brave.

They were composed and did not feel threatened at all by his presence. At a point, they stopped and waited as he continued to move in their direction. They took notice of his Appaloosa ponies, and they came to understand that a Nimipu brave was approaching. They gave the sign for peace and rode up to him. Their first action was to escort him to Many Arrows, who also owned an Appaloosa stallion.

Many Arrows was thrilled to see his Nimipu brother. Shadow was filled with the affection that had been working its way to the forefront of his thoughts every day that drew him closer to this place and moment. They embraced in a respectful and dignified way.

"I know why you have come to our country, but I feel honored that you have come to my home so soon," said Many Arrows.

"It is so that I have another purpose for being in these lands, but it is also a pleasure to be here with you now," replied Shadow.

"Come to my lodge and rest and refresh yourself, my friend," Many Arrows requested.

There was time spent resting and catching up on events that had transpired since they had last been together. Shadow made it known that he had taken a woman to be his and that they got along well together. Many Arrows let him know that he was glad for him, and then he went on to inform Shadow how he had had the good fortune to take a couple of sisters into his lodge to be his companions and a help to him. Shadow had certainly noticed the young women and now understood their relationship.

The time came for Many Arrows to ask the question, "What is it we can do for you while you are here?"

Shadow let him know. "I would very much like to visit the place of the smoking water."

Many Arrows was happy to hear him ask that and, without hesitation, agreed to take him there.

Many Arrows made the arrangements, and it wasn't long before Shadow, along with a small escort of Absaroke braves, headed to this mysterious place, led by Many Arrows.

The following lighttime, they had come to the perimeter of the land that never slept. When they actually entered the area of the many smoking pools of different colors, Shadow felt that those of his homeland would think it must have been a dream that he was telling of. He himself was thinking, *This is very strange. What kind of power is in this place?*

He did not want to get too close, for it all made him very uneasy. While he stared and contemplated and was deep in thought, a large jet of water came bursting toward the sky. Dancer reared, and

Shadow nearly came off his back, being very startled. Many Arrows roared with laughter as did the other braves, having lured Shadow to that very spot in anticipation of the coming event.

"How did you do that?" Shadow exclaimed! He was thinking it was some kind of joke that they were able to pull off.

"I did not do anything but bring you to this place, but I did know that it does that quite often and hoped it would. You should have seen your face," replied Many Arrows, and then he burst out laughing again.

After a while, Shadow recovered and had a good laugh at himself as well.

Many Arrows suggested that they continue farther in the same direction because there was a mountain range that he wanted him to see, and he felt Shadow would appreciate it. They made camp after some more travel. Shadow was somewhat amazed at how much buffalo, bear, elk, wolves, ravens, ducks, swans, beavers, and other small fur-bearing animals inhabited the area. No one should go without in this place, he could plainly see. Also, he could see how they would always have to fight to hold on to it. Any who had less would desire this land of plenty.

The following lighttime, they came into view of the Knife Edge mountain range. Again, Shadow was impressed, almost beyond mere expression. Finally, he added, "This is a wonderful sight to be enjoyed. Thank you for bringing me here. It is in my heart as a thing of beauty to recall in my reflections of places and times."

"I am glad to hear you say that, my friend. Let us make camp here and rest before our return trip," Many Arrows replied as he gestured toward a nearby location while looking for any movement about them other than their own.

The ponies seemed to be restless at times during the darktime. When they awoke, Many Arrows stated, "I believe there are others besides ourselves in the area." It immediately caused Shadow to be on the alert for some evidence of what Many Arrows had inferred.

Soon after breaking camp and hitting the trail, the others came into view. Many Arrows proclaimed, "Utes, just move along as if we aren't concerned with their presence."

That was what they did while the Utes, who outnumbered them, looked on, apparently no more concerned about their presence. They kept on their way as if the encounter never happened.

It didn't take too long to make it back to Absaroka, and there, Shadow again spent his time resting and visiting with his friends, which included spending time with Long Hair, seeking any wisdom that he might impart to him.

The time came for Shadow to say his goodbyes, which he graciously did, thanking them profusely for their kindness and goodwill. He expressed his hopes that they all should meet again.

He made his way out of their village, passing the Absarokes' excellent herd of ponies, when there was a bit of commotion within the herd. He then turned to look, as did his stallion and gelding. They all gazed upon a lone Appaloosa stallion in a show of recognition to some of his parting family. They watched as he whinnied and pranced about.

"Sparrowhawk," Shadow said. "You make us proud." His heart swelled. Then to his surprise, Dancer and the gelding neighed back to him in response. "What a close family we have, my children!" he exclaimed with joy. "Enrich the herd, Sparrowhawk!" he added as they proceeded on their journey.

Not long on the trail, Shadow began to reflect on his parting discussion with Many Arrows concerning the mission that Shadow was set upon. Many Arrows had implored him that if he was going to attempt to end Gray Wolf's life, he should be sure and provide himself a way of escape. Even Shadow had to concede that it presented a very real doubt if this could be done with any degree of certainty.

After several sleeps, Shadow was coming into the vicinity of where Little Bear had met his untimely end. He made his way to the exact location, wanting to pay his respects to his longtime close friend. There was still a remnant of his robe in the tree, where Many Arrows and he had placed Little Bear's corpse. It wasn't anything that could be recognized, but it did not matter, for he had passed on to the other side. Shadow said a few words to his missing his companionship, ending with "I'll see you on the other side, my brother."

Shadow then moved into the forest at the base of the mountain range. He wanted to get out of the open and find somewhere to stop and prepare himself for the trial of his wits in the endeavor he was about to undertake.

Dancer carried him as far as he and the gelding could travel due to the steep climb in elevation. They managed to get near to the base of some tall rocky crags that Shadow felt would shelter them from the wind and was not a place where wayfarers would be passing through.

After he had set up camp, he began to reflect and found himself thinking about his friend Spotted Feather and their first meeting not far from where he was now. He very much would like to be able to pay him a visit, but he felt that he wouldn't most likely due to the circumstances surrounding his objective and the probabilities of its outcome.

The following lighttime, while waiting around camp, he made the decision to climb the crags that were near and seek the higher ground for the benefits that inhabit such places.

CHAPTER 14

THE RECKONING

He hobbled the ponies with every intention of not being away from them for long. He began to climb what appeared to be an animal trail he had found. Higher and higher he climbed, all the while feeling the exhilaration that came with the freshness of the higher elevation. Yet still higher he climbed to where the view became intoxicating. How he enjoyed the high country as he had come to understand through experience.

Finally, he arrived at a place where he decided to stop and seek after more inner strength to carry out his intentions. He let himself down onto a flat location, sitting cross-legged in a meditative manner. He began to recall the attack by Gray Wolf and his fellow braves on the Nimipu hunting camp and their attempt to murder them all at that time, as well as the needless death of his beloved pony, Sun Dancer. The pain that he felt and the vow he made to avenge the violation of their right to exist all came back to him in the form of righteous indignation that was seething.

It wasn't long after he felt he had succeeded in putting himself in the frame of mind it would take to accomplish his task, which was to make Gray Wolf regret the attack he orchestrated on his people.

He stood and adjusted himself physically, then prepared to descend in return to camp. He took a last look around, and once again, there appeared a family of goats among the steep cliffs above him.

They were farther away this time, but when he looked upon them in their daring trek through life, he was wholly filled with encouragement. "Lead me," he uttered while he continued to watch them make their way out of his line of sight. He felt a lift from the encounter and took it to heart throughout that late time.

When he awoke in the early time, he was ready to proceed toward his destination.

He traveled all that lighttime and got to the place where he knew that he was near to where he had left an arrow in the base of a tree, with every intention that Gray Wolf would find it and spend his time wondering if the owner would return to confront him.

Shadow held up under cover and waited until the darkness would conceal him. He was overcome with an anxiousness that he knew would not let him sleep. Throughout the darktime, he slowly and painstakingly made his way closer to the exact location where Many Arrows had told him he would find Gray Wolf's camp during the hot time.

When he felt confident that he was in proximity, he hobbled the ponies and proceeded closer on his own. He made his way to a place where he could remain until the light would once again allow a person to see. As the darkness slowly began to recede, the first thing he was able to determine was that there were people camped at the location he had staked out.

As his visibility became clearer, Shadow began to focus his attention on any activity he could make out. Within a relatively short period, he saw someone moving about, whom he believed could be Gray Wolf. As he continued to watch, he became convinced that the figure he saw with a slight limp was indeed the one he sought.

At that point in time, he couldn't see any way to get nearer to him without being found out. He tried to formulate a plan that would allow him to pull off an ambush for his intended target.

As he continued his observations, Gray Wolf made his way to a tipi lodge and entered. While Shadow waited, Gray Wolf stayed put, not making any showing of himself. Shadow had the uneasy feeling that he had probably just come out to make water or waste, and it was going to be sometime before he would come out again.

"Now what?" he whispered to himself. Then something unexpected happened. He watched a young woman of tender age slip out of the lodge carrying something in her hands.

Shadow was intrigued and stayed on her every move with his eyes as she made her way in his direction. Suddenly, he understood that she was heading for the nearby creek to get water. His mind was racing. "What to do, what to do?" he thought out loud in a whisper. Then he committed himself to an immediate course of action. He was going to abduct her. He pulled off his deer skin shirt and began to slice at it with his flint blade. After he felt he had what he needed, he waited until she knelt to draw water. So as was intended, he managed to abduct her.

Now Shadow was running for his life, from the pursuit of Gray Wolf and his braves, ever since his daughter Rain had arranged for his escape from captivity and a certain brutal demise.

There was a lot going through Shadow's mind. First and foremost was to get away, as far and fast as possible. But then he said, "What am I doing? I came here to take revenge on my enemy, and instead I'm running away." Shadow brought Dancer to a stop, along with the gelding, and made a sharp turn toward the lands of the Salish and his good friend Spotted Feather.

Gray Wolf was putting in every effort he could to catch up to Shadowhand. When he came to the place where his tracks had shown him stopping and then making an abrupt turn, he was surprised and suspicious of this sudden change of direction.

There was someone else who was in the chase, unbeknownst to the others. Rain had been fast on Gray Wolf's trail since he and the other braves had set out after Shadowhand. The reason why was a bewildering feeling to her, but it definitely was an obsession that seemed to hold power over her in the absolute.

Gray Wolf was in one train of thought: Shadowhand must die. This business of having someone out for his blood had gone as far as he was going to let it. The abduction of his only child was unforgivable. This must end, and he was going to end it.

Rain was filled with the thoughts from the inception of the capturing of Shadow that she had to prevent her father from killing him. She also did not want him to kill her father. After spending as much time with him as she had, she felt that the possibility of that was plausible.

Shadow was losing ground to his pursuers, and he was well aware that danger was stalking him. He was encumbered by the gelding and the burdens it bore, being Shadow's possessions. He was in no way inclined to let him or what he carried go in his haste.

He was also feeling bad about leading his enemies in the direction of the village of his friends. Although in assessment, he just naturally hoped for some form of assistance.

He pressed on, as did his pursuers, along with Rain, the one who held out hope for some acceptable outcome.

Finally, Shadow knew the time had come to make a stand. He believed that the Life Giver was aware of his plight and was not without faith that something could yet be done on his behalf.

He was traveling on open ground, but there were wooded areas on both sides of him where one could seek concealment, but he was well aware that they would track him to any place he sought to hide.

He came to a stop and dismounted. He then removed his war club from its place, along with his flint knife. He didn't want to get into an exchange of arrows with Gray Wolf and his men. He couldn't bear the thought of his beloved ponies being struck down. He hobbled the ponies where they stood and began to pray for strength and courage.

Within a relatively short time, the pursuers came in to view. Gray Wolf immediately came to a halt and pondered what he was seeing. He gave instructions to the braves that were with him to follow him nearer to where Shadow stood but not to attack him.

In the meanwhile, Rain came on the scene, still not known to anyone but herself. She dismounted and made her way along the forested area in the direction of Shadow.

There was also another party that looked on at the developing scenario on this narrow strip of open country. These onlookers happened to be the inhabitants of these parts, consisting of Spotted Feather and a fellow band of hunters.

Spotted Feather had already read the situation, that the brave with the Appaloosa ponies was indeed his good friend, Cloud Shadow, and that those who were slowly approaching him were Siksika, and their intentions looked ominous. He was working at deciding what would be the best course of action, when he decided that he and his companions would come into view, so they could bring a change of circumstance to those who were about to enter into mortal combat.

They slowly rode out of their concealment to the perimeter of the forested area, opposite of where Rain was still remaining out of sight.

When the Siksika saw the Salish band make their presence known, again they stopped. By this time, Gray Wolf was within walking distance of Shadowhand. He dismounted as well.

He collected his flint knife and war club and moved closer toward Shadow.

Shadow thought, *It all comes down to this.* Gray Wolf had an obvious unmistakable limp. They both locked eyes with one another. A more determined look was not possible by either opponent. With a war club in one hand and a knife in the other, they faced each other. Shadow was younger and taller, with plenty of strength. Gray Wolf was stocky with a barrel chest and broad shoulders and was powerful looking. His bangs were cut straight just above the eyes, making his large head appear somewhat square, with a firm wide mouth and small piercing eyes.

Shadow didn't feel intimidated though. It wasn't the first time that he had looked into those eyes. The others stood their ground, looking on.

Rain was frantic with the feeling of impending doom.

Gray Wolf charged at Shadow, bringing his club in a high and wide downward swing, aimed at Shadow's head. Shadow attempted to block the strike with his own club, and it was pulled from his grip with the impact and landed at their feet. He also brought his knife up at the same time. And as Gray Wolf's arm continued downward, it came across the blade. The blade cut his arm badly and caused him to drop his club as well. He then lunged at Shadow with the point of his blade directed toward Shadow's heart. Shadow managed to sidestep his forward motion and drive his elbow into his oncoming face, stunning Gray Wolf quite thoroughly. Shadow then kicked his feet out from under him, and Gray Wolf went down onto his back. As he went down, Shadow retrieved a club from off the ground. While Gray Wolf struggled to focus his eyes and recover his senses, Shadow raised the club to deliver the final blow. At that moment, there came a piercing scream that could not be ignored, and then a closer cry of, "Don't kill him! Don't kill him!" Rain was pleading.

Shadow didn't feel he had time to look around as he drove the club with all the power he could bring to bear onto the elbow of Gray Wolf's strong arm. Gray Wolf could in no way refrain from shrieking in agony, as all who were present knew he had just had his elbow shattered beyond repair. For a time, all was still, except for Gray Wolf's suffering.

CHAPTER 15

THE PRICE EXACTED

Rain slowly approached the spot where the combatants were. She was torn in her loyalties and emotions. The primary feeling that came over her was gratitude to Shadow for sparing her father's life. She also believed that overall, Shadow had been in the right and her father in the wrong. She grabbed Shadow's arm and placed her head on his shoulder.

Then a couple of Siksika braves dismounted and brought Gray Wolf's pony over and managed to get him mounted. Gray Wolf looked at Shadowhand and Rain standing together and glared at them both with hatred. Rain dropped her eyes, not in shame but that she did not want to enter what her father was attempting to convey. He was defeated. She knew that, even if he did not want to admit to it. Then the Siksika turned and rode away. Rain did not let go of Shadow. At that, Spotted Feather and his companions came to where they stood.

Spotted Feather exclaimed, "You never cease to amaze me, my friend!" And then he asked, "Who is this woman that holds you like she will never let you go?"

"How good it is to see you again, my good friend," replied Shadow. "This is my second wife, Rain."

"Your second wife? I didn't even know you had a first," stated Spotted Feather.

"We have much to get caught up on since we last saw each other," Shadow responded.

"Come and rest and refresh yourselves," relied Spotted Feather.

When they arrived at the Salish village, they found time to engage in specifics. Shadow began to convey all the subject matter of interest from the time that Spotted Feather and Many Arrows had left out from the Palus band encampment up till then.

Spotted Feather followed the tale with keen interest, and when it had been told, he retorted, "So you weren't even going to stop here and visit your old friend?"

"Of course, I wanted to, but the need to move on was important for a better chance at success," Shadow excused himself in a good-humored way.

"I forgive you. After all, here you are to share yours and your lovely wife's company with us," Spotted Feather concluded.

Shadow had kept Rain close by his side. He knew that she had been somewhat traumatized for a relatively lengthy time. He wanted to help her regain some feeling of security. He knew that until she did, it would be hard for him to come to know her in a more composed manner, which would show her true nature. Therefore, he would continue to try to help her become more adjusted to her new life with him as well as he could.

After the passing of some sleep times, Spotted Feather asked of Shadow and Rain to come on a not so long trek to the Salish Lake. He simply stated, "You will enjoy it there."

Rain and Shadow appreciated the offer, and the following lighttime, they left on their sightseeing trip. Spotted Feather was riding Storm, his Appaloosa stallion who typically spent his time at stud. In honor of Shadow's appearance among them, he brought the prized pony along.

By the time the sun was high, they came to the lake, and they spent a very pleasant time there. Shadow complimented the place profusely, being the very large and beautiful lake that it was.

Off in the distance, there were the obvious snowcapped mountains. Spotted Feather noticed Shadow peering toward them and said, "In those mountains are some wondrous places. I would also like to show you those places as well." Rain seemed to give some recognition to the topic.

Shadow stated, "I hope that will be possible for us someday also, my friend. It would be a fine time for us. I look for an opportunity that would allow it. Due to the time of the seasons, Rain and I will need to be leaving for home soon."

"Of course. Some other time, my friend," Spotted Feather replied.

Spotted Feather didn't speak it, but he had his concerns at the probability of being able to spend that time together. Shadow was also a little skeptical at that prospect. However, they both held out hope that there could be circumstances that would provide the opportunity.

When the time came for their leaving, there was a certain somberness attached to it. Although being matured individuals, they put it behind them and embraced the time for their sincerest appreciations for one another's friendships, with well wishes for the time to come. With that, Shadow and Rain said their farewells and left on their long trek home.

Shadow felt a lot better about the circumstances of his leaving buffalo country now as opposed to his previous attempt. "Guidance," he muttered to himself while getting a quizzical look from Rain. He smiled to her, and she in return smiled back.

They went along on the same course that he had taken with his companions, Many Arrows and Spotted Feather, some time ago. They stopped often, enjoying their time together. Shadow could not help but slip into periods of thinking on his relationship with Running Wild, still caring deeply for her.

Rain hadn't traveled all so far from the places of her memories, but being on a journey in an entirely new direction was a wonderful feeling to her. If a person were ever really free on this earth, she felt about as free as one could possibly feel.

Shadow felt a sense of freedom as well just by getting out of the self-imposed mode of revenge he had put on himself.

The lighttime was sweet, and the darktime sometimes sweeter. Rain was showing obvious signs of unwinding from the extreme stress she had been under. She sometimes referred to Shadow as good medicine. Mostly, those occasions occurred under the robes.

Shadow took time to do some exploring of areas unknown to him. He was of a mind to go to areas where others didn't or seldom do. Rain was more than willing, as long as Shadow was with her.

They had a fine time, bathing in many creeks and rivers, at times lying in the sun to dry themselves. Maybe they would travel some, maybe they wouldn't, but eventually they had completed that phase of their trip and began to come into the territory of the Nimipu.

After not much more travel, they came to the place where the Kooskia band made their home. As he had found it the last time, they pretty much wandered in with not much notice from the inhabitants. Once again, he inquired after his cousin, Yellow Jacket. This time, he was told that Yellow Jacket and a group of other braves had left that early time in pursuit of a band of Shoshone who had stolen away with a substantial number of Nimipu ponies the darktime before. At hearing this, he and Rain left the village to see if he could pick up the tracks of the pursuers or the thieves.

Shadow felt if he could be of help, he would. The tracks were not hard to find, and he and Rain followed at a fast pace. Rain was an excellent rider. There wasn't any need to slow down as they trailed after those who had already gone before them. She had her own pony, and he, riding Dancer, brought the gelding as well, not knowing how long this would entail.

As their chase took them in the direction of the old Nimipu trail that Shadow had taken to search for the Absaroke village, the sun began to set. He and Rain then came to a place where the Shoshone had held up to rest. It just happened that from where he and Rain had come to, they were not only able to see the Shoshone camp but could also make out where Yellow Jacket and his party were stopped as well.

Shadow believed that the Nimipu were waiting until first light to then try and swoop in and recoup their ponies.

Shadow began to formulate a plan. He and Rain would make their way around to the other side of the Shoshone camp and position themselves for the time so that when Yellow Jacket and his men swarmed in, he and Rain could already be driving their ponies back toward the Kooskia braves. It would allow his fellow tribe members to be in the position to deter any attempts by the Shoshone to stop the recovery of their ponies.

The primary obstacle that they were facing was the fast approaching darkness. He felt that if he and Rain were going to have a chance of getting to the desired location, they needed to do it right away. He indicated to her to follow him as he left out.

It took some patience, stealth, and hard work to get into position before the dawn, but they managed.

Shortly after they arrived and the light began to make an appearance, the area erupted into cries of challenge and surprise, along with the sounds of galloping ponies.

Shadow and Rain were poised for action, and they came racing from cover, directly at the confused herd, and began to drive them back in the direction they had come.

The Nimipu didn't initially know who they were, but upon seeing a man mounted on a Appaloosa with another in tow, along with a woman, both waving hides and hollering with the herd on the run in their direction, it seemed to be a positive thing.

The Shoshone mounted as quickly as they could and wanted to pursue after the herd, but with Yellow Jacket and the others rushing at them, they hightailed it in the opposite direction, not stopping for some while. As the Kooskia Nimipu gave up the chase, they headed back to lay claim to their stolen ponies.

When they caught up to the herd, Shadow and Rain were trailing behind it.

"You never cease to amaze me, cousin," Yellow Jacket flatly stated.

Shadow went on to explain how it was that they had come to be there, adding, "I'm sure you could have taken care of the problem yourselves, but we just thought we might be of some help."

Yellow Jacket responded with "You did well, and we thank you for your very helpful good timing, and we very much hope that you and your companion will pay us the honor of staying with us to rest and refresh yourselves, that we may hear of your other movements." He glanced over in Rain's direction.

While at camp, Shadow went on to tell of his exploits in the buffalo country and how it was that his traveling companion happened to be with him. Also, he went on to introduce her as his second wife.

"I didn't know you had a first wife," Yellow Jacket responded. It gave way to Shadow's telling of his taking Running Wild of the Palus band to be his wife not long before his departure to the buffalo country.

After Shadow had gotten his state of affairs up to Yellow Jacket's approval, Yellow Jacket went on to add how he was very impressed with Rain's participation in the plot to get back their ponies. He finished his oration by stating, "She is a woman to take pride in." Shadow helped Rain understand the compliment, and she appeared noticeably pleased.

The following lighttime, they left from the Kooskia village toward the home of the Palus band. Rain was once again enjoying the travel and changes of scenery. Shadow couldn't help but think about what the reaction of the village and his family, especially Running Wild, were going to be when he showed up with Rain. It wasn't all so uncommon for a man to take a second wife, but that usually happened after being sometime in the first relationship. At least several winters would be helpful. The idea being that the second wife would be of assistance with the many chores to be done.

Although, as with his first marriage, he hadn't planned either one of them. Rain had expressed similar concerns while on their long trek to Shadow's homeland, but he had assured her that all would be well. Although he felt certain that she had her doubts.

One thing his family had come to understand was that he had become a man not to be trifled with. If he said it, if he did it, one should take heed that he acted with authority within the space he occupied.

After some sleeps, since they had left the Kamiah area, they had gotten to a place where they could see the Palus encampment. The time of confrontment was fast approaching, and he and Rain were feeling the pressure.

They saw riders coming out to meet them. Shadow recognized one as his younger brother, Talon. He had done some springing up since he had last seen him. There were calls of "It's Shadow! It's Shadow! And there's a woman with him!"

"Who's that?" Talon asked as he drew near.

"I'll tell you later," Shadow responded as they rode into camp.

Rain felt awkward and out of place, like she knew she would. Right away, Black Eagle, Fawn, and Running Wild came up to where Shadow had dismounted.

"Who have you got with you?" asked Fawn while Shadow looked at Running Wild with a strange little smile on his face that portrayed his uneasiness.

Running Wild had a look of confusion and stubbornness at the same time. Shadow, without speaking, walked over and helped Rain off her pony. Not that she needed the help, but he thought it might help to reassure her. Then he walked over to Running Wild and placed both his hands on her shoulders and stared into her eyes to show that he saw only her. Then he took her hand in his and slowly walked over to where Rain stood. He took her hand into his free hand and spoke the word "Sisters."

Running Wild wanted to act out in some manner in protest, but only her deep feelings and respect for Shadow kept her from it.

Shadow looked around at the crowd that had gathered, and they looked stunned. Then they all heard the words "Oh, good, another sister!"

Shadow looked over at the source of the voice. He saw his little sister, Brook, standing there. Somehow, when everyone heard those words, a sense of relief fell upon the whole episode. Then for most of them, it was all about Shadow being home again.

Chapter 16

Shadow's Triumphant Return

When Black Eagle got close enough to Shadow to speak quietly to him, he said, "You are a brave man, my son." Then he patted him on the back.

Of course, there was much explaining to do, as the occasion permitted, and eventually it all came out, almost all.

The picture was painted for them to see, and everyone who heard of the telling was even more in awe of this one called Cloud Shadow. Everyone loved a good story, and this tale would be told around the lodges for ages to come.

Then there was the new family order within the Cloud Shadow lodge. It didn't come easy, but over time, Running Wild and Rain did become sisters.

Shadow stayed at home for several winters, not traveling farther than the nearby vicinity. Sometimes he would go visit Red Dreamer, with the Waptailmin. Sometimes Red Dreamer would come to visit at the Palus camp.

There were babies born to Running Wild and Rain. He had a daughter with Running Wild, for she had been with child while Shadow was away. She gave birth not all so long after his return. Then Rain gave birth to a son at the appointed time, since she had been living with the Palus band. Then Running Wild had just given birth to a son in very recent days.

The family of Cloud Shadow's lodge was growing, as was his herd of fine ponies. Life was good.

Running Wild named her daughter Beautiful Flower, and Shadow named Rain's son Raven, inspired by the gleam of his black hair. Then Shadow named Running Wild's son Wild Wind, for there was a tumultuous wind the night he was born, and to give recognition to his mother.

One lighttime, not long after the warm time had come once again, Dreamer came to their camp with a Waptailmin hunting party. He plainly stated that he and his companions were going to take the trail to the buffalo country.

He wanted to counsel with Black Eagle and Shadow concerning things to watch for on the journey and to inquire if there were any who wanted to accompany them on the hunt.

Black Eagle, by this time, was well along in age and didn't entertain the idea. Shadow stated that he was too involved with his family affairs at that time but wished them well, saying, "May the Great Spirit go before you and be an ever-present help in all you seek to do."

There were some younger Nimipu who very much desired to go. One of them was Talon, speaking confidently that he knew that it was right for him to go to the buffalo hunt at this time.

Black Eagle simply said, "Watch, for there is much danger in that place. Go and do well."

Shadow added, "Follow wisdom and avoid foolishness." His mother, Fawn, hoped he was up to the undertaking.

After final preparations, they left on the perilous journey, escorted by a host of well-wishers to a point where they were left to their own accord.

Shadow felt an uncomfortableness as they went out from among them at not being one of the hunting party, but not for long. He was surrounded by his wives and children, and he quickly went back to enjoying his home life.

It had been a pleasant warm time, with all contributing to the work that needed to be done so that it wasn't too difficult for anyone in particular. Life along the rivers was going well for those that called it home, and home it had become to Rain. She stayed busy with being a wife and mother and partner in all things pertaining to the band's activities. Learning the language was a naturally progressive occurrence, of which she became fluent.

As a mother of the village, it was necessary that she could give the proper verbal scolding when the many little urchins began to try and gain the mastery over any they could, as they were often inclined to do. Like the time when Beautiful Flower and Raven and several other children released a rabbit they had caught near several sleeping dogs. They did, so the curs would run through Rain's hide scraping project. They released the rabbit, and the dogs gave chase. Rain, as intended, was ran over by the pack. At one point, she was seen laying on her side, fending off the beasts with her scraper. It all made for some great fun and a lot of laughs at her expense until she regained her composure. Then those rascals got an earful of some of the sharpest Nimipu upbraiding that had been heard in that village for a long time.

All in all, things were peaceful, and everyone seemed content with their simply structured lifestyle. With the rising of the sun and the setting of the same, the circle of life provided for all, as the Life Giver intended.

Before the cold time had fully come, the hunters returned from the buffalo country. Dreamer and his Waptailmin party continued toward home. Talon and the other young Nimipu hunters had much to tell. There also was a lot of festivities in honor of their safe arrival back with their families once again.

When the telling of the events of their hunt came out, it all took an interesting turn as it unfolded. They told of when they arrived in a favored location. It was very busy with many hunters of different tribes. They all managed to come to a consensus of sociability and cooperativeness. After a lot of interaction between the tribes, they came to understand that Shadow, Cloud Shadow, Shadowhand was becoming somewhat of a legend among all the tribes there, even the Siksika.

Sometime later, Red Dreamer paid a visit to the Nimipu encampment confirming what Talon and the other young men had been saying.

In a way, all the talk made Shadow feel uncomfortable, because deep down inside, he was actually a humble man. He was humbled by what he knew to be the real story—that the Great Spirit was in control of the destiny of them all.

He brought some up and others down, and some who rose to high places could be subject to fall the furthest. He smiled at what he heard said and then put it away from himself.

The cold time was fast approaching, and it was again time to make certain that they were fully prepared to face it. With the return of the hunters also came the bounty from their efforts. The large store of dried buffalo meat was very much appreciated. Along with the good supply of dried red fish would keep them well stocked with the food stores they needed.

So as the cold took hold of the land, they were able to feel comfortably secure in their village. They were spending their time with the production and repair of clothing, along with production and repair of tools and weapons, of which they could work at within their confines, along with the craft of storytelling, whether factual or fiction, or a mixture of both.

The children who could not be contained seemed to usually not concern themselves with minor issues like cold weather. They typically would go outside, unless conditions became too severe.

For the adults who were looking for their opportunities for intimacy, the times of their children's outside recreation activity met that interest.

As the cold time began to show signs of relenting to the change that always came against it, Shadow began to make plans for another hunt, trap, and venture.

He wanted to go in the direction of Cold Wind Grandfather, at times following the Mother River. He hadn't yet brought this area into his experiences, of which he was very much interested to do.

He spoke to his brother Talon about his idea and invited him to join him. Talon accepted without reservation.

Shadow and Talon left together on the bases that it was meant to be a time for them to have a brotherly experience. Just them getting to work together on accomplishing the many aspects of such an exploration.

CHAPTER 17

BLACK EAGLE'S POSTERITY AT WORK

They took several pack ponies with them, always with the intention of hunting for and returning with sustenance for the people at home.

To a certain degree, as Shadow and Talon traveled along the area, it was quite familiar to them, to the extent of a full lighttime's journey where they went about stopping for the approaching darkness. Shadow knew that at some point the following lighttime, he and his brother would be entering new lands for them. It was exciting for them to go to these areas that were not part of any previous experiences.

The land was very desolate in places, but continuing, the landscape had subtle and drastic changes that gave a variety that they enjoyed. It also was not without its challenges, which they craved as well. There were areas of soft sand, deep gullies, and sharp loose rocks, along with its share of rattle snakes too. As they continued their travels, Talon appreciated his older brother's invitation to come along, and the both of them had privately been entertaining thoughts that between the pair of them, they made a very able and daring duo. After all, they were the sons of Black Eagle.

They slowly veered away from the Mother River as it angled off generally toward the rising sun at that point. They stayed within sight of the mountain range that they purposed to parallel as they loped along. It had taken several sleeps to get to the place that they had already come to.

They began to climb out of the flat land, and the landscape was becoming more forested. It was suitable to Shadow, as the general climate was more refreshing to him as their trek continued to take them higher in elevation. It was a fine place to be, with so many promising locations to pursue.

They had taken a deer earlier in their travels and were now once again looking to make camp.

When they had chosen a spot, they dismounted, and Talon immediately arranged a span pole between a couple of trees. Then he slid the doe off the pack horse to hang and skin. They had gutted it right after it had been killed, but they planned on taking the hide of every animal they took. They wouldn't waste one anytime they had control over the matter.

After the deer had been skinned, they butchered it, wrapping the meat in the hide. They kept out enough for their evening meal, as well as for the next time when the need arose.

Shadow tried not to hurry when the occasion allowed. Of course, as it has always been in life, one has to take advantage of the situation when it presents itself, which typically means when able, but when there was an opportunity, he took it.

That evening, they took their time and enjoyed a relaxing period roasting venison on slender green limbs, talking about family and any subject matter that came to mind. Shadow talked at length of making the effort to trap for smaller fur-bearing animals like fox, marten, mink, otter, beaver. To them, the value of these pelts was in their softness. Life was rough enough without everything that was put against their skin being coarse and irritating. They all desired some softness and comfort in their lives. It was just an intuitive thing to do so.

It wasn't the best time for the quality of the furs, but it was an opportunity to check into their availability.

The following lighttime, they ventured farther and higher yet. They then both agreed that they should set up their extended hunting camp in that vicinity.

That next early time, they went out to look for sign and make some plans for locations to set up trip snares, as well as low-hanging snares, to catch whatever they were able to.

They had taken the time to build a crude pen to contain the ponies while giving them a little space to move about. Now they were on foot to make their maneuvering of the terrain more advantageous.

They set more than a few traps and checked them every early time. Every time they checked, there were some animals caught.

When they weren't involved in the traps, they hunted, taking bear and elk and deer. One of their hunt times, Talon felt that there was another presence close by his area of sight and was searching for what it could be. With his keen senses, he discerned some movement over his strong shoulder and above him. When he quickly turned to get a clear look, he briefly had a view of a stalking mountain lion. As soon as he had had a sighting, the animal crouched in the rock cover he was using. Talon could just make out its twitching tail where it lay concealed. He nocked an arrow then picked up a small stone and tossed it right into the spot where the predator awaited. When the stone hit, the big cat leaped in the direction of another large rock to flee. While in midflight, Talon's arrow met its mark, dropping it to the ground not far from where the hunter stood.

"If you would have leaped at me instead of away from me, you may have had a chance, but now it is too late for that. Hunter of these parts no more," Talon pronounced as he looked down at the dead panther, feeling satisfied with the outcome.

In the evenings, they spent time along some creeks that were the residences of many beaver families. They took a number of them with arrows. At times, they were able to kill them with sticks.

One of the facts of life is death, and for these men, to kill was the way of life from time immemorial.

It was approaching the time that they felt they needed to be leaving on their return trip. They broke camp after a lot of preparations with the care of the pelts and hides and butchering and packing.

Shadow and Talon made a wide sweep back in the direction of the rising sun, hoping to possibly get a look at where the Mother River got its origin. They didn't want to go too far out of the way, because they were loaded down with the bounty that they needed to retain.

It was a practice that Shadow was adopting, to try and travel in a roundabout fashion so as to take in a bit of different return sights, even if in the same vicinity. There was much fine country to see, and they both felt enriched by the experience. They never made it to the origin of the Mother River, but they took in considerably more of its length than they had any idea of before this endeavor. It was satisfying to have more of the country within their knowledge.

Shadow began to think about a trip along the Mother River sometime all the way to the place where the sun set.

He had heard tales of how it went on to what was known as the Big Water. He purposed in his heart that if the Great Spirit would grant him the opportunity, he would make that trip.

For now though, he needed to focus on what lay before him. To return safely with the bounty was the pressing thing at hand and not letting the ponies get too close to some of the precarious ledges they found themselves near to at times, with the pack animals so weighted down.

Eventually, they found an area where they would be able to cross the river. It had widened there, to the point that the current slowed considerably, and the water level could be traversed by the ponies with only a short swim at intervals.

After several more sleeps, they had come within close proximity of home. Shadow spoke to his brother. "It has been a fine time with you on this hunt, my brother, and it is right that we should feel proud of our efforts and thankful as always for the favor of the Life Giver. You are a fine companion on such an undertaking."

"I, too, have had a good time, and thank you for this chance to grow in the ways of gathering these needed goods," Talon let his brother know, as they drew closer to the end of their journey.

CHAPTER 18

THE PASSING OF A PATRIARCH

The brothers returned to their village with the carefully packed meat to now be thinly sliced and placed on drying racks right away.

All the hides were being distributed to those with the most obvious need. They withheld the pelts for their families to be turned into some of those soft comfortable items that they had been intended for.

Several more cold times had passed, and Raven, Shadow's first son, was becoming very interested in spending time with the ponies. Shadow began to teach him to sit on the older more docile ponies to help him get his balance and learn to grip the pony's sides with his legs. They were both enjoying their time together in this way. The Nimipu had progressed into a renowned horse people and the owners of vast herds of ponies. Dancer Too had matured into a prominent stallion and was much to be desired by any who looked on him, and with many fine offspring.

The men went about separating the animals for select breeding or gelding or breaking, which included many other forms of training. At times, they went through much ceremony, with racing events and acrobatics while on horseback, with Raven always in attendance. It was a fine opportunity during this period for the Nimipu boys and girls. There was access for the women and girls to spend time with the ponies, too, although they were kept quite busy with family needs.

SHADOW OVER THE LAND

The rivers were always an ever-present provision, with appreciation by all who were their beneficiaries. There was plenty of access to the rivers for cleaning and bathing and swimming. The men and boys were able to take down some waterfowl with arrows at times if they were persistent. Of course, there was always the fishing.

The laughter of the children, chatter of the women, the bellowing of the men, and the barking of the curs, along with the neighing of the horses, all added to the pleasant atmosphere of the village life.

The people had always been here since their inception and always would be. No one could say differently. Their lands were the finest on earth. If someone didn't believe that, all they had to do was just ask them, and they would tell them so.

That cold time, Shadow and Talon, as well as Raven and Wild Wind, tried their hand at making snowshoes. It was something Many Arrows had gone into detail about while he stayed with them that season. He never did make them due to the lack of snow during that time, but this cold time, there was deep snow. Shadow prayed that it wouldn't last long, because the pony herd was struggling to reach the grass below. They weren't able to assist them in any way, not being able to even cover any distance outside the encampment. That was when he began to recall Many Arrows's telling of the shoes for walking on snow.

They managed to construct a pair for Shadow and Talon, then they set out to use them. They consisted of a looped oblong limb held together by strands of crisscrossed hide. When they had secured them to their feet, they felt excited when they found themselves walking on top of deep snow, with barely any sinking to trouble them. Soon there were many hands at work making them in their village. They got some good use out of them in being able to move about. Although by the time the snows had cleared, they had lost many from their herds. It was a very sad time for the Palus band. All they could do was hope and pray that they wouldn't see that type of cold time again. They still had more ponies that survived, and they made a good comeback with time.

That hot time, the Waptailmin and the Nimipu had another joint hunting venture. Raven was given an almost grown pony for his own, and Wind was in training to become a horseman too. Beautiful Flower was becoming a big help around the lodge, even at her young age. Talon began to take other Nimipu braves with him to run trap lines for pelts in the country where he and Shadow had gone sometime before. Rain had a daughter she named Lovely Butterfly, remembering that there were a lot of butterflies about at that time.

Not long after the cold time had set in again, Black Eagle was overcome with illness. He was confined to his lodge, laid out on his back for some time, unable to stand or to walk. And then he passed on to the other side.

He had words for his family before his passing. He spoke at length with his wife, who stayed by his side throughout his debilitation. He also spoke with each of his children in turn. When he spoke to Cloud Shadow, he said, "My son, I am going away soon to the place where my ancestors wait for me. I have lived well and have no regrets. I leave you to watch for the family. I am proud that you are my son. Trust the Great Spirit to show you the way."

Shadow assured his father that he would do as he asked, saying, "I will do these things as you have said and will look for you in the place where you go when my time comes. Thank you for being a leader for me to look to in this life. Be at peace, my father."

Not long after, he passed in the same way he lived, dignified and honored by the people and his family.

When the weather allowed for travel, Shadow made a trip to the Wallowa band to inform Big Cat of his father's passing. He took Raven with him, believing the boy was up for the trip. It was a proud time for Shadow, having his son along with him as a traveling companion.

Raven wanted to know everything about this new land that was before them, as well as who these people were that they were going to see.

"If they are our family, why didn't they live where we lived? Or why didn't we live where they lived?" There were lots of questions to be answered and puzzling things to be resolved, but Shadow did his best, with much patience.

Shadow felt it would be a good place for Raven's first trip away from home. It was so diverse with its fine mountain range as a background, along with forests and valleys and casual river flowing from the mountain-fed lake that sat at the base of the mountains as a centerpiece to the perfect portrayal of this wonderful place. It was another asset of the Nimipu lands.

While loping along on their journey, Shadow decided that it would be a good time to talk with his son concerning right and wrong and the facts of a spiritual realm. That the Great Spirit would teach them what was right, if they desired it. He told how if they were peaceful toward others and they toward them, then they were friends. He went on to explain that there would always be some who would not be peaceful toward other peoples. They were people who followed after wrong spirits, and it was important to know the difference and to not be fooled into a false sense of security.

That it was because these unpeaceful people were in this life also that the peace-seeking people must be prepared to defend themselves.

He spent some time speaking of the weapons of a warrior.

Then he began to explain that the Great Spirit created everything, and with each part of life, there was a counterpart. That the Great Spirit knew all and saw all, even that which was in their hearts.

Raven came back with, "Mother told me that when she was a child, she was told that the god of power was the sun, and if she needed anything in life, you asked it of the sun god. She also told me that later, she came to believe, because of something that happened to her, that the Great Spirit was stronger than the sun."

Shadow went on to teach Raven that the Great Spirit made the sun and the moon and the stars, and that he decided who and what had power. He went on to say, "Take care, for there are many dangers, but do not be afraid to live the life that has been given to you, looking to the creator to provide what is needed."

"I will seek the wisdom of the Great Spirit for my life, Father," Raven responded.

"That would be the best way to live, my son," Shadow said in conclusion.

After several sleeps, they came to the Wallowa River. Shadow made a special effort for Raven and himself to bathe in the river. Then they built a sweat lodge and had a good sweat. They bathed again, all in a ritualistic manner. Shadow instructed Raven that what they did was in memorial to the passing of a generation, in reference to Black Eagle. Also, it was a form of new birth, that they might begin anew.

The following lighttime, they came to the village of the Wallowa band and the home of Big Cat. Shadow was no stranger to the village, and so within a short time, Big Cat appeared, giving his welcome. "Come, rest and refresh yourselves," he offered.

After they dismounted and a fuss had been made over Raven and how he had grown, they settled in to speak of important matters. Shadow didn't mince words but got right to the telling of Black Eagle's passing. Big Cat was visibly shaken. He also didn't look like he was feeling very strong in these times himself.

CHAPTER 19

CONDOLENCES GIVEN

Big Cat talked at length about the times Black Eagle and himself had had together. While they listened, Raven received an education on his grandfather's legacy. Shadow also added stories that came to mind from over the years. And afterward, it ended up being a fine tribute to Black Eagle.

After spending sometime there with the people, Shadow excused himself and Raven, letting it be known that he and his son were going to spend time touring about the Wallowa domain.

Shadow felt privileged to be showing off their country to Raven, always with the emphasis on it being given to them by the Life Giver. That no one had the right to it but them. That the land was a heritage that they should always cherish with the utmost pride.

They hobbled the ponies and hiked in the mountains, something that was a new experience for Raven. Shadow told the story of his vision quest as they climbed, speaking of a chief among the mountain goats, his spirit guide, who overcame the next to impossible as a routine. As he spoke, Raven scanned the horizon for a possible glimpse of the dignified creature his father had described. It made no appearance, but that didn't take away from what he came away with, feeling it a wonderful experience.

"This is a fine place, Father," declared Raven.

"I suggest you come here from time to time. It will do you good," replied Cloud Shadow.

"I know that you are right, Father, because it has already done that for me, and I will never forget it," responded Raven.

After they had returned to the Wallowa village, they continued there for several more sleeps, wanting to make Big Cat's time more cheerful. Shadow understood how closely his uncle and his father's hearts were tied together.

It did do Big Cat's emotions a lot of good, to have Black Eagle's son and grandson there with him over that time of hardship. He was very proud when he looked on them, knowing the story concerning the blood feud between the Nimipu and Gray Wolf, the Siksika war chief.

The way that Shadow had taken it upon himself to settle the wrongs that were done against the people, and the irony of Raven being a descendant of Gray Wolf too. It all seemed amazing that it could be so, when he considered the beginnings of the feud and then the way it was put to an end.

The time came when Shadow decided that he and Raven would depart. At one time, Shadow believed that his son would become overextended in his strength and stamina and would long for a return to their home. Instead, upon learning that other Nimipu bands were located not all so far away, he all but insisted that they go to visit them. They parted with much sweet sorrow all around, with a very respectful goodbye to Big Cat.

When they moved out of the Wallowa area, they went in the direction of the rising sun. Their destination was the Red Fish river, but before they could get there, they needed to cross the Winding River once again. It made Shadow uneasy at times crossing the rivers, but there was no need to worry, because Raven did it with skill and daring.

Shadow had explained to Raven concerning the bands, that there was the Lower Red Fish band and the Upper Red Fish, and then the Kooskia and the Wallowa, and of course their own band, the Palus.

After they had crossed the Winding River, they entered an area of tall grassy hills and sometimes steep inclines. They were going to visit the Upper Red Fish, and first coming to the Red Fish river, they continued toward the land of the rising sun, which was the direction the river flowed from.

They took a sleep before proceeding the following early time. After, they had a meal and looked to their grooming, which included bathing in the river, something that contributed to their general health and well-being.

They traveled for some time. Then when the sun was high above them, they came to the village they sought. The inhabitants didn't take an immediate notice of their approach, but there was something about Shadow's pony that always caught the attention of any who saw him. He was a direct descendant of Sun Dancer and Dancer Too, and not consequently, his name was Dancer Also. With his prancing gait, he was always exuding confidence in a very demonstrative manner.

Before long, the people began to congregate, having begun to take interest in their visitors.

When Shadow had spoken to Big Cat of coming to visit with the other bands, he was told to ask for White Owl when he came to the Upper Red Fish band's camp. He was made to know that White Owl was a chieftain and knew Black Eagle and to speak to him about his passing.

When Shadow had the people's attention, he spoke out, "I have come seeking White Owl to give him news concerning Black Eagle of the Palus band."

As soon as White Owl's name was mentioned, some went to tell him of the visitors. Within a relatively short time, a group of young men gathered around a not so young but dignified man came strolling up to where Shadow and Raven remained mounted.

"You have come to speak with me concerning Black Eagle?" asked the old chief.

"Yes. I give greetings from my uncle Big Cat. I am the son of Black Eagle, Cloud Shadow. This is my son Raven, and we bring word of Black Eagle's passing."

The old chief stood silent for an extended moment and then spoke, asking, "Are you also called by the name of Shadowhand?"

"Yes, some have given me that name," replied Shadow. There was a murmur among the people gathered there.

"Come and rest and refresh yourselves," White Owl responded.

Shadow and Raven dismounted and led their ponies in the direction they were shown. While they were walking along, White Owl placed his hand on the shoulder of a brave near him and said, "My son, Bull Elk."

The man turned toward Shadow and nodded a greeting. Then the old chief signaled to a boy nearby, around Raven's own age, to come to him. "Grandson, Cunning Fox," he stated. After that, the boy grabbed Raven by his arm and pulled him after him, and they ran off with a group of other boys.

Then White Owl led Shadow along with Bull Elk and some of the other men of the band into a fine large tipi lodge, where they all began to seat themselves among the soft supple pelts that were strewn about.

Shadow couldn't help but notice that the other men were looking at him in a manner that seemed unusual to him. He couldn't relate to it.

Bull Elk, not being able to contain himself, blurted out how he and other hunters from their village had been in buffalo country the hot time, last, and had heard tales concerning a Nimipu brave named Shadowhand, and they had been anxious to meet him.

Shadow had heard a similar story from his brother Talon as well as Red Dreamer, and now this. There was a question-and-answer series that proceeded, and in the end, they were all in agreement that it was a very good story that they all enjoyed, and indeed this was the Shadowhand.

White Owl also thought it interesting that the story began with Black Eagle and Big Cat. When he inquired after them, that was when the details of the passing of Black Eagle came out.

White Owl expressed his regret at the news and his condolences to the family. Then he began to tell of his initial meeting of them both. They had come to the village to visit their fellow tribe members as young men, venturing through the Nimipu territory. He talked of how they both were very full of assurance that if a thing could be done, they could do it. After they had been around the camp for some time and had begun to get to know each other, it was proposed that they have a pony race. The race would be open to any who cared to participate. He went on to say that when the race actually took place, there were so many ponies and riders, they could hardly see the contestants for the dust. And when the race was over, Black Eagle had come in ahead of everyone.

Then occasionally, they would find time to visit one another over the passing of the winters.

It came up by a mention from a member of the group there what a fine pony Shadow was riding. Shadow went on to tell of his history with the stallion. While he told of those things, White Owl appeared to be pondering on some matter. Then he began to speak. "I would very much like to have a colt from that stallion."

Shadow let him know that he would be happy to make him a present of Dancer Also's male offspring.

White Owl went on to say, "Why not have a pony race, and if your pony wins, you can chose a pony from my herd? If my pony wins, you give me a colt from your stallion."

Shadow responded, "I'm not interested in racing my stallion myself. I would rather be a spectator."

Bull Elk interjected, "Perhaps our sons would like to ride the ponies in a race?"

White Owl looked at Shadow then asked, "Would you allow your son to race?"

Shadow felt confident that Raven would be able to stand up to the rigors involved to stick to the mount under such pressure. "I think that sounds like good fun," he countered.

White Owl told Bull Elk to go find the boys and to tell them to come to his lodge. Bull Elk found them at the river swimming. He yelled to his son, "Cunning Fox, bring Raven and come to White Owl's lodge right away!"

Within a relatively short time, the boys made their appearance, where they were informed of their roles in the upcoming race. White Owl, Bull Elk, and Cunning Fox already knew what pony Cunning

Fox would be riding. They all made plans at that point. The race would be held the following lighttime.

There was a celebration and merrymaking throughout the late time. The people were making much to do about having Shadow as their honored guest. It was all more than he imagined could happen. He felt that his son was somewhat confused about the stories of his exploits. He took Raven off by himself and told him he would fill him in on what it was all about and what the people were referring to. Shadow thought it important that he hear the truth of it without the possible embellishments and exaggerations he might be subjected to. Raven had complete trust in his father's words and knew he meant what he said, so he just let it go for the time being.

CHAPTER 20

THE RACE

The following lighttime finally arrived, and all the boys in the village were up early. Everyone was talking about the race, but the boys in camp seemed to be intrigued about it the most. All of them imagined that it could be them about to face off in this contest of skill and courage and speed. For Cunning Fox and Raven, it really was them who were about to become the center of everyone's attention. They and the chosen ponies that were deemed exceptional rivals.

By this time, Shadow and Raven were getting a bit curious of the animal that Raven and Dancer would be up against. Shadow made mention of it to White Owl, and then White Owl summoned that Lightning be brought forth.

Not long after, Lightning appeared, led by a group of revelers. Lightning was a white stallion in his prime and obviously full of himself. He was a grand pony who would surely be up to the task.

Raven had never ridden Dancer, but they knew each other quite well. Raven had spent many long periods around Dancer and had always showered him with affection. Shadow felt comfortable that Dancer wouldn't have any issues having Raven ride him.

Shadow decided not to tell Raven about being able to choose a pony from White Owl's herd if he won. He thought that in case things didn't go well, perhaps he wouldn't take it so badly if he didn't know that part of it.

White Owl stipulated that the ponies be ridden bareback, just horse and rider, nothing else. The course was a wide-open area, not too rough but not altogether flat either, in a rather large circular shape generally.

When the time came, they brought Lightning and Dancer near the area where the beginning of the race would take place. Being a very horse savvy people, they knew not to let the stallions get too close to one another as they waited for the race to begin.

They didn't want any fights between them.

As Raven and Cunning Fox came into the area, Shadow couldn't help but think that his son was starting to take on some of the physical characteristics of Rain's father. He was stocky and wide but powerful for a boy. Shadow was also feeling very proud of such a fine son. He could tell that Bull Elk was having similar thoughts as Cunning Fox strolled by, looking poised and ready.

They both walked up to their mounts, running their hands along their flanks. Looking at the boys would cause a person to question their ability to be able to get on their ponies, but each grabbed a handful of mane and hoisted themselves onto the backs of their steeds.

Both ponies seemed to sense that there was something big about to take place. They pawed at the ground and tossed their heads about. Then Dancer did something that Shadow hadn't ever seen before. He reared onto his hind legs and gave a hop, then another, all the while Raven clung like it was just the natural thing to do. When Dancer dropped back down, Shadow thought, *Well, if he can hang on through that, he'll stick the rest of it.*

All the people were pointing and smiling and feeling they were being treated to a show. Even White Owl was grinning with delight.

Shadow and Bull Elk led the ponies to the starting point. There were a number of men out on the course serving as points to be rounded when the racers reached them. Raven and Cunning Fox were to go around the course and then repeat it again. The pony with rider to cross the starting point after that would be the winner, if either made it that far.

There was some distance between the stallions, and they were ready to run. It was hard to keep them back. White Owl stepped to the side of the racers to where he could be clearly seen. He raised an arm, looking at the boys, and the boys watched him closely. Then he dropped his arm, and they were off and running.

Every now and then, Raven felt like he was slipping to the side, and it seemed to him that Dancer would make a slight adjustment that helped him get centered again.

Raven had never ridden this fast before, but he was loving it. The air was swishing through his eyes so hard, it was difficult to get a decent view of what was ahead, but he could see just well enough.

Lightning and Cunning Fox were right beside Dancer and himself. He couldn't resist hollering out, "Ai-ye, ai-ye, ai-ye!" in a high-pitched sound over and over. He felt like a warrior in full charge, and Dancer was very much in the hunt. It was good to be alive! What fun and excitement. He knew the opponents felt the same way.

When the ponies dropped into the low areas of ground and then came back up, he felt his belly dropping and rising. Every now and then, Dancer would give a short leap to avoid something. They had rounded all the men in their places and were passing the starting point.

It seemed to Raven that it was hard to tell who had been ahead. It was that close.

Raven and Cunning Fox had a chance to glance at one another off and on. Something they both portrayed was that they were having the time of their lives.

At a point, Dancer stumbled briefly, and Raven almost went over his head, but he clung, and he dug his knees and heels in and stuck as well as anyone could hope to.

They were rounding the last bend before the finish, and Raven felt quite certain that they had fallen behind slightly over that last stumble.

With all his heart and will, he hollered out, "Ai-ye, ai-ye, ai-ye!" At the same time, he lowered his head and laid his heels into Dancer's flanks. Feeling a leaping surge, he slowly but surely passed Lightning and Cunning Fox. When they reached the finish, they were clearly the winners.

When it was all said and done, everyone agreed it had been a fine race with no disappointments.

Shadow, within a short time, let Raven know he had won himself the pick of White Owl's herd. He also went on to inform White Owl that whenever he could send someone to collect it, he would provide him with a colt sired by Dancer. All was well with the entire village that day as the celebration continued.

Raven went with Cunning Fox to browse through his grandfather's herd, with great expectations on Raven's part how wonderful a thought of being able to choose the one pony that most appealed to him. Although it was told to him that Lightning's value as a primary stud source took him out of the agreement. Apart from that though, the choice was free for him to make.

After looking for some time, he set his sights on a young colt that had caught his attention previously. It wasn't old enough to break yet, but it was weaned from its mother.

The colt struck Raven as a pony like none he had seen before. It had the Appaloosa spots on his rump with a white background, but the rest of the pony was a light gray, with the mane and tail a mix of the colors. Yes, that was the pony for him, he had decided.

"Well, Black Eagle is still having his way in this village," stated White Owl. "There isn't another man I would rather lose to, him or his children. I am very glad to have had you and your son's company and would be happy to have you with us at any time. It is good and right that you are going through the different bands to inform us of his passing. I hope that my family would treat me with as much respect."

Bull Elk was standing by and overheard what his father had said. "I promise you that I will do the same for you, Father, when that time comes."

"Thank you, my son," White Owl said, acknowledging what Bull Elk had promised.

Raven and Cunning Fox said their goodbyes as well, and as they made their way out of the camp, the people gave them a respectful farewell.

They then moved off in the direction of Cold Wind Grandfather to visit the Lower Red Fish band.

Raven began to talk of the race and the prize that he had won. "You know, Father, I believe I could feel the presence of the Great Spirit with me during the race, guiding me to do what it took to come out the winner."

"I know that feeling that you speak of, my son," replied Shadow.

"I prayed that the Great Spirit would be with me, and I believe he was," Raven said.

"I think that is so, and what a fine prize you have received," Shadow responded. "And what will your pony be called?"

Answering his father's question, he went on, "I'm going to name him Ghost."

"Ghost? What do you know about a ghost?" Shadow asked.

"Well, I remember Grandfather told me once that a ghost can be seen if it wants to, but if it doesn't, it won't be seen. I like that idea, and when I look at him, he makes me think of the ghost," Raven answered.

"That seems like reason enough to name him, and because he is your pony, you can name him whatever you like," said Shadow.

"Good. His name is Ghost," responded Raven.

"Son," Shadow continued the conversation. "I feel I need to tell you a story involving you, your mother, and myself, and a lot of others as well."

"Does this story have to do with the people calling you a legend of the people?" asked Raven.

"Yes, that is the story I refer to. I want you to hear it from me and to know that what I tell you is the real story."

"Yes, Father, I will listen to what you say and remember your words," Raven replied while they loped along.

Shadow began by telling what he had heard as a boy concerning the conflict between the Siksika and the Nimipu, starting with the attack on Black Eagle and Big Cat while with the hunting party all so long ago. The following attacks all resulted in deaths and injuries on both sides. The needless death of his beloved stallion, Sun Dancer. After all these occurrences, he determined to take revenge. Eventually, it all came out concerning the abduction of Rain, the battle with Gray Wolf, and the taking of his mother as his wife. He told him how there were a lot of witnesses to the fight between Gray Wolf and himself, which, as it turned out, to be to his victory. Shadow went on to say that he had spared Gray Wolf's life that day, even though it was clearly his to take, that those who witnessed it found so fascinating and worthy of the retelling. So it had been told to many, and the people had decided that it was an important thing to them, for this story to be remembered.

"That is a big story," replied Raven. "And to think I am a part of the story to me means that the story continues with me."

"Yes, that is right," responded Shadow, surprised at his son's reaction.

At that time, there was a stirring behind them, and they turned to find Bull Elk and Cunning Fox approaching. Bull Elk signed a greeting, and soon they were a collective group. Bull Elk explained that they wished to travel with them, which was happily agreed to, and so together they traveled.

Raven and Cunning Fox quickly joined into conversation, as did Cloud Shadow and Bull Elk.

The Nimipu tribe was a family wherever they might come together. It was obvious to Shadow and Bull Elk that their sons had grown close in a short time, and it did their hearts good to see it.

During their time of traveling together, the stories of the buffalo country and other related stories concerning those places got the better of Raven and Cunning Fox, and they blurted out in unison that they wanted to go there and experience that place of wonder themselves. Shadow and Bull Elk tried to make light of their sudden intense interest, but through stubborn persistence, eventually, it was suggested.

"Maybe when the cold time ends, we may go," stated Bull Elk after a discussion with Shadow.

That was all they needed. From that moment on, it was all the boys could think and talk about.

The following lighttime, they came to the Lower Red Fish band's encampment. Bull Elk and Cunning Fox were received there as close neighbors would be, and soon it was found out that Cloud Shadow was among them, the one who had acquired a name that was fast becoming a name of renown. He drew much attention and caused much excitement about the village.

The chieftain of the band, Rising Moon, appeared and extended his greeting. "Come and rest and refresh yourselves. It is good to have such honorable guests to visit us."

The usual stories were told as they got acquainted with one another. The story of Shadow and Rain helping the Kooskia band retrieve their stolen ponies from the Shoshone sometime back surfaced. Bull Elk and Cunning Fox hadn't heard that one, and when they all understood that Rain was Raven's mother, it all took an even more interesting turn for them.

The passing of Black Eagle was spoken of and received with the respect due to the elder.

Everyone enjoyed the recent pony race story that was followed by the story of Black Eagle's previous race there long ago, along with more questions and answers concerning the tales of Shadowhand. It was a festive time for all who were there and would become one of memories in later times.

The following lighttime, Shadow and their party moved on toward the Kooskia band's village, where once again they received a warm welcome.

Yellow Jacket and his family were very glad to have Cloud Shadow in their midst once again. After some time spent on their initial greetings, it came out concerning the passing of Black Eagle and the family's desire to tell of it to the tribe.

For Yellow Jacket, the news had a personal significance, Black Eagle being his uncle. Growing up, Black Eagle always had a bigger than life presence to him. It made him feel vulnerable in some way, realizing that even Black Eagle was subject to a death.

Rather than spend their time mourning him, they chose to celebrate his life and their honorable guests. Again, there were festivities and ritual dancing. There was all the best food stuff that could be provided, along with more all-important storytelling.

Chapter 21

The Concerted Effort

There was more talk of a trip to buffalo country that developed into some plan making for such an event, which excited the boys to no end. Yellow Jacket and other members of the Kooskia band had made it known that they were certainly interested in being a part of such a trip if it were to take place.

Bull Elk informed Shadow that he and his son wanted to continue with them to the home of the Palus band. Shadow and Raven welcomed their company.

The following early time, they left for their return home. Raven, having never been away for any length of time before, was very much looking forward to the reunion with family members.

When they came within visual distance of the Palus encampment, a group of, on the smaller side, riders came out to meet them. They turned out to be his sister Beautiful Flower and brother Wild Wind, along with a host of other boys and girls, calling out, "Raven's home! Raven's home!"

The shouting and laughter that followed was raucous, and it continued right into camp, where it reached a whole new level of volume as Fawn, Running Wild, Rain, and many others joined in.

The return of Cloud Shadow and Raven was a happy occasion, being understood but not spoken of that there was a general concern for the young man's well-being. Seeing him happy and well was a great relief.

Cloud Shadow was also missed as a respected and appreciated headman of the band.

Wind was right in the middle of it all, asking questions, almost without end. "I want to hear everything that you saw and did," he told Raven.

"Well, there's much to tell," replied Raven. "But I'll try."

Shadow was enjoying embracing with his mother and wives and children. Just having them close again gave him much happiness. It was good to be home.

Bull Elk and Cunning Fox were enjoying watching the Palus band's interactions with Shadow and Raven.

The following day, Shadow and Raven, along with Wind and several other Nimipu boys, took Bull Elk and Cunning Fox out to look over Shadow's herd. Shadow showed several colts that he knew to be sired by Dancer. He told Bull Elk to pick one out for White Owl as Shadow had promised him. After a short time, there was an agreement made on a particular one, and it was a good pick on a fine young colt, one of the finest that ever lived.

That lighttime, Shadow noticed there were too many stallions in the herd. The following early time, he and Talon and Bull Elk went about separating a certain chosen group to be gelded, just for the purpose of reducing the amount of injuries from violent clashes that occurred too often with a large population of stallions. It was a lengthy process, but eventually, they finished the work, and Shadow felt better for it.

After a series of sleeps had passed and there began to be a change in the weather, with the cold time beginning, Bull Elk let Shadow know that he and Cunning Fox would be returning to their village not long hence. Cunning Fox and Raven had been completely absorbed in working with the ponies. Raven had been working almost nonstop with Ghost, getting him ready for their coming trip to buffalo country.

He was sad to see Cunning Fox go, but they were sworn to ride together when the weather broke. There were lots of fond farewells and see-you-soons when the time came for their departing.

Not long after Shadow's return, he was informed that Red Dreamer had come calling, looking for his friend Shadow. Shadow had purposed in his heart that he would go visit him as soon as he got the opportunity.

Within a short time after the departing of Bull Elk and his son, Shadow asked Raven and Wind if they would like to accompany him to go and visit their friends, the Waptailmin.

Of course, they could not be contained. They were mounted and ready within a very short time, so short that their mothers hadn't even had time to prepare a few things for their trip. It wasn't long though, and they were on their way and dressed warm, for the times were getting colder.

After some sleep overs, they came within a relatively closer distance to the Waptailmin village. They slept over again. Then in the early time, they proceeded the rest of the way.

After making the river crossing, they had to change their leggings and moccasins. They entered the village shortly after and went on to Dreamer's lodge, where they were received most welcomely.

Dreamer expressed surprise at seeing Wind with Shadow and Raven. "Wild Wind is on the move in these parts, I see, and what a sight it is," Dreamer jokingly stated.

"Yes, it is an exceptional traveler," Shadow quipped, following Dreamer's line of humor.

Wind knew they were talking about him but wasn't quite sure about the references being used, but he was appreciative of the attention.

Dreamer saw to it that they were well fed and thoroughly warmed for their journey's efforts. There was much to relate after the extended break in their communications.

After going over different stories and events, the subject came around of the coming trip to buffalo country. Shadow didn't hesitate to ask Dreamer to come along and any other Waptailmin braves that would care to join in.

Red Dreamer expressed his sincere interest and made it known he felt it would be a pleasant distraction to contemplate during these coming cold times and much time spent inside the lodge.

It was obvious that the invitation was uplifting to him, and Shadow was happy for that.

Shadow and his sons stayed on for several more sleeps and were treated to the fine hospitality of their close friends and allies.

After leaving, they had a good return trip, with Wind and Raven becoming more proficient horsemen over every bit of distance they traveled.

Back in camp, there was the usual business of preparing for the fast-approaching cold time—preparing and storing of the roots and berries and red fish harvests, the constant making and mending of the clothing and of tools and weapons, the fortifying of the lodges and looking over the herds concerning any problems that might present themselves, such as lameness, open wounds, or eye irritations. Sometimes they could be helped with a cleaning and applications of certain herbs and poultices. They would do what they could if such problems were found.

As the circle of life would have it, the cold time set in, and the people took shelter, taking life as it came to them. Things were going well enough, until it was found out that Fawn was taken ill.

The family' first reaction was to beseech the Great Spirit for her recovery, but she seemed to have a different idea for herself. With a longing to be with Black Eagle in the next life, and within a relatively short time, she passed on, having given her wishes for the family to continue to look after one another and stay close in their relationship.

Her death was followed by a burial and period of mourning. She would be missed by all, being a revered matriarch, such as she was.

Shadow's wives were especially affected with her passing, and of course the grandchildren.

Brook had married recently and was absorbed with her new family yet understandably very saddened with the loss of her mother. Shadow and Talon tried to be stoic about it, but her departure definitely hurt them.

Shadow reflected on the last words from his mother, when she expressed what her thoughts were concerning her eldest son. "Cloud Shadow, you have been a delight to me from your first moments as our child till this moment we have together. I foresee an importance in your existence that far exceeds the help and comfort you have been to my life. Leave yourself open to the destiny that awaits you, for the Great Spirit is preparing the way, of this I am sure, and your sons will follow in your path. Know that you are a cherished individual and are under the protection of the Life Giver. Continue to live upright, and all will be well." With that, she seemed to fall asleep, and she was never heard to speak another word.

After the passing of Fawn, Shadow began to consider that he was going to take his entire family on the trip to buffalo country. He also had the idea to encourage the other men of his band to do likewise. He even went so far as to make the effort to pass the word to the other bands as well through the little contact with some who passed through their territory.

With much anticipation, the cold time gradually began to come to an end. Already, the members of the band were doing what they could in preparation for the journey and an extended stay. The general consensus was that if they went up for the hunt by families, they would stay through the cold time in buffalo country.

The more news that began to come by messengers, the more it sounded like this was going to be the largest nomadic shift of the Nimipu people in anyone's memory.

Of course, there were those who would not consider leaving the homeland, as it was in all the bands. Their hereditary territory would remain intact as always. Also, all who dared to venture away had every intention of returning.

It came about that all the bands sent messengers to the Palus band, desiring to hear Cloud Shadow's opinion on when and where the bands should gather. He obliged them by stating that they should meet at Kamiah, that sacred site of their origin, at a certain time which he conveyed.

Something that had begun as a conversation between Shadow, Bull Elk, and their sons had caught hold and had become a major undertaking. Shadow could see how the process of getting the vision, formulating a plan, and then making it happen worked. It all seemed good and bold and positive to everyone who embraced it.

There was much work to be done, but the tasks had all been undertaken and were being accomplished quickly and without drudgery or complaint but rather with an uplifting feeling of pride and purpose.

Dreamer was informed of the enormity of what had initially been conveyed as a much smaller endeavor, but he sent word that all was good with him. That he and his people would be ready at the appointed time.

Finally, the preparations were completed. Those who were not leaving stayed near those who were. In the midst of the excitement, there was also a somberness that had a hold on the band. It was the same throughout the entire tribe across the territory as well. Although there was no consolation to be had, there was an understanding that existed to fill the void.

It had been suggested by Shadow to his brother, Talon, that he remain behind with the others who had elected to stay in the homeland. It was a hard decision for him to make, but in the end, he conceded to do so.

Right at the appropriate time, Red Dreamer and his fellow hunters arrived at the Palus village. They came with the same amount of men and provisions that they had originally proposed, not feeling any need to alter their plans for themselves, even though the Nimipu had enlarged the scope of their intentions.

The following early time, there came the departure of the Palus band toward their rendezvous with the other tribe members. Even the dogs, whose masters were leaving, came along. Shadow had planned to be leaving as soon as possible, for he knew travel would be slow with the arrangement they had undertaken.

A lot of the wayfarers spent their time surveying the surrounding homeland as they were moving away from it. Emotions were running high, but for the most part, they were feeling positive concerning their adventure. Rain could hardly contain her thoughts concerning this return trip toward her former place of habitation and memories. Running Wild had never been away from the homeland and was apprehensive yet intrigued like she had never known before.

Raven and Wind were altogether thrilled at the prospects. So onward they went, toward those wide-open possibilities.

Some who weren't coming on the extended trip followed along for some distance before turning back. Also, there were some tears that were shed by not just a few.

There were several camps made on the trail to Kamiah. When the Palus band came near the sacred place, it was apparent that others had already arrived before them.

Yellow Jacket and his family were already there, and members of the Wallowa band, who also brought news of Big Cat's passing, were received with the reverence due to his memory.

Soon after, Bull Elk and his family arrived. Then Rising Moon along with his family arrived, and there were many others from each band.

When Raven spotted his friend Cunning Fox, he was treated with the pleasant surprise of seeing him mounted on Lightning. "How is it that you are mounted on Lightning?" asked Raven.

"My grandfather made him a present to me," answered Cunning Fox.

"That is a great honor your grandfather showed to you," responded Raven.

"Yes, it is, and it is good to hear it coming from you, my friend," said Cunning Fox. "When you say it, it seems to make it even more so," he continued.

"I really do think that," Raven went on. "He is the type of pony that is kept like a treasure, so I am sure your grandfather cares very deeply for you."

Then they paired off and began to look about the encampment. The atmosphere was becoming more festive with every new arrival.

It was agreed that they would stay over for some sleeps till they felt that all who were coming had made it there.

There was developing a special bond between all those who had chosen to come along on what had become an event without precedence. It was primarily the idea that they were there for each other no matter what until they all returned safely home.

While they were encamped at that location, Shadow made a point to make known that Red Dreamer and his Waptailmin braves were good friends of the Nimipu and were to be treated with the utmost respect.

Once again, there was much feasting and dancing to the rhythms of the incessant drumming, and of course, the storytelling. The favorite entertainment were the ancestor stories, which were not complete without the tale of their origin.

In the lighttime, they would gather around the heart of the monster and pray and sing and dance with much thanksgiving to the Life Giver for his particular goodness to the people. They were also thankful to have Cloud Shadow with them and other highly respected members of the tribe.

CHAPTER 22

THE LEAVING

At last, the time came when it was decided that any who were coming had already arrived. The following lighttime, they broke camp. The large exodus was finally underway, with the barking of the curs, the nickering of the ponies, the laughter of the children, the general murmur of voices, and an occasional shout here and there as they all moved toward the Lochsa River. As expected, travel was slow, but no one was concerned about it. They were primarily just enjoying being on the move once again. Only this time, they were actually leaving out of the place of their lands to those distant lands that always drew the tribes with its allure.

Shadow received some loving smiles from his wives while looking over in their direction. It caused him to reflect to the time he was bringing Rain to live with the people of the Palus band, having no idea how it was going to work out. Now, being able to have the knowledge of the outcome, he found himself feeling well pleased. Rain had provided him with a fine son and beautiful daughter, as well as being received as one of the people.

Lovely Butterfly still wasn't able to ride a pony on her own, but she spent her travels doubling with her mother or Running Wild or big sister Beautiful Flower.

The people had plenty of fresh mounts for all as they drove a sizeable herd along with them in their journey. All the people had the privilege to ride a fine pony in a fine country. It was their heritage, and they grasped the gifts of the Great Spirit with zeal.

As the time grew late, they stopped to hold over and rest. Ahead lay the rising hills that soon would become mountains. Where they camped at, there were steep embankments that contained the Lochsa River, along with lots of rocky outcroppings. Shadow and a number of the other experienced travelers knew that this was a less alluring part of the trail to be traveled yet with many splendid views to come.

As the moon began to make its appearance, along with the innumerable stars, it once again became apparent to the people that it was a different experience to be camping on the trail with such a large group away from the homeland. Although, they were masters at making themselves at home wherever they happened to be. They all spent a very pleasant darktime, and in the early time, they bathed and prepared a meal. Then again, they got it all together and continued along the way.

As the travel progressed, they definitely were beginning to experience some gain in elevation and quite a transformation in the landscape. With the large granite boulders protruding out of the river, in the many varied shapes and sizes, along with the thickening of the forestation and general varied plant life along the river's edge and upward into what could now be called the base of a mountain range.

Again, the time called for a stopping and a stay over camp to be made. Rain and Lovely Butterfly went walking along the river, collecting wood for a cooking fire. As Rain stooped, loading her arms with wood, she heard a sharp cry and then a splashing sound. She immediately dropped what she had in her arms and ran to the river's edge, where she knew her daughter to be standing just moments before, just in time to see Butterfly being swept away by a fast river current. She began to scream toward camp, which was in the direction that Butterfly was traveling. Running Wild was keen to the sound of Rain's voice and began to focus all her attention toward the river. Right away, she saw Butterfly moving swiftly along with almost no chance of getting free of her perilous plight. Without hesitation, Running Wild began running as fast as she could, trying to head Butterfly off. Eventually, the current slowed into a deeper, wider place. The embankment was quite high, but at a full run, she launched herself into the air in the young girl's direction. When she hit the water, she began swimming with all that was in her and managed to reach the young girl.

Then it took all her effort to be able to hold on to her and swim toward shore too, but the river was taking them away.

Finally, in a last chance effort, she locked her teeth into the back of the young girl's scalp and skull and laid out on her back. Then with both arms free and legs furiously kicking, she fought her way to the shore.

Running Wild dragged Butterfly onto dry land and laid her down on her back while looking down on the apparently lifeless body.

At that moment, Shadow had managed to get to where his wife and child were. Immediately, he grabbed his child and turned her onto her chest and then picked her up in the air by holding her at her waist. Butterfly folded over head down and evacuated all the water in her lungs. Then she coughed and coughed some more and then began to cry.

The relief was overwhelming, but it only took another moment for everyone to grasp the suddenness of the life-threatening danger they had just witnessed. Much thanks was given all around, and especially to the Life Giver.

Lovely Butterfly did remarkably fully recover in a relatively short time, as well as learn not to walk so close to the edge.

The following lighttime, they began to encounter snow on the trail. It was no surprise, as the trail continued to climb in elevation, and it was still early in the warming time. It certainly was more snow than they cared to try and travel in.

They made camp sooner than they had been with the intention of holding up for a time. They decided that it would be helpful overall to take a delay and allow for the snow to subside. They had no way to know if the trail was passable until they had had a look. Now they knew there was some waiting that needed to be done.

Once again, they went about the work of creating a home where there was no home. Soon they were all comfortable with the means that they either brought with them or acquired where they stayed, and typically it required both.

They had all things in common, even the hardships. They were kind, generous, high-spirited, brave, and playful. They felt fulfilled within their very existence.

They continued for an extended time, sending scouts out ahead periodically to check on the condition of the trail.

Eventually, on an occasion, the scouts came back with a promising report that led to a decision to continue the following lighttime.

It was a well-received word to know that they would soon be on the move again.

The next lighttime began the clamor of a large group in motion once again, along with an atmosphere of excitement and jocularity. Even the animals seemed to be happy and having fun.

There was more travel yet on the pass trail to be completed of mostly climbing and areas of steep descent as well. Those among them that had never made the trip before spent a lot of time gazing off into the beautiful surroundings. Even those who were quite familiar with the area could not help but be impressed with the fine country all about them.

There was an unusual abundance of mountain lions in that location they were in, being heard frequently in the late time. The curs were intimidated as well as emboldened by the big cats. One night, there was a loud disturbance of lion screams and barking dogs, along with the frantic crying of a pony. When some men were able to investigate, they found a pony had been attacked and severely injured. They then had to put him down, not being able to save it.

The people weren't above eating horse flesh under such circumstances, but it wasn't something they cared to do, given a choice.

Onward they pressed, sometimes agonizing, other times exquisite, and all the points in between. There was no complaining. It wasn't done. Whatever they had to do, that was what was done, any time, all the time.

Eventually, it was said throughout the traveling band that they were close to the end of the mountain trail. It had been a memorable experience, but they all looked forward to the considerably flatter terrain.

After coming out of the mountain pass, they made a sharp turn toward the land of the thorn plants. They were told that the party was destined to a place to stay at known as the place of the ground squirrels.

It was a longstanding campsite of the Nimipu hunting parties for generations, a very fine place for crazing and foraging with a slow meandering river and nearby forest as well.

A couple more sleep overs and they would be there. When they did arrive there, the whole gathering was delighted with the location. At a glance, it appeared to provide all they could need for a temporary homeland. There were few among them who had been to this place before this time, but that had changed now to being many of this generation of Nimipu becoming familiar with these surroundings.

There were traces of a camping site from past visits that seemed a good choice. It was mutually agreed that they would occupy that same area, and then they proceeded to do so.

As the women went about creating the camp, the men began to discuss a plan for locating the buffalo.

CHAPTER 23

BACK IN BUFFALO COUNTRY

The sooner they got started, the sooner there would be plenty of fresh meat in camp.

They weren't planning on hunting that lighttime, but they hoped they would find their prey and be able to set out in the early light, fully prepared to kill and butcher and transport the meat and hides.

Shadow and Dreamer and Bull Elk left in the direction of the place of the rising sun. After some long hard travel, coming over a rise of land, they located a large herd. With high spirits, they quickly turned for their temporary new homeland.

When they arrived and told of their find, it brought about a celebrative mood with much anticipation.

All the women were adept at butchering, but it had been many cold times gone by since the Nimipu women had been to buffalo country.

Once again, these strong and proud women would take on the task of field dressing the fine beasts that the Great Spirit would provide for them.

The Nimipu were second to none. Their willpower would prevail. The Creator had made them so.

The following early time, most of the group left to the hunt. They didn't have the means to keep all precautions. They had to have some confidence that things would be all right at camp while they focused their efforts on a successful organized excursion in this initial attempt.

Raven and Cunning Fox were given permission to come along after some pleading. It would be no game, but to imply that there would be no fun to be had would not be true. The thrill, in some ways, was incomparable. Shadow and Bull Elk were certainly not the type of fathers to keep their sons from this source of excitement.

Shadow stated plainly his position to the boys. "You are not to cast your arrows in the hunt. You can follow, but stay clear of the men. Maybe before this hunt is over, you will be able to try your hands at the killing, but you must stay clear of the men."

Raven and Cunning Fox both gave their recognition that they understood what they had been told.

The party had brought plenty of pack ponies, and they were all to a person prepared for the task at hand.

They approached the rise where they had gotten their view the previous lighttime. Shadow halted the procession as he moved forward for another look. There before him was a great herd of bison, more than he had remembered ever seeing before.

He returned to lay out the strategy they would undertake. The women would stay behind the hill along with the pack ponies. The hunters would make a wide sweep to come in on the herd's flank.

The hunters left and over time arrived in position to make their pursuit.

Shadow had chosen a pony he had been working with, beside Dancer. He felt confident that the pony had what it took to carry him into the killing range that he would need with the agility and speed to get him safely away from the stampeding beasts, if necessary.

They had come to an area where there was somewhat of a division between the herd. Shadow thought to charge into the gap that separated them, isolating the smaller group from the main herd and driving them apart into a more manageable size.

He asked the majority of the hunters to follow along the outside edge to keep the herd from scattering.

He told Raven to go with them but to stay out of their way.

He and Bull Elk and Dreamer would cut the smaller group from the larger.

Bull Elk and Dreamer charged in and began the process, and Shadow followed behind. At first, it seemed to be working well. The separation was taking place, but then unexpectedly and without any apparent reason, the larger group of bison bolted in the same direction as the smaller group. Within moments, the larger group began to converge with the smaller, catching Shadow and his pony right in the middle of the crush.

All the hunters had instinctively already begun the killing.

Raven and Cunning Fox were getting a show like none they had ever seen.

No one was watching as Shadow's pony went down in the stampede.

Eventually, it was obvious to everyone that there was a very large herd stampeding toward them, grabbing the attention of all who were there.

Then to everyone's surprise, they witnessed a sight like none had ever imagined. It was Shadow racing along on the back of a large buffalo.

Shadow had managed to jump before his pony went down and scrambled onto the bison's back with all the clinging tenacity humanly possible.

Now he was hanging on for his very life, for if he fell into that collection of stomping hooves, he would die. He held and he held. Then there was a break in the congestion, which made some room between the animals. And just as Shadow felt he could no longer remain on the beast, Bull Elk came alongside him at a full gallop, and he and Shadow were able to lock arms, which allowed Shadow to be maneuvered off the bison onto Bull Elks pony.

Immediately, Bull Elk drew away from the stampede so he could come to a stop and allow Shadow to get to the ground.

Shadow then dropped to his knees and thanked the Great Spirit for preserving his life. He stayed where he was for some time, not feeling any need to move.

Bull Elk had asked him right away if he was injured, and Shadow had replied that he was not.

He then had a little while to himself to collect his thoughts before others came to the place where he sat. Raven arrived and dismounted and then came over to his father and blurted out, "You never told me you could do that, Father." Then the others that were present began to laugh. Shadow laughed also.

"Oh, yes, I do that every time I hunt the buffalo. It is very exciting," Shadow replied.

"I think you better make that the last time," Raven went on. "That seems to be a dangerous thing to do."

"I think you are right, my son. I am not going to do that anymore. Now help your father up," Shadow asked of him.

Shadow's pony was found trampled to death, a testimony to the destructive force that had been generated at the meeting point.

In a relative short period after the buffalo riding incident, there came the women and pack animals into the area of the dead and dying bison.

At first, they knew nothing of what had occurred, only learning of it over time.

Of course, Running Wild and Rain were concerned about Shadow when the story became clear. Shadow assured them that all was well, and the work proceeded as it had to.

It took time getting back to camp. A darktime passed and the following lighttime before arriving at their temporary homeland.

That darktime, the story of Shadow's ride on the rampaging buffalo dominated everyone's attention.

Shadow didn't give it much thought at that specific point, but that incident would attach itself to what would later become the legend of Cloud Shadow.

As time went along, they continued to hunt the buffalo with a more successful outcome than their initial effort.

There were roots to dig and berries to pick, and life was full and good.

Their group, in its entirety, hadn't been bothered by any marauding bands from other tribes. Everything was going well. As they had already decided, they wouldn't be leaving right away. They were going to hold out in this location through the cold time.

One darktime in camp, as different individuals talked of places and things and any other tales that came to mind, Rain began talking about her homeland that she remembered. It was a story of interest because it wasn't familiar to anyone else.

Shadow had some understanding of where she spoke of, but it was very limited.

She spoke of the mountains of enchantment that were in these lands she recalled. She wasn't certain where they were located in relationship to where they were encamped, but she believed that they weren't all so far away.

While she spoke, Shadow was thinking that these were the same mountains that his friend Spotted Feather had spoken of, telling him that there were many wonders there. Rain went on to tell of the spirits that inhabit that great place and that the young men of the Siksika nation took their vision quests on those mountains. She told of huge rivers of ice coming down from the mountains that were the color of the sky inside, with many large beautiful lakes and many fine animals, such a place to be experienced. She made mention of a mountain called the Chief Mountain, which was especially desired for those on a vision quest.

Through all that was said, no one appeared to notice that Raven was becoming mesmerized by the picture his mother was portraying.

For most of those hearing what was being said, it was no more than another interesting tale, but for Raven, it would become an obsession.

As more time passed, the weather began to get colder. Shadow and Red Dreamer and Bull Elk began to formulate a plan to make a hunt into the nearby forest just for a change. Yellow Jacket and Rising Moon let them know that they would also like to come along as well. Raven and Cunning Fox talked their way in also, and there were other hunters that got involved too.

There weren't any particular animals designated as their primary objective. Deer, elk, bear, or panther, it didn't matter. It was a hunt.

The following lighttime, they left, and there was a light snowfall in the air. As their trek continued, the amount of snowfall increased, although they didn't concern themselves with it.

After some time, one of the scouts reported that he had come across a herd of elk not much farther on.

Having a substantial number of hunters, they agreed to attempt to enclose the elk in a man-on-pony net.

Shadow let Raven know that he was free to cast all the arrows at the prey as he was able. The same was told to Cunning Fox by Bull Elk.

The snow began to fall more and more as the hunters began to close their net, directing their ponies around the open area where the elk were congregated.

When they were of a distance to see the elk clearly, the snowfall was so heavy that they still couldn't make them out very well.

Then the elk detected the hunters and panicked, seeking to run, but every direction they made for they soon realized was cut off from escape.

Then the hunters began to unleash their deadly missiles upon the desperate elk.

Shadow and Bull Elk held back watching Raven and Cunning Fox on their technique and skill level. It was apparent that they had not been neglectful in their practicing. They also possessed the strength needed to draw the bow to its full power. Their arrows struck true, along with a lot of others, with many elk being taken down.

Now though, they were faced with a decision to make—to try to take the elk back to camp at that time or hold over till the following early time.

The snow was falling even heavier, and the temperature was getting colder.

They had to discuss it. Some seemed impatient to be going. Others felt it would be a mistake to leave that location at that time. Finally, the majority decided that they should stay put.

Once they had come to their decision, they set about to find burnable wood. The most suitable were the lower dead branches off the different evergreen trees that surrounded the area.

It had become survival mode of a dire sort, given the rapid and severe swing in the temperature from nothing to be concerned about to death-defying.

After they had collected all the burnable wood that could be found in the remaining light, Shadow suggested they round up some of the elk carcasses and collect them together to make a mound of which to build their fire.

"If we don't," he added, "the snow will drown it out." It sounded doable to everyone present, so they proceeded to gather the carcasses as needed.

Then they gathered the ponies and placed them between themselves and the ever-relentless blowing wind.

They then built their fire as it was fast becoming dark. They then waited and endured.

The cold was so bad that no one could sleep. Instead, they focused on keeping their fire alive with little benefit. It finally stopped snowing in the middle of the darktime, and immediately, at first light, they broke camp.

It wasn't their way to leave unbutchered game behind, but they were just glad to be getting out of there with their lives. The predators would have a feast. The hunting party was finished with their hunt. Sometimes the prize to be taken was the subject learned, if you survived the lesson.

Soon the cold time set in, and the Nimipu people in their temporary homeland were settled in for the duration of their limited movement, being all so predictable in this part of the world. With plenty of provisions and buffalo robes, they all fared well enough.

While they were held up together in their close quarters, Raven started in on Shadow, pressing to travel to Siksika country. He told Shadow that he felt compelled to go there on his vision quest. It was no mystery to Shadow as to where that idea came from, but he couldn't deny that Raven was feeling what he claimed. He understood how those things got ahold on a young man and that the importance of it couldn't be questioned. It wasn't just that Raven had brought it up to him one time, but it began to take preeminence over all else from his point of view.

As time went on, Shadow began to formulate a plan to eventually end up in these places of Raven's heart and intent. The place that had been spoken of by Raven predominately was Chief Mountain.

Shadow's first order of business when the weather would permit was to take down more buffalo. He felt it could be done in a relatively short time, and then the people could be freed to return to their own country.

After that, he would set out with a party of the willing to first visit his friend Spotted Feather and the Salish people and seek council there concerning their next step. He relayed these thoughts to Raven, who responded, "I am very happy to know this and believe that it will be so. I hope to hunt the buffalo with you as well, my father."

"I think you are ready for that also, my son. I look forward to that for you, for it will be a test of manhood, an important step to be taken," replied Shadow.

Raven had to tell Cunning Fox what his father had told him. Right away, Cunning Fox approached his father with the talk of Raven participating in the coming hunt. And then he pleaded his case to also be allowed to hunt the buffalo. Bull Elk couldn't bring himself to say no and agreed to it. It was settled. He and Raven would participate in the next hunt.

The time passed, and it was now the time to scout the whereabouts of a bison herd. On a clear lighttime, Shadow and others left to seek the location of their intended prey. After some travel, they found a substantial herd. They returned with the information and decided to leave right away to increase their chances of finding the herd close to the same place.

Within a short time, the hunting party was on the move. When they got to the place where the herd had been spotted earlier, it was nowhere to be seen.

The hunting party began to follow the trail that had been left by the bison. After another lighttime of travel, they once again located the herd.

The plan of attack was much the same as had been used on previous hunts. The women and pack animals stayed back in concealment while the hunters circled wide and came in on a flank of the herd. Cunning Fox was riding Lightning, and Raven rode Ghost. Shadow went with Dancer Also, his trusted steed.

On signal, the chase was on. The primary necessity was to get in close but not get overrun. Ghost had matured into a fine, strong, intelligent animal with no shortcoming.

Raven had full confidence in the pony's abilities. Ghost drew up beside a fat cow, and Raven let fly his arrow, making a good hit that toppled his prey as he moved on. Ghost had sought out a bull this time, and again Raven drew his bow to its full draw and buried his arrow deep within the area of its heart. Then the bull collapsed.

Things were going well, as the other hunters were taking a substantial number of buffalo too. Cunning Fox had also taken down a cow, and Lightning was pursuing a young bull. Just as Cunning Fox began to draw his bow, the bull made a surge toward Lightning. When he did, Lightning adjusted quickly. Unfortunately, it was too quick for Cunning Fox to adjust with him, and he took a tumble to the ground.

It was a very hard hit, and Cunning Fox lost consciousness. When he came to and evaluated his overall condition, he found that he had acquired a leg injury that lingered long after the accident. The hunt, all in all, was a huge success, except for the Cunning Fox incident.

It was because of this injury that caused Bull Elk to make the decision that he and his entire family would return to their homeland with the rest of the hunting party when the time came.

After discussing his plans to go toward Cold Wind Grandfather to visit his friends, the Salish, and then possibly going on from there to the Siksika country, Shadow found that the willing party he had initially had in mind turned out to be Running Wild and Rain, along with their children. He didn't feel any sense of letdown but simply excepted the outcome as the will of the Life Giver, not just for his family but also for the Nimipu people.

When the time came for the parting of their directions of travel, it came out somewhat spontaneously that the Nimipu people were reluctant to have Cloud Shadow and his family go on another course than they were going.

It actually took some prompting from Shadow to get the others to accept the outcome he proposed. In the end, they all said their farewells with much emotion and parted company from the place that had served them well as a temporary home.

Shadow was especially appreciative of his friend Red Dreamer, who, along with his braves, worked tirelessly toward any task that they were asked without exception. He wanted to continue with Shadow but felt the need to stay with his fellow Waptailmin and see their trek through as he had originally stated to them.

Now it was just Shadow and his family making their way through this rich and often hostile country.

Raven was fast becoming a man, which was comforting to his parents at times, but it also brought on some feelings of uneasiness as to how well the transitions from boy to man would take place. How well Shadow understood that with manhood came many challenges. Often, one did not survive the contests over the elements and obstacles that presented themselves as sure as the coming of the next sunrise. Although so far, Raven had been an overcomer, and that was an encouragement to all whose lives were interwoven with his. It certainly was obvious to anyone who observed Raven that he was filled with confidence.

Chapter 24

Throughout the Land of Big Medicine

Running Wild and Rain had their hands full keeping up with their responsibilities, but they both were feeling glad for the opportunity at these experiences of the journey and did not want for it to be any other way. They all proceeded with contentment and high expectations. It was several sleep overs before Shadow began to feel that they were nearing Salish territory. As they proceeded, it came to be that they were met by some mounted braves that Shadow recognized as members of Spotted Feather's tribe. When these riders noticed the Appaloosa ponies, they had a good idea who they were. Within a short time, the travelers were being escorted into the village of their destination.

The reception that they received was not without honor and respect, for the legend of Cloud Shadow had been kept alive amidst this encampment.

Before they came to a halt, they were greeted by Spotted Feather and other men of renown.

"My good friend Shadow and his family have come to visit. What a wonderful surprise to see you!" exclaimed Spotted Feather.

"I could not stay away any longer," responded Shadow. "I needed to spend some time with my Salish friends again."

"Come and rest and refresh yourselves, our revered guests, and welcome," continued Spotted Feather.

Their younger children, Wind and Butterfly, were immediately absorbed into the throng of other children, whereas Flower and Raven continued with their parents. They were shown into Spotted Feather's lodge, where they were waited on by a host of generous servers.

Spotted Feather was so taken by Rain and her now matured son, knowing the details of their story.

Of course, he was surprised to find that the Nimipu had come to the area in a large number the last hot time as well.

He then went on to proclaim his joy that Shadow hadn't left the area before he came to pay a visit to his friends.

Spotted Feather was amused to hear Raven tell the story of his father riding on the back of a poor distressed buffalo.

"That sounds like your father," he replied. "Always looking to do something to stand out from the others."

They all had a laugh after that quip.

The conversation came around to Rain's reminiscing over her memories of the Siksika country and how Raven had taken hold of the thought and had become determined to see it for himself.

Spotted Feather seemed to have lapsed into a deep line of thought after hearing that being said. Finally, he spoke, saying, "I would like to lead you to the places you speak of, going by way of the mountain trails of the Land of Big Medicine." It was plain to any who heard Spotted Feather speak on this very important subject, as he believed it to be, it was sacred to him.

After spending some time banqueting with the Salish people while Shadow and Raven and Spotted Feather discussed the plans for the journey ahead, Rain started to come to the understanding that she was not included in their planning. It began to boil up in her contemplations until it couldn't be contained any longer.

She proclaimed, "Do not think that I am not going with you to my father's country. I cannot come so near and not visit that place."

By the look on her face, Shadow knew she was serious as could be. Knowing Rain's strength and ability and general durability, he couldn't think of any rational reason why she wouldn't be suited for the trip. When the matter was brought up to Running Wild, she agreed to wait at the village with Wind, Flower, and Butterfly until their return. It was settled. Now to set a time of departure.

Although there was a feeling that some key factors had been determined, Spotted Feather brought up the point that the snow and temperature in the places they were bound for was not yet accommodating to travel there.

While they were about the business of socializing, there came word from a Salish hunting party that an Absaroke hunting party was camped not even a sleep away. Normally, the headmen of the tribe wouldn't concern themselves over this news. The Salish bands weren't particularly aggressive toward other tribes' interests in hunting wherever game might be found, even if it was in their territory. The thing that did cause some genuine interest among them was the possibility that Many Arrows could be connected to this party. It was quickly agreed between them to go and inquire of the hunters on any information pertaining to Many Arrows.

The following early time, Spotted Feather, Shadow, Raven, and several of the Salish braves set out for the Absaroke encampment.

Spotted Feather rode an offspring of his Appaloosa, Storm. He wasn't a full Appaloosa but had many of the characteristics. Spotted Feather spoke of how he cherished Storm as much as any other pony he had known, for being a gift from a great friend and for being an excellent pony. He always had free range to mate with any of the mares owned by the Salish people. These words made Shadow and Raven proud, and even Dancer Also seemed to appreciate it.

All the Salish braves made a fuss over Raven's stallion, Ghost. He had some unique characteristics about him that any horse-loving individual could not help but take notice.

Near the end of the lighttime, they came within sight of the camp they sought. Spotted Feather had stated his opinion concerning the fact that because the Absaroke had been willing to camp so close to Salish territory, he felt it gave him more hope that Many Arrows could be among them.

As they came nearer, Spotted Feather made known that the party should hold up and that he and Shadow would proceed into their camp. Within a short distance, they both noticed one of the tipi lodges had a pony tied at the entryway that was Appaloosa looking in its appearance. They both smiled at each other as Many Arrows, along with a group of other Absarokee braves, strode in their direction.

There was no sense of unease among them. For one thing, they were mounted on Appaloosas. Who else could it be but friends?

There was much joy between the men being united again. Within a relatively short time, Raven and the Salish braves came into camp also. It was another festive occasion, the legend of Cloud Shadow not being lost on the Absaroke braves either.

Many Arrows was very impressed with Raven, having never met Rain but hearing the story from others, like a fable of much intrigue. He recalled how Shadow had stated that he would exact a price from Gray Wolf then the tale of the abducted maiden Rain, Gray Wolf's daughter. Then Shadow found with his captive and taken back to the Siksika camp. Then the amazing escape and the chase that followed. Then the showdown with Shadow being the victor and Rain the unexpected final payment. Yes, it all made for some fine storytelling. Here now was the young man, the son of that fanciful union.

Many winters had passed, and here they sat, companions apart for so long, together once again. The storytelling went on long into the darktime. Raven once again brought up Shadow's thrilling ride upon the buffalo, which everyone enjoyed hearing. They heard of the passing of Long Hair, as well as Black Eagle and Fawn and Big Cat. Finally, it came around to the plan for a complete passage through the Land of Big Medicine. Many Arrows made it known that he had never taken that trip before and was very interested in the idea of it.

The camp managed some sleep, and in the early time, Many Arrows told Shadow and Spotted Feather that he would like to accompany them on their planned journey. Of course, Shadow and Spotted Feather were very happy to hear Many Arrows express to them that desire.

"We will be honored to have you as our traveling companion," proclaimed Shadow, with Spotted Feather echoing the same.

Many Arrows let them know that he would remain with the hunting party for several more sleeps then would come to meet up with them at the Salish village. When Shadow left from the Absaroke hunting camp, his heart was full. The plan to divert toward his Salish friend's home was beginning to develop into much more than he had even hoped. Shadow began to reflect to the time long ago when he and Little Bear had parted from their hunting party, leaving the protection of his father and others of the more experienced braves to travel with the Absaroke to their encampment, for the reason of wanting to begin to try and establish a friendship and alliance with other peoples. The feeling he had that it would be important as time went by. Now he knew that it had been by the direction of the Life Giver that he had followed that feeling, for he certainly did cherish these friends and allies whom had come about in his life while striving to establish an alliance through trust and goodwill.

When they arrived at the Salish village, there was more planning and preparation that would be done as they bided their time.

The lighttime that Many Arrows arrived, all the preparation was complete. The warmer weather had been coming on more intensely, and Spotted Feather, speaking from experience, had concluded that it was indeed time to embark on the expedition. Even though he had looked upon these places before, and he knew that they were in for a trip fraught with peril, he also knew there would be unequalled adventure and beauty. A small group of Salish braves sought to come along to be of assistance in any way they could. They were welcomed by all that were already set to make the journey. The following day, they left, with the tribe bidding them farewell while keeping their concerns contained. Even Running Wild tried to show a positive display as they departed.

Raven was enthralled with the possibilities. Rain was filled with anticipation for the sights and experiences she knew awaited them and for those she could not foresee. Shadow, as always, looked forward to the adventure but not without some reservation, having known the power of adversity. Many Arrows, Spotted Feather, and the volunteer Salish braves mostly felt a sense of responsibility to see

Shadow and his wife and son through, providing whatever effort that was needed.

So onward the stalwart hearts went, with as much determination as could be mustered at any place or time and with any other group of people. Off in the direction of Cold Wind Grandfather they went and soon came in sight of Salish lake, a grand beautiful lake. Then they pushed farther beyond in the same direction. It became all so apparent for any who looked that there was a strongly marked change of geography looming in the distance.

At this point, it had become late evening, so they stopped and had their meal and slept.

At first light, they proceeded once again, continuing to make progress in covering the distance that lay before them. They came to a place that Spotted Feather indicated would be the trailhead to be taken as the starting point of going to the sun. By which he meant in the direction of the place of the rising sun. Although it almost seemed he was implying that they would be drawing closer to the sun. Either way, it had an alluring quality to it. It was a long hard trail they took on that leg of their trek, with Spotted Feather pushing to make contact with the first of several large lakes that they would come to in their travels. It was becoming dark when they came within sight of the first lake. They managed to get to the closest shore of the lake and make camp with still some ability to see their immediate surroundings.

Once they got settled in, Spotted Feather promised that they wouldn't make any more long grueling pushes. He did go on to say it would yet be grueling, but he would keep from making it so long, if he could help it.

"We all want to have an enjoyable time if possible, so let us make the effort to do so," Shadow interjected. It was a pronouncement of sorts, meant to set a standard for the continuing intervals of the trip. They all made an agreeing contribution to what had been purposed, thinking that it sounded like a good way to proceed. They lingered at the lake's edge for another sleep before leaving once again. They continued, following the lake for what seemed a long time.

They stopped again at what appeared to be a sighting of the lake's end, which was confirmed by Spotted Feather.

"The lake does end not far from here," he said. "Then there will be much travel before we come to another."

Rain knew that this area was the same from her past recollections. Where they now stood, she didn't know it in particular, but she still was overcome with an overall appreciation at having arrived at this gateway. It was part of who she was, spending time in this fine country as she was becoming old enough to develop her thoughts and memories. With her life's experiences that she had come to know, she was able to bring to image a vast scope of travels, some more endearing than others. These places were locations of fond memories with her family while growing up in the Siksika tribe.

Everyone in the party was beginning to feel a sense of clarity that seemed to permeate the atmosphere about them and caused one to take in deep breaths of the purity and freshness. It could be smelled and tasted as well. It was a fine place to be, weather permitting. They looked out over the expanse of pristine water, forests of nobility, mountains of grandeur. The Great Spirit had provided the occasion, and it was a time of thanksgiving.

They held up to rest and take nourishment. Everyone was taking in the pleasantries that this place provided for them.

For Raven, he had an idealistic nature that welled up inside of him, along with a wanderlust for the next horizon. He had a genuine sense of being exactly where he was meant to be. He was seeking the next experience that would help to prepare him for manhood, which was his own personal quest.

He was grateful for the company he was among. He truly felt he couldn't imagine better.

The time came when they all mutually agreed to proceed with the traveling. Having secured their gear and provisions, they began again. As they moved in the direction that the journey was taking them, during an early period of the lighttime, they had to divert their eyes somewhat to avoid the glare of the rising sun.

Relatively soon after departing, they began to pass between a couple of mountainous ridges, being enveloped to an extent. Spotted

Feather encouraged them to move along to ensure that they would come clear of the enveloping mountain faces before they could come to a stop from this leg of travel.

Shadow spent a bit of time, while being so closely surrounded with these mountains, studying the higher elevations for signs of movement. He believed that in more than a sighting, he saw either goats or sheep. Sometimes, he would imagine that he had the same view as they did and what it might be like from those heights. Finally, after a good effort of pushing through as Spotted Feather had prompted them, they came to what was a large open place with a splendid expansive vista of more fine forest and vast mountainous terrain. It was a location to stop and rest.

When they entered the area with the large vista opening, Rain exclaimed, "Aha! This is a place I recall. This place is part of my cherished memories!" Rain began to chatter excitedly with her realization. Shadow and Raven were happy for her because it was apparent that it was a joy to her, while she continued to look about at the many sights before them.

CHAPTER 25

THE WELCOMING PARTY

Spotted Feather pointed toward the distant mountains, saying, "The trail takes us along the edge of those mountains, where after some sleeps, we will come to another large lake."

Rain just peered off in the direction that Spotted Feather had indicated while grinning profusely. She did feel very happy in a way that made her feel younger, with all the reminders of her youth.

Raven was also grinning, enjoying each progression toward their destination, while looking at the frozen rivers of ice that descended from the recesses of the mountain tops.

Shadow was grinning as well, seeing the pleasure on his wife and son's faces. He also could not keep from being glad just for the opportunity to be in this splendid place. He looked forward to what lay ahead.

That darktime, it was clear and starry, along with a lot of moonlight that showed off the snowcapped peaks and a glimmering river, creating a softness to the shadowy forest.

They kept their fires small, not wanting to attract attention to themselves. The understanding that they were in the country of the Siksika was a fact that they dared not ignore.

The following early time, Spotted Feather suggested a change in their routine. He made it known that he thought it best to deploy a pair of braves to take the lead of the party so they could observe any development, being much less detectable that way. He also suggested another pair to stay to the rear of the party, watching that no one was trailing them and that they should continue to employ this strategy for the rest of their trip. They all agreed that it sounded like a wise plan.

Again, they packed up and proceeded with their travel. The Salish braves who had volunteered for the advance scouting and rear guard moved to take up their positions.

After hearing the plan of Spotted Feather, Raven made a point to remember it and the sound judgment involved, which again reinforced his opinion on the quality of his companions.

Shadow, as always, never ceased to scan his surroundings with an understanding of the potential for trouble. It was when nearing the end of that interval of travel that a forward scout returned, informing them that they had come across signs of another group of people's recent presence in the vicinity. The news was disturbing but not altogether unexpected. With this group of strong-willed individuals, the idea of turning back was not even considered. It can be said that sometimes bravery and foolishness are closely related. Although it shouldn't be recommended that one be afraid to do whatever was needed to pursue their objectives in life. So such was the reasoning that caused them to press on, even when the probability for success was suspect.

Not long after they had received the information concerning others nearby, they stopped for the time to hold over. They made an effort to contain the light from their cooking fires. They didn't have to have fires, but they figured they were in for too long of a trip to be doing without. Although they would work to keep them less conspicuous throughout the rest of the expedition for expedience's sake. So as it goes with brave souls, they set out the next early time venturing into that uncertain place, steeling themselves for whatever may come.

Again, toward the end of that particular leg of travel, the rear guard caught up to them, conveying the news that they were being trailed. The forward scouts returned, reporting that they had seen much sign of others nearby.

That late time in camp, there was a common understanding that they were about to encounter the inhabitants of the area.

"I think that we as a group should not pose a threat to these people. We have not been hunting. We are medicine seekers," stated Spotted Feather.

Rain spoke up, saying, "They are the tribe of my father's people. I will speak to them of our purpose."

They ended their late time giving themselves over to their fate, asking the Great Spirit to look on their plight with favor.

The following first light, they again proceeded on their predetermined course. This time, they all left together. After a relatively short time, they could again see a large lake on the not-too-distant horizon. They also began to sense that they were not alone in their immediate location.

Then, as if by appointment, they found themselves surrounded by a host of Siksika braves, exceeding their own number by many times over. It was good that it was no surprise encounter and that the interceptors did have them very much overpowered, for there was no tension from fear on their part.

Although it did feel altogether precarious for the small band of interlopers, based on the uncertainty of their encounter.

The Siksika held their places while Spotted Feather signed that they came in peace. At that, a pair of braves rode toward them. When they came up rather close, a single brave gave a general salutation. He then made a verbal inquiry, not understood by the group.

Then Rain responded, "Nimipu, yes, Shadow Hand. I am Gray Wolf's daughter, Rain. This is my son, Raven. We are seeking medicine. We come in peace. We will take nothing from these lands."

The brave seemed amused at this discovery, as did his partner. The brave then went on to inform Rain that her party must come along with them and that they would hear more of this tale.

Rain went on to translate what was conveyed, and it was made known to all the wayfarers. Before long, they were being escorted in the direction of the lake up ahead.

The Siksika led the small group, needing to stay over a couple of sleeps along the way. They were traveling beside the large lake and then turning toward the Land of the Thorn Plants. They again stayed over a sleep before finally arriving at a large Siksika encampment. It was very large and daunting. The entire camp was in a frenzy over the arrival of their men with captives.

They, in their entirety, were led to a location in the center of the village where they came to a stop outside of a very large tipi lodge. The lodge was embellished with a large depiction of the sun.

There was a lull that fell over the gathered throng. Out stepped Gray Wolf, along with several other prestigious-looking elders.

When Gray Wolf set his eyes on Shadow, he immediately pointed at him and yelled out, "Seize him!"

At that outburst, Many Arrows, as fast as it could be done, nocked an arrow on his bow and had it at full draw and aimed at Gray Wolf's heart. Then an elder who had stepped out of the tipi lodge along with Gray Wolf walked in between Shadow and some who began to act on Gray Wolf's command. This man was Big Sun, a major chief among the Siksika nation.

Big Sun began to speak, and all hearkened to his words.

"I was there that day Shadowhand challenged you to mortal combat. I witnessed the fairness and bravery and mercy that was shown to you by this man. I cannot allow that he would enter this place and be disrespected in this way."

Gray Wolf, although attentive to the words of Big Sun, was also very much focused on the arrow he knew was serving him a death sentence at that moment. When Big Sun finished speaking and all kept their place, Many Arrows withdrew his posture of aggression.

Big Sun continued speaking. "It seems obvious to me that these who have come among us have not posed a threat to us. I call for calm and respect for these visitors unless there is a reason to think otherwise. Come and rest and refresh yourselves," he offered.

At that, the crowd, for the most part, began to disperse, and the band of wayfarers began to dismount. A lot of the Siksika braves continued to linger nearby. They were somewhat fixated on Shadow, for he had also become a legend among their people.

Gray Wolf had been put on hold in his initial reaction. Although in his advanced age, his hatred and rage did not burn as intensely as it once did. After surveying the group before him, he found himself being more overcome with curiosity than any other feelings. He was certain that this, now a woman, was his daughter. He had told himself that he had disavowed her and would concern himself with her no more, but it was easy when he believed that he would never see her again.

Rain resisted trying to approach her father, being totally uncertain what he was feeling or thinking, especially after his aggression toward Shadow.

Big Sun recognized Rain and approached her, asking, "What brings you here?"

Rain respectfully replied, "I once again desired to look upon the place of my father's people. I expressed this to my husband, Cloud Shadow. While I spoke of these things, our son, Raven,"—she indicated who he was—"began to take interest. I told of the Place of Big Medicine. I spoke of the Chief Mountain and how the young men of the Siksika people desired to seek their vision and spirit guide quests there. Afterward, our son began to feel compelled to go there himself, and so it is that we have come here."

While she spoke those words, Gray Wolf stood by and listened intently. He also could hardly withdraw his gaze from upon Raven after hearing that he was her son. Raven resembled Gray Wolf in a lot of ways, being stocky, broad shouldered, barrel-chested, with a wide mouth with small piercing eyes.

Rain, as it came to be, was Gray Wolf's only child. His only wife had died young, not so long after the birth of his daughter.

He felt something coming over him that he had not known before. It was compassion, as he thought about Rain's reason for returning and looking upon his grandson standing so close by.

Raven was aware of Gray Wolf's unyielding focus toward him. Mostly, it made him confused as to what the reason might be yet also recognizing the likeness.

Gray Wolf, without reservation, spoke. "You have a fine son, my daughter."

At those words, Rain moved before her father and placed a hand on his shoulder and replied, "It makes my heart glad to hear you speak those words, my father."

At that, he placed his hand upon her shoulder. When Raven heard their exchange of words, he also walked up to where they stood. Raven spoke, "Grandfather whom I have never known." Then he placed his hands on the shoulders of his mother and grandfather, and then all of them moved in a step closer and placed their heads together. There were sounds emitting from their tight enclosure that could only be construed as sounds of extreme and pure emotional release.

There were a pair of individuals who weren't participants in this special reunion who were also very much appreciative of the scene taking place before them. They were Shadow and Big Sun. Big Sun was a man who had been Gray Wolf's closest friend in his life and had been a witness to all his trials and tribulations, of which there were many. Of course, Shadow had an entirely different reason to be thankful. He hadn't cared for the fact that Rain and Raven were estranged from Gray Wolf.

From his own personal point of view concerning Gray Wolf, he felt no more animosity toward him. He had paid the price and then some. Shadow could not help but notice that Gray Wolf still walked with a limp and obviously could not bend what used to be his strong arm.

The venturing party continued their stay at the Siksika encampment, having a very memorable time there. Gray Wolf and Raven spent their time communing for long intervals at a time like a couple of long-lost best friends that have been reunited. Rain simply spent her time looking on with deep satisfaction.

Although the time did come when it was agreed that they should proceed on their journey. Raven promised his grandfather that he would return to see him again before leaving the area. Rain and her father pledged their undying love for one another, no matter what their lives held for them. Shadow and Gray Wolf never exchanged any formal gestures toward each other, but it was evident that Gray Wolf didn't feel it necessary to hold any further grudge.

CHAPTER 26

A Spirit Guide

There was a bittersweet parting, and then they moved on in the direction of Cold Wind Grandfather. There was some discussion before they departed about an escort by the Siksika for protection. It had previously been told that there had been some incursions by the very hostile Kenistenoag, who were principally inhabitants of the country of the Cold Wind Grandfather and were sworn enemies of the Siksika people. They also seemed to relish the opportunity to harass and murder them whenever they were given an avenue to do so.

Although even Gray Wolf felt that given the nature of their guest, a large party wouldn't be appropriate. So they continued as they had begun. They proceeded with several more sleeps of travel before they came in view of Chief Mountain, with its sheer face and somewhat flat top. Before the sheer face, there was a gradual solid rock base. It had a majestic look about it, calling out, "Come and see what you can find of me." Raven looked on, as if under a spell.

Shadow motioned for a halt and conveyed that he thought they shouldn't proceed any farther. It should be for Raven to traverse the final leg of the journey. While the party were still the guests of Big Sun's encampment, the topic was of the vision and spirit guide quest that had been discussed in Raven's presence. The cleansing of the body, along with meditation and prayer for more wisdom and inner strength. The bodies cleansing coming about through fasting and a good sweating.

Gray Wolf had presented Raven with a pouch containing dried cedar shavings to mingle with the coals in the sweat lodge, creating a sacred incensed smoke to be directed onto the body to help make the flesh more acceptable to the spiritual realm.

All these things Raven had purposed to do before setting out on his quest.

Everyone present was helpful in any way they could but tried not to interfere with the intent and purpose of the ceremony of one.

The time arrived for Raven to depart. He felt ready within himself. He left on foot. All things considered, he believed it best.

The first obstacle he had to overcome was a river flowing from the mountains into a lake. He managed to find a place where the water was relatively slower, and he also located a somewhat large piece of dry wood. He stripped off his clothing then placed his bow and quiver of arrows, along with his flint knife and clothing, on the piece of wood. He then pushed till he could no longer stand while continuing pushing as he kicked for propulsion, guiding his float to the opposite shore.

Once there, he pulled the piece of wood to shore and placed it where he could find it for his return. He carried his belongings without dressing, allowing the air to dry him before he placed his clothing back on. Then again, without delay, he proceeded, with Chief Mountain always beckoning. Before he reached the rock base, from where he stood, he watched the sun recede directly behind the peak of his objective mountain. Now he would hold up because of the darkness.

At first light, Raven left again after a meditative waiting period, with the mountain looming overhead. With solid determination, he pressed on. Finally, he could reach out and touch that which was the base of his goal. He immediately began to plot his course to ascend to a place hopefully of a more perfect understanding. He soon found himself studying segments of crags, some certainly offering only impossibility. After a period of searching, Raven gave himself over to a place where there was a deep fluted section where he believed he could place his feet against one side and his back up against the other. And then by pushing with his legs and arms, he could work his way up to a location that he had viewed and would, as he was counting on, be able to stand. He also felt that from that point, there appeared to be some access to more movement upward.

He set out on the task at hand, moving the objects on his back to his front. He began his ascent with confidence. It was slow going and very difficult. After much agony and effort, he managed to reach a plateau, where he lay out as if dead.

Much later, he came awake to his situation. He could tell by the location of the sun that he had been in a deep sleep for a long period. He made himself stand and then remained in that position for a while before taking a step. He began again, finding that he could indeed move along as he suspected to be able to from farther below. He did so for a while, climbing higher with each stride. Later, when he had come to another place of difficulty, he decided to stop for the time, because again it was beginning to get dark.

That darktime, after a long period without food and having had little water, he experienced the knowledge of being a spiritual being and having no sense of his bodily needs. He began to have thoughts that were unfamiliar to him, such as life after death and a feeling of a presence of deceased ancestors. A direct and continual relationship with the Creator, the Life Giver, the Great Spirit, being one in the same.

That there existed an influence of violence that was part of this time that he was born into. That it would end sometime, but not during the time of his life, so to expect it and be prepared for it when it happens, to be able to stem the tide in his favor if it be possible.

His thoughts moved along throughout the darktime. Eventually, the light began to make its presence so that he could find his way once again.

To find his way was foremost on Raven's mind. So he found it hard to believe as the light began to focus his attention on a location he hadn't taken any notice of prior to then that appeared to allow for farther ascent from where he previously believed there was no way. Without delay, he moved on to reach that higher ground.

He proceeded along when, at a certain place in time, he arrived at a point where there, directly in front of him, was a pinnacle of modest stature, and cradled at its base was a huge eagle's nest. Something deep inside him made him to know that this was his destination. He didn't know why or for what reason he was there at that particular place. While his mind was seeking an explanation, at the time appointed, there arrived a large black shape that began to manifest into the form of an eagle in a full-on attack posture with shoulders back, wings outstretched, talons extended wide open, and beak agape, causing a momentary shock to Raven. Then the shape came to a stop as it brought itself to alight upon the pinnacle.

It wasn't a brown eagle of which Raven had seen many, but was black, black as a raven's wing. Raven found himself speaking out, "Black Eagle?" Then the strangest thing he had experienced thus far happened to him. He knew that a voice within other than his own began to address him.

"You have come a long distance and with much difficulty to find your way to this place. Now hear me as I tell you what you need to know. You are never alone. You are greatly loved. Be strong and take courage. Your reward awaits you. Uphold those who cannot stand without help. Yours is an honorable place in this life, so press on and do not falter, for I will be near. Think on these things to help you when the way gets hard."

At that, the eagle once again took to the air and was gone. Raven knew it was time he was going also and turned back toward the place from which he had come. Feeling full in every way possible, he made his descent to the place of mortal men and all the challenges that awaited him there.

It was late the following lighttime when Raven returned unexpectedly to his family and companions. There was much rejoicing upon seeing him unharmed and happy. They were happy that he was back, happy of his success, happy because he was greatly loved, and happy to be able to continue with their lives together.

While Raven was being provided for, he began to expound on all the things that he had seen and heard. Of course, Shadow found it all most interesting, especially the part about the black eagle.

CHAPTER 27

TRIUMPH AND TRAGEDY

When the wayfarers departed from that place of medicine, it had already been decided that they would stop at Big Sun's encampment. Raven told his grandfather that he would, and they all, to a person, felt it would be too strenuous and lengthy to return through the mountains.

Again, they stopped over to rest from their travel. The following lighttime, after a short time on the trail, a forward scout returned to them with the news of a party of what appeared to be Kenistenoag waiting in ambush for a party of approaching Siksika. He went on to tell that he did not believe that they were aware of the movements of their party as of yet.

After hearing these things, they began to formulate a plan to ambush the ambushers. First, Shadow and Spotted Feather and Many Arrows sought to get a closer look at the situation. At that, they hurried off, having the others wait for their return.

They came to find that the Kenistenoag were not far from where the venturers had received word of their presence. As Shadow and the others took a concealed position to view them, things became unraveled. At the same time that they looked upon the concealed warriors of the Kenistenoag, they sprang on the Siksika, who had just come within range of their ambush. Also, unbeknownst to them altogether, there was another group of Kenistenoag that had been watching the venturers' every move. At the same time the one group sprang on the Siksika, the other attacked the venturers' party.

A lone Salish brave with the sole intent of informing the forward observers of what just took place raced away from the attack. The Salish brave reached Shadow just before he and the others headed into the fray taking place before them.

Something that was working to the benefit of those being attacked was that the Kenistenoag hadn't embraced the horse culture for themselves, so they were wholly afoot.

Many Arrows hadn't noticed the approach of the Salish brave and proceeded with a charge toward the Siksika struggle.

Shadow and Spotted Feather immediately turned back toward the place where they had come from. Within a short time, they arrived to see Raven and Rain, along with the Salish braves, fighting for their lives. Several of the ponies had already been brought down by enemy arrows and spears. Raven and Rain were still mounted and were staying close to the fight, swinging their war clubs for all they could summon. Some Salish braves were still unleashing missiles of devastation upon their attackers.

Shadow and Spotted Feather flew in upon the enemy, bringing forth more lethal punishment. Suddenly, there was a signal from a Kenistenoag attacker, and they that were still able broke and ran for cover among the forest.

Shadow surveyed the scene before him as he and Rain and Raven came together. Rain and Raven had some superficial wounds, and there appeared as well to be a couple of the Salish braves who had lost their lives to the onslaught. Spotted Feather had been struck in the shoulder by a spear. It was a bad wound with the potential to be deadly.

Shadow asked Rain to tend to Spotted Feather and for the others to stand guard while he went to see how the Siksika party had fared.

He rode off in the direction of the other attack. Without hesitating, he moved toward the battle site. On arriving, he could see that it, too, had come to a conclusion, but with more casualties than the other fight. Right away, Shadow noticed Many Arrows's pony standing near what appeared to be Many Arrows laying on the ground in a fetal position, not moving. There were other bodies strewn about him. There also were a number of Siksika braves moving around the area, along with some mutilating of the dead and dying Kenistenoag taking place.

Shadow quickly dismounted near to where Many Arrows lay. He knelt over him, speaking his name.

"I hear you, my brother," he understood Many Arrows to whisper in response. Many Arrows went on, "I looked for you. I did not see you near."

"I had to fight to save Rain and Raven," Shadow replied.

"Did you save them, my brother?" he asked.

"They are well, my friend," Shadow answered him.

"Good. I am glad for all of you. Keep them safe and cherish them," Many Arrows responded.

"How is it with you, brave heart?" Shadow asked. There was no response. He asked again with more forcefulness. Again, there was no response. Shadow felt a deep sadness sweep over him, along with a great sense of loss. He later learned that Many Arrows had put up an amazing fight, so much so that the enemy determined that he had to be stopped. Eventually, and with much effort and sacrifice, they had managed to run him through with a spear. Shadow made it known that he and he alone would take responsibility for caring for his body.

Once the venturers caught up to the location of the other battle scene and the wounded had been cared for, all the victorious survivors made way for Big Sun's encampment. The deceased warriors were drawn on travois. There was a heaviness that stayed with the returning party throughout the trek.

Raven couldn't help but recall the vision impression concerning the acts of violence and being prepared to meet them when needed. The tragic loss of Many Arrows represented the fact that there was no promise for tomorrow. They needed to live each day with thankfulness and responsibility, making the effort to try not to be an unnecessary burden to others by way of holding up their end of the task at hand in every avenue of their lives, if possible. He couldn't see any responsibility toward acts of foolishness or deceit. One certainly had to be vigilant in all things. He also recalled his mother's efforts at holding off her attackers. She inflicted much damage on those who were careless enough to come within range of her club. It seemed obvious to him that being the offspring of Shadow and Rain was a sound beginning to being an overcomer. Rain and Shadow likewise were very proud of the way Raven had stood his ground in the struggle, with never any indication of relenting his aggression toward the attackers. It was do-or-die, and he brought to bear all that was needed to help repel the onslaught.

Then there was another thing that caught Shadow's attention as he took that moment to look after Raven's efforts during the fighting. He felt certain that he had seen a low flying eagle nearby. It appeared to be black. Finally, they arrived at Big Sun's encampment. There was a stirring at their arrival when it was perceived that there had been a serious attack with fatalities. Big Sun and Gray Wolf were present when they wearily made their way to Big Sun's lodge. At a glance, Gray Wolf could see his daughter and grandson seemed to have fared reasonably well. There was a wailing that began to prevail over all other sounds in the camp, resulting from the realization of the deaths of their tribe members.

The venturers dismounted, and Gray Wolf approached Rain, inquiring of the details of the assault upon them. Shortly after that, Rain made the point to her father that she was going to need to direct her attention to working with Shadow to help him prepare for the taking of his good friend's body back to his people. At that, she left conversing with her father and went to help Shadow tend to Many Arrows's preparation. Cloud Shadow welcomed her efforts and abilities, realizing he needed the assistance.

Rain worked with Shadow, rewrapping Many Arrows's body with hides to hopefully allow it to be transported on the long journey to Absaroka. Shadow didn't care to contemplate the thought of prolonging the trip at all. He let Rain know that he would be leaving right away. He also let her know that he wanted her to return with Spotted Feather and the remaining Salish braves to their village and to wait there with Running Wild and the children for his return.

Within a short time after they had spoken, Shadow left on his sorrowful mission.

Rain informed Spotted Feather that she would be leaving with him to his home whenever he felt able. Spotted Feather was more than ready to be at home to rest his very painful and debilitating wound.

Then she returned to her father and the discussion they were in previously. As Raven stood nearby, he heard her tell his grandfather that most likely at first light, she would be leaving with the Salish back to where her daughter, Butterfly, and others of Shadow's family were waiting for their return. Gray Wolf asked that she stay with him sometime yet, and she replied that she could not. Upon hearing the discourse between them, Raven responded, signing as he spoke, "I will stay and spend more time with you, Grandfather."

Rain countered by asking, "Are you certain of what you say?"

Raven replied, "I feel that it is right for me to stay and come to know my grandfather. With his time in winters, now is the time to spend with him."

Rain just smiled at them both and said no more.

The following early time, Gray Wolf and Raven were there with Rain and Spotted Feather right before they departed. Again, emotions ran high, but things were settled between them as they said their farewells.

Raven told his mother, "Don't worry. I know the way home. One lighttime you'll look, and there I'll be." She embraced him and her father and then mounted her pony and left for their destination. Raven turned away after exchanging waves with her to enter the experience of living among the Siksika.

Shadow looked off at the far horizon as he contemplated the task that lay ahead. He also continued to mourn the loss of a true friend and cherished companion while trying to maintain a positive outlook.

Rain had much to reflect on, not having her husband or son with her on her return trip to meet up with Running Wild and the children. There was all that had transpired while on their venture, and then she would dwell on the thought of her father and son being together at this time in their lives. Then her thoughts would shift to Shadow and the burden that he was under. There was certainly plenty to think about as she traveled along. Running Wild, in the meanwhile, had been anxiously waiting, hoping to hear some word concerning the rest of her family. She also was anxious to tell Shadow and sister, Rain, that she was expecting another child. The symptoms began to take place almost immediately after Shadow and Rain and Raven had departed. It hadn't been easy keeping up with the work of caring for the children and dealing with her morning sickness too. She recalled when she mentioned to Flower, Wind, and Butterfly that they would be getting another little brother or sister in the not too long of time. They all acted excited about it, and it made her smile to herself. She thought, not for the first time, what a pleasant family she was part of. She thanked the Great Spirit for that, as she often did. The very next lighttime after Running Wild's most anxious time, Rain, along with Spotted Feather and the remaining Salish braves, returned.

CHAPTER 28

A Vision of Consequence

The entire village came to greet them and look after their needs. Running Wild and the children were on hand as the small procession made their way to the center of the encampment. There was much excitement and turmoil as it was made obvious that all was not well. There was no Shadow or Raven, Spotted Feather with an apparent grievous wound, and a pair of Salish braves bodies on travois.

Rain quickly dismounted and immediately went to Running Wild and the children. "Shadow and Raven are fine" was the first thing out of her mouth. She knew beforehand that it would be Running Wild's first concern, and the look on her face confirmed it. Running Wild hugged Rain and wept. Rain, in turn, held Running Wild in a comforting embrace for an extended time. When they let go, Rain gave her a reassuring smile. Rain then went on while holding the children close to her to tell of the reason for Shadow and Raven not being with them yet. They were all sad to hear of Many Arrows's death. As Rain continued telling all that had happened, it made for a most interesting yet tragic tale.

Eventually, Running Wild got an opportunity to let Rain know of the coming new addition to the family. Rain showed that she also was happy and excited to hear it. Raven was feeling good about being with his mother's people. Gray Wolf also was feeling a happiness that was quite rare in his life. He was waking up in the early time with his grandson, whom not long before he didn't even know existed, having him there with him, sharing their time together.

Shadow arrived at Absaroka after several sleeps. As before, it was a large encampment, and shortly after his coming into view of the camp, a group of riders came out to meet him. He motioned to the travois and uttered that it was Many Arrows.

At that, a single rider turned and hurried toward their village. By the time Shadow came into the camp, everyone already knew why he had come.

Many Arrows's father, Long Hair, had passed on already, he knew, because Many Arrows had told him so. He was met by his wives and children and close friends. He conveyed to them of how he had been killed in battle against the Kenistenoag and that he had fought bravely until the last. Several of the Absaroke braves thanked Shadow for returning Many Arrows's body to his people. Shadow let them know that he thought of Many Arrows as a brother and that his death was a great loss to him.

Shadow sadly turned and made his way out of camp, with the sounds of wailing being heard around the village. Not long after his departure, he could hear a rider approaching. He halted as a boy on a pony trotted up to him, holding Many Arrows's bow in his hands, gesturing for Shadow to take it. Shadow knew what a fine bow it was, backed by mountain sheep horn. It was a bow that was loved. He also knew that it was a special present from his family. Shadow grasped it then pulled it to his heart and gave the boy a wide smile. The boy smiled back with a face that reminded Shadow that Many Arrows lived on.

When he arrived at the Salish village, a happy reunion awaited him there. His children rushed up to him first. They then escorted him to his wives, where he received fond attention.

"Where's Raven?" Shadow inquired.

"He chose to stay on with his grandfather," Rain explained as she peered into the quizzical face of his father.

"For how long?" he asked, still looking perplexed.

"I don't think he knows yet," Rain responded. "He said he knows the way home, and sometime, we'll look up and there he will be."

Shadow appeared to ponder that for a moment and then replied, "Good."

Then he heard a small voice saying, "Father, were going to have a little brother or sister before long." It was Lovely Butterfly with a very smug look on her face.

"We are?" responded Shadow. "Who said?"

"Running Wild did," replied Butterfly.

Shadow looked at Running Wild, and she looked into his eyes and nodded in agreement to what her spokesperson had just informed him. He then put his arm over her shoulder and placed a hand on her belly and his head against hers. He responded, "I am glad to know it. It is good." He was very tired and emotionally drained.

Shadow continued there with Spotted Feather for several more sleeps. Spotted Feather was gradually recovering, and he and Shadow were once again saying their farewells. The entire Cloud Shadow family had been received into the Salish tribe. It had become common knowledge that they would be leaving the following early time. There was a feast and dance that late time in honor of their friendship with well-wishing all around.

At first light, they packed their belongings as well as some provisions and gave their final parting hugs and thankyous. Even Spotted Feather had managed to be present for the occasion. It was a fine time as weather conditions went. They all mounted and began to proceed on their way, with some final waves of goodbye.

Shadow, in parting, had the thought of how good it had been to spend that much time with his close friend. He also couldn't help but reflect to the time not all so long ago when they were approaching the Salish camp with so many hopeful expectations and now being able to have the memories of those expectations fulfilled. Although it was at a cost that they couldn't have conceived.

Meanwhile, Raven sat with Gray Wolf and Big Sun, along with other tribal elders, smoking the ceremonial pipe and hearing words of experience from the prominent heads of the village.

Part of the reason for the meeting in Big Sun's lodge was concerning Raven. After he had returned from his vision and spirit guide quest, his grandfather had questioned him on what took place. He explained as well as he could, and Rain had assisted him in any details that needed clarifying. When the describing had ended, Gray Wolf was well-informed. Then the story was retold to Big Sun by way of Gray Wolf, and so now they were going to reiterate before these elders, mainly because it was thought to be that interesting of a tale.

Raven knew that he sat in a privileged place, just being allowed to sit among this group of renowned tribesmen. He also began to develop an understanding that he was not of these people. Not that he didn't respect the Siksika culture, but that it was not his culture.

Something Raven hadn't been aware of previously was that the symbol of the black eagle was big medicine among this band of Siksika. The fact that Raven had returned with a story of a black eagle who spoke to him was most curious indeed. Although he didn't hear the words emitted from the eagle's tongue, he felt certain that the thought impressions were issued from the living entity that was before him. He also recalled his father telling him that the same thing had happened to him concerning his encounter with the mountain goat.

Big Sun began by relating the story as told to him by Gray Wolf. As the others who were gathered there listened intently without interruption, he continued to convey from the time that Rain first mentioned Chief Mountain to Raven up to Raven's return to the Siksika village after receiving his vision. There was also mention of a sighting of a black eagle present at the battle with the Kenistenoag, apparently seen by several witnesses. When Big Sun had finished, they all turned their eyes toward Raven, although he had been aware of them taking glances at him during the telling of the tale.

Raven wasn't sure how to respond to the attention that was now upon him, but before he did anything, Gray Wolf spoke, saying, "My grandson did not tell this story to me looking for any kind of attention. He just told it at my asking. Big Sun felt that it should be told again, that you could also know of this taking place. That is all."

An elder called Talks A Lot responded, "This is a strange tale to me. I will think on it some more." With that, the others seemed to concur. Then they all stood and began to make their way out of the lodge.

Then there was just Big Sun, Gray Wolf, and Raven remaining. Big Sun then spoke, "If this vision did not involve a black eagle, it never would have been retold. It is a story that makes us to wonder on the importance of such a thing coming into our village. I will ask the medicine man of our band for his thoughts about this matter."

After Big Sun had made that statement, Raven noticed Gray Wolf's countenance take on an uneasiness. Something Raven didn't know, because nothing had been said in regard to it, was that this band of Siksika were very superstitious, thus the reason for Gray Wolf's concern for his grandsons well-being.

Later that lighttime, the medicine man, along with a large congregation of the band, gathered near Big Sun's lodge as Big Sun greeted them there.

The medicine man began his speech. "I have asked of the familiar spirits concerning this thing that faces us about a Nimipu brave in our village who claims to be guided by a black eagle, and I have gotten guidance that he should be put out from among us."

Big Sun, although a head chieftain within the Siksika nation, was not an overlord of the people. He was respected for his intelligence and bravery. He was made chief, but not to make demands of the people. He knew that this was not a group to be trifled with. He went on to address the crowd. "I have heard your words, and I do not question what you have spoken of. All I ask is that you allow me to take charge of the matter. I will make this clear to Gray Wolf and his grandson. Go and be certain that this will be done as you say." At that, the crowd dispersed, and Big Sun went to speak with his friend Gray Wolf.

Big Sun entered Gray Wolf's lodge, where he found grandfather and grandson conversing. They looked up at Big Sun as he made his presence known. Right away, Gray Wolf knew there was trouble by the look on his friend's face, bracing himself for what he was about to be told. Big Sun was not one to mince words, so he got right to the purpose of his visit.

He began by saying, "Things have not gone well concerning the matter of Raven's vision. I do not hold with this people's fearful ways, but I know how they are when it puts its hold on them. They have decided that Raven has to be put out from the village."

Raven looked over at his grandfather with a look of concern and sadness. Gray Wolf had a look of stubbornness and determination. Then he spoke. "So we both shall leave then."

Big Sun and Raven both questioned him on his pronouncement, but he was adamant about it.

CHAPTER 29

BITTERSWEET REUNIONS

The following lighttime, the pair made all their preparations and left with only Big Sun to see them off.

Raven had let his grandfather know that the only destination he had in mind was the Palus band encampment. Gray Wolf responded, "Good. I will see my granddaughter." Something Raven did not know was that they were only a few sleeps behind the rest of the family.

As they moved off into the horizon, Big Sun stood in place, looking on, thinking that he should not have mentioned Raven's vision to others. But what he didn't realize was that it had all been predetermined. Gray Wolf felt an unexpected feeling of excitement come over him as he peered off into the vast distance. He was off on an adventure with his grandson, a thing that he could never have imagined not so long ago. Raven also felt good about traveling once again, of which he felt came to him naturally by way of his father.

*****

Shadow looked on at his wives and children who were out ahead. Wild Wind was beginning to look less like a child and more like an adolescent, as Beautiful Flower had not so long ago. Flower would be absorbed into the women's ways soon enough, but Wind would need to be looked to by himself, along with the help of Talon and Raven, so that he would gain the right skills with understanding which would prove to be necessary. As his thoughts went to Raven, he felt a twinge of anxiety and then said a prayer for his safekeeping. Of course, he couldn't know that he was happy and healthy and very much enjoying his time as he progressed along with his grandfather not all so far from where he was at that moment.

Then his thoughts went to his brother, Talon, who had stayed behind. He was asked to stay behind to help provide for the band's needs, whatever they might be. Shadow followed that thought with a mental image of Talon enjoying a leisurely time around their village. It was ironic that he should be having an impression of that sort, because instead, at that moment, Talon was struggling for his life.

His brother sometime earlier had traveled with a small group of other Nimipu braves a considerable distance toward Cold Wind Grandfather, looking to trap for pelts. They had traveled the same route that Talon and Shadow had when they went on their trapping expedition. Only this party had exceeded that distance. Something they were not expecting to find was a very nomadic band of Kenistenoag in the same area as themselves. They had no suspicions. They had never heard tell of any conflicts with hostile peoples in these parts.

The Kenistenoag had been dealing with extended periods of extreme cold, and a migration toward a somewhat more moderate climate, wherever it could be found, had been underway. This group of wanderers had ended up directly in the path of Talon and his fellow braves.

The Nimipu had been trapping for a while now and had pack animals laden with a bounty of pelts, along with a substantial herd of ponies, which, to the Kenistenoag, represented food. They were in a fixed position, having already sighted the unwary hunting party coming directly toward their place of concealment.

It was a full-on rout by the Kenistenoag. The unsuspecting Nimipu were surrounded. Talon was at the rear when the attack came. It all happened so fast. All he saw was the surge of moving bodies on foot with spears and clubs being flung and swung and he himself being hit in the side of the face by some heavy object. He was mounted on a young spirited stallion, a descendant of Sun Dancer, who instinctively reared onto his hind legs while flailing his forelegs aggressively toward the attackers. When they came down, he and his pony bolted away from the assault with Talon clinging for his life.

The stallion ran while Talon held on. Within a relatively short time, he pulled up his pony and tried to view the onslaught behind him. He could see no one still mounted. It appeared all was lost. He himself was bleeding heavily from above and below the eye. He felt sure that there was nothing that he could do for his companions. Even though in that feeble state, he had a fire burning for retaliation.

With deep sadness and regret, he turned for home. His foremost regret was that they had come on this excursion at all, although knowing full well that it was a point of futility, being too late to change the outcome.

After some distance traveled, he stopped and cut a piece of deer hide to fold into a pad, along with a long strip to secure it with. He then compressed it against his face, wrapping the strip a couple times around his head before putting it into place. As he once again left on his arduous journey, he could feel a significant change taking hold on the temperature toward the colder side.

*****

As Raven and Gray Wolf continued their trek, there were some small sparse snowflakes drifting through the air. Where Shadow was along the trail, they also were experiencing some light snow activity. The cold time was coming early, it seemed. The going was slow for Shadow and his family. For Raven and Gray Wolf, the pace was more brisk.

Shadow held over an extra sleep due to high winds. Raven and Gray Wolf pressed on. While they were still making headway, they spotted a group of ponies and a small camp ahead. As they approached, it became obvious to the campers and the approaching riders that this was to be a reunion of family members.

What a pleasant occurrence to take place in this unlikely location. Rain was quite overcome at the sight of her father as well as her son. Again, the embracing and utterances of deep emotion erupted from among them. The encounter was uplifting to everyone. It wasn't until a little while later that the story of why Gray Wolf and Raven were on this trail, at this time, came out.

Gray Wolf was quickly introduced to the other children and was particularly pleased to make the acquaintance of his granddaughter, Lovely Butterfly. She likewise was happy to have this grandfather in her life. They got off to a good start right from their initial meeting.

Gray Wolf made the statement to Rain, "It is good to begin a new life at this late time." It had certainly been a turn of the course of his existence. With this happy occasion, they all felt freshened and invigorated.

This was not the case with Talon, who was weak and exhausted. He plodded on with his inner strength and prayers to keep him going. Sometimes, he slept while riding as his highly intelligent pony stayed on course. He slowly progressed on his trek home, and his mind pondered each moment that passed. He began to ponder his growing relationship with his pony, who up till that time had not been given a proper name. He decided to endow this faithful friend with a name that was fitting. While he contemplated this matter, the light had since faded, and a lone bright star made an appearance, causing Talon to utter to his pony, "Bright Star, you surely are my bright star. Lead on."

There were times when the snow would accumulate on the ground, and Shadow, along with his family, would shelter for a period. The full force of the cold time had not come yet, but it would present itself more often than not, particularly at this elevation, which was still far above the lowlands. Now it was becoming slow going for them.

As for Talon, he also was facing a lot of freezing temperatures while Bright Star continued on course. In one place, he found a partially eaten carcass of a coyote. He stopped there and rested while managing a fire to cook what meat he scavenged.

At first light, he began his journey again, knowing the hardship of the remaining distance yet to be traversed. With his great pony and determination, they pressed on toward their goal. Anything edible Talon could muster, he consumed. More than on a single occasion, he trapped some small fish in shallow pools along the river's edge. He ate any insects he could get in his grasp. He brought down a small bird with a stick. He also was able to snare a rabbit while he held over for a rest period. He broke open pinecones for their seeds. Whatever he could do, he did. Onward they trudged, relentlessly, purposely, onward. Eventually, they covered the distance. When they came within sight of their destination, Bright Star caught scent of the herd and began to trot. And shortly after, Talon encouraged him to run. They came toward the Palus encampment at a fast pace, finally slowing upon entering it, where Talon collapsed from exhaustion.

When he awoke, he was looking into the faces of Shadow and Raven. As it turned out, he had laid unconscious for several sleeps. He had awakened just shortly after they had gotten home. No one yet knew why he had showed up alone, although it did not look good. What had happened to him and the others was still a mystery. There had been a young woman kneeling beside Talon when they had entered the lodge. She got up and went out after they had come in. Now she returned with a meat broth to spoon into Talon's mouth. Talon sensed the nourishment as it came near. He took in a spoonful, then another.

After some more moments of silence, he spoke. "Dead. All dead."

CHAPTER 30

READY FOR A RECKONING

Shadow, being very torn at the sight of his brother in that state, asked, "What happened?"

"Ambushed, murderers," replied the extremely weak individual lying before them.

Shadow responded, "We'll talk later. Rest and take some more broth, my brother." He then patted him on the shoulder and went out from Talon's lodge.

Eventually, Talon grew strong enough to tell the entire story. They all wanted revenge, but they knew that they would have to wait. The weather was controlling their actions for the time being.

There was a great mourning like none any could recall in their lives. The deaths of that many young, strong Nimipu braves at one time was unheard of among the Palus band.

When Talon finally recovered, he had changed in his behavior, appearing restless and dangerous. The wide pronounced scar stretching from the top of his face to the middle of his cheek added to his menacing appearance. The only one who was able to have any success with consoling him was the young woman who had nursed him back to health.

Little Wing was her name, and she possessed that special balm to treat her man. And he took her to be his wife.

Talon also enjoyed spoiling his great friend Bright Star. He usually kept him tied to a stake near his lodge to keep an eye on him, but he did not neglect to give him his play periods and exercise each lighttime. He also worked with him a lot just to sharpen their interaction for that moment when it had to be there. Bright Star had saved his life, and he felt that it was very possible that he would need to do it again. Talon understood that his mount in battle was every bit as important as any weapon he might carry.

The cold time had set in with its full besieging capability. There was plenty of time to discuss the inevitable search for the attackers of the Nimipu hunter, trappers. Talon's description of those responsible caused Shadow and Raven to feel close to certain that these perpetrators were of the same tribe that had attacked them also and ultimately were the killers of Many Arrows as well. This realization only heightened the zeal they had for a reckoning.

Raven had an idea that had taken root in his core—to make himself a shield that he would carry. He also intended to create a symbol of a black eagle on the face of the shield. It wasn't wholly an original idea, for he had seen a shield in Big Sun's lodge that had a depiction of the sun painted on its face. Gray Wolf had volunteered to help him construct it, for he had made several shields in his time.

It was also a time to repair and make snowshoes, something that Many Arrows had introduced to the Palus band while he was among them. It certainly appeared to be shaping up to be that type of cold time. There was already a significant amount of snow accumulated.

After Raven's shield was completed and had been dry-cured, he took some charcoal and sketched his design. Then he proceeded to finish it with paint. It filled the entire face of the shield, the outstretched wings, the top of the head, to the tips of the talons being edged with a red border. Raven began to revere it as part of his medicine.

All who looked upon his creation had to comment on how impressive a piece of art it was. Raven felt sure that he had been aided in his creative abilities by his spirit guide.

Of course, there was more to life than a man's pride, and a very pregnant Running Wild was another. She had carried her expected child over long distances and through severe weather conditions, and she now felt that the time was near for her to deliver. She was home now and among friends and family, all looking forward to the birth of her next child, as she was.

The day came when she went to the lodge reserved for menstruating females and the birthing of children. Shadow was nearby, along with Gray Wolf, with Rain assisting her in any way she would need. It didn't take long before there was an unusually loud howling noise, and it wasn't from Running Wild. It was from a newborn. Shadow and Gray Wolf gave each other a look of "What was that?"

Immediately after that initial cry, Rain hurried out of the lodge and came directly over to Shadow, saying, "You have another fine son, my husband."

Shadow exclaimed, "Are you sure? I thought I heard a howling wolf!"

Gray Wolf smiled and replied, "I thought so too." So it was that Howling Wolf was born that day.

He was indeed a fine boy, and his mother was appreciating him much more, having him in her arms as opposed to having him in her womb. He was certainly living up to his name. He was a louder baby than anyone could recall. However, he received plenty of attention, which helped to keep him pacified.

The cold time lingered. Life was more difficult. There were essential functions that had to be done regardless. There were sufficient provisions, but as always, during these hard continuing conditions, there began to be a strong desire for fresh meat rather than the dried, smoke cured meat they had to resort to.

Eventually, the weather began to turn. After some more lighttimes, the wind calmed, the sun shined, and there was a significant amount of snow melt. As the time passed, there began the expected new growth of the grass and flowers making an appearance.

Shadow felt it was time once again to visit with the Waptailmin people. He longed to see his friend Red Dreamer and council with him. He let it be known to Talon and Raven, as well as Gray Wolf, that they would be leaving for the Waptailmin village soon.

Preparations were made, and in a relatively short time, they all left together to meet with their friends the Waptailmin. To all except

Gray Wolf, it was a place that was very well-known, but to Rain's father, it was all part of his new life.

After several sleep overs, they arrived at their destination, being very much welcomed at the Waptailmin camp. Then they continued to Red Dreamer's lodge, where they were warmly greeted. They dismounted and then made their way into his spacious and comfortable lodge. There were several other elders present as well. They smoked and had small talk, using sign and words combined. It was apparent that Dreamer was extremely glad to see his friend, Cloud Shadow. Dreamer retold the story of Shadow's amazing ride on the buffalo, which once again was well appreciated. Gray Wolf had previously heard the tale from Raven and was continually learning to regard Shadow more highly, despite his earlier reluctance to do so.

After all the usual formalities had come and gone, the time came when Shadow began to communicate on a more serious note. "We have come to speak with our friends the Waptailmin people concerning attacks on our people by the Kenistenoag. Attacks that have resulted in the deaths of a party of our hunter, trappers, Talon being the only survivor, also the death of Many Arrows and a number of my wife Rain's people, along with some Salish escorts as well. In the not-so-distant time from now, we are going to the area where Talon and the others were attacked to seek revenge. We tell you this knowing that you may want to join us in this war party."

The Waptailmin elders, as was their way, let Shadow know that they would discuss the matter further and send word soon of their decision. With that, Dreamer gave Shadow a nod that let him know that no matter what, he would accompany them.

The visiting party of Nimipu stayed over at the Waptailmin camp before leaving not long after first light. Shadow felt certain that some Waptailmin braves would join them. The plan for a retaliation against a hated enemy was already understood within the Palus band. There were already a significant number of Nimipu braves committed to the war party. Talon and Shadow wanted a strong reprisal capability when they went, so there would be no question of the outcome were they to come upon the enemy. Shadow knew that he could draw on many warriors from the other Nimipu bands if he asked, but he felt it was important to act as quickly as feasibly possible. Several sleeps after the Nimipu party had returned, a Waptailmin messenger arrived at the Palus camp, bearing word that the Waptailmin would provide warriors for the effort of revenge and that they were wanting information on when they should be ready. Shadow let them know that they would be leaving out in so many sleeps, as he made a certain number of marks on the ground. The messenger acknowledged he understood and would convey the message as it had been presented.

The Palus band entered a time of preparations, which included prayer and contemplation, along with ritualistic dancing, accompanied by distinct rhythms created by their drumming, combined with chanting. It became a time of seriousness and somberness like none any could recall before this time. The men looked to their personal weapons, that they were honed to their satisfaction, going about their readying with the utmost gravity.

Just as surely as the rising of the sun, the time for departure was at hand. While the Nimipu went about their needed steps before gathering to leave out, there arrived a large contingent of Waptailmin warriors, much more than they thought to see.

It raised emotions for Shadow as Red Dreamer approached him in salutation with his palms showing. Shadow showed him the same. Both smiled broadly.

Once they all finally were moving in the direction of Cold Wind Grandfather, they truly presented themselves as a formidable force on a mission for a righteous purpose. Talon led the way, his scarred face peering out into the distance with complete resolution. Raven carried his shield, evoking the might of the black eagle. Shadow, Red Dreamer, and Gray Wolf all looked very capable of doling out a plentiful measure of pain and death on their foes. Gray Wolf had his limitations, but he could still grip the pony's mane with the hand of his injured arm while swinging a club with the other. He wasn't going to miss the chance to confront his hated enemy, the Kenistenoag, if at all possible. These people had been a vexation on the Siksika existence since time immemorial, and then for them to attempt to kill his daughter and grandson, he was not about to stay behind.

The route that Shadow had asked the war party to take was to follow the Mother River toward her head waters. He explained that once they had gotten that far up into Cold Wind Grandfather country, they would sweep toward the setting sun, casting a net over the area as they moved through.

The war party's collection of ponies was close to impeccable. A finer selection of horse flesh may never have been gathered together. As usual, there was a need to keep some degree of separation between these fearsome four-legged warriors. Bright Star, Ghost and Dancer Also were up front, followed by a parade of highly trained, proud, and spirited animals who would rather die than quit on whatever was required of them.

CHAPTER 31

THE TURNING OF TALON

The avengers traveled for several sleeps with a forward scouting party made up of some of their keenest men. Not long after they had stopped to hold up for the dark time, a scout appeared, informing them that they had surprised several men on foot. A fight had subdued them, and they held them captive up farther ahead. It was interesting news, and after questioning the scout on these men's appearance, they felt fairly certain that they were indeed Kenistenoag. Then the scout offered another bit of information that sealed their fate.

"There was a war club found among them, of the Nimipu," he stated.

The war party left at first light to set their eyes upon these despised wretches. When they arrived at the location that the captives were being held, the whole party dismounted and encircled the bound individuals. They all had some amount of blood on their person. A scout pointed out the culprit that was in possession of the Nimipu war club. They did most definitely fit the description of the Kenistenoag. Talon stepped up to the one who had been singled out and crushed his face in with his club. He died instantaneously. The fear that swept over the remaining pair was almost palpable.

Gray Wolf stepped up to the frightened pair and began to converse through sign and some verbal exchange. Afterward, they began to nod and point in a particular direction. Then Gray Wolf communicated with Raven, and then Raven, in turn, to Shadow and Talon, that he had made them to understand that they were to show them their camp location. Gray Wolf had had more contact and experience with these peoples than any of the others. The captives agreed to lead the party to their fellow murdering clan. The warriors bound the captives onto pack animals and then proceeded.

The Kenistenoag camp the war party was searching for contained a rather large group of these nomadic people, led by a man named Bad Moon. It was fitting for a man who knew no compassion and led by intimidation and fear. As a whole, this group had no understanding that there was any other way. They were a backward lot who would stop at nothing to achieve domination over man or beast. Unfortunately for them, they had committed an atrocity against humanity that was about to bring about their ruination. Bad Moon was being his usual cruel self, beating a young woman who shied away from him when he began to grope her. These things and other unpleasantries the scout observed as he peered in on the camp, before he left to report that he had found the group they were searching for.

When he arrived back to the awaiting avengers with the information they were waiting on, Talon, as if by design, walked over to the trussed-up captives who were still slung over the backs of the pack animals and grabbed each one, raising their heads and slitting their throats. Then they were untrussed and dragged away from the gathering place and left for the scavengers. No one said a word regarding Talon's actions.

The band of warriors at this time began a ceremonial painting of their faces, with varied personal touches that they felt important. When it was finished, they presented themselves as the fearsome lot that they were. Then there was a strategy discussed and arrived at. They would approach the camp in a wide circle, enclosing on it thoroughly, trying to avoid killing women and children. Every man, young and old, would be put to death. They would take down as many as possible with the bow and arrow. Any remaining would be dealt with accordingly. This band of Kenistenoag were about to face the wrath of the Palus band of Nimipu and their Waptailmin allies.

The unsuspecting enemy encampment carried on as if it was just all things as usual. Their minds filled with all desires for pretty much everything, being that they had next to nothing. If they could receive it through murder or theft, so be it. They had been raised to enjoy harassing and killing, and such were some cultures in the world, but what was given would be received.

At a point, a few individuals in the camp noticed riders approaching, not understanding that it was a noose that was being drawn to their calculated end. Someone in the camp yelled out in warning. Then instinctively, weapons were readied for their defense, which were mainly spears and clubs. Within a moment's time, there began an onslaught of arrows that cleared the camp of many who were standing. The sounds then of war cries, screams of hysteria, and panic was everywhere.

Bad Moon was inside a lodge, and seeing the carnage taking place, he hid under a pile of hides.

Several riders were pulled from their mounts, and others dismounted voluntarily to combat their foes. There were beatings and stabbings and slashing at a vicious level, but no quarter was given and none asked for. It became hard to spare the women because they also joined in on the fighting. If they interfered with the judgment being given out, they were not shown any leniency.

Talon stayed mounted, making contact with a war club on a horrible scale, being inflamed with destruction. He used the same club that had previously been found on one of the perpetrators. Bright Star seemed to be hunting as well, like a good buffalo pony on a buffalo hunt, getting close and positioning for the kill. At one point, there was a surge of enemy fighters coming at them, and Bright Star spun to gain some distance. And then with a few quick steps, he leaped over several of the Kenistenoag and a large fire pit to remove Talon from danger, landing in the fray of another contest for mastery. A couple more of the enemies were toppled over and destroyed. Those that had pursued Talon were confronted by Shadow and Raven, who also remained mounted. Raven had delivered several blows that he believed to be death blows thus far. Gray Wolf leaped from his mount onto a pair of Kenistenoag, who had been getting the best of a Nimipu warrior. The enemy combatants were thrown off-balance, providing Gray Wolf and the warrior he had aided the opportunity to give them death for their reward.

Not long after Gray Wolf's leap of salvation, the battle quickly subsided. The remaining women and children had stopped resisting. Talon had dismounted and asked that the remaining enemies be bound. While he stood there glaring at those who still lived, a young woman approached him, pointing to the lodge where Bad Moon was hiding. She made it clear that she felt that there would be something worth finding in there. Gray Wolf took an interest in this development, signing to her a question, to which she responded, "Headman."

Gray Wolf relayed her reply to Raven, who informed the others. Moments later, Bad Moon was dragged out and deposited on the ground. The young woman walked over to a cooking fire and grabbed a firebrand, brought it over to where Bad Moon laid, and shoved it into his eyes. She didn't seem to have any more regard for herself. Taking that act of retaliation was all that mattered to her. Everyone figured she had her reasons. As Bad Moon lay there in agony, Talon picked up a spear off the ground and shoved it through his heart. He then passed from bound enemy to bound enemy, slitting their throats. When he had finished, there was not a man alive among the Kenistenoag camp.

Gray Wolf signed to the women and children that it was finished. With the avenging warrior band, there were injuries, but none that were life-threatening. It had been a total victory, and they gave their thanks to the Great Spirit for his protection and guidance. It was time to go home.

Shadow pondered the events leading up to the actual retaliation and thought on the hoped-for result—the survivors would pass on the message that there were dire consequences for killing any inhabitants of this region.

Talon, while on their return journey, seemed to be deep in thought. He sided up to Shadow and spoke out, saying, "Brother, I hope I never have to kill another human being. I've ended the lives of more men than I've imagined I ever would. I felt driven to do it, but now I feel that it is out of me, and I want it to stay that way. I only want to be helpful to others and to take care of my family."

"I think that it will be that way with you now, my brother," replied Shadow.

They gave one another reassuring smiles as they continued.

CHAPTER 32

The Return, and Raven Departs!

Gray wolf sided up to Shadow, and in a somewhat understandable Nimipu dialect, he stated, "You good man."

Shadow did appreciate his sentiment and responded, "You're a good man too." It was followed by consensual nodding, confirming their spoken words. There was certainly an amount of forgiveness that had to have taken place to achieve these declarations between them.

Shadow became distracted as his thoughts were focused back home with his family, thinking about not being so young anymore and his spirit of adventure not as keen these days. He was enjoying images of his new baby boy and thoughts of spending more time with Wind to help shape his priorities.

While he thought on these things, Red Dreamer sided up to him. In his tongue, he expounded, as he signed, "Bad people gone, good people live on. Nimipu good people. Friends help to end bad people."

Shadow responded, "Yes, Waptailmin are good people too. You are our good friends, and the Nimipu thank Red Dreamer and the Waptailmin people again for their help and friendship."

"We are pleased to be able to do this, and now we have made secure our lands against raiders. It is good for us all," Dreamer concluded.

It had been a long journey, and every man was glad for it to be nearing its end, and so it was with long treks. There was no place like home. It was a place to rest and grab hold of the next vision for the time to come, to visualize it and then make it happen. It was simple enough if you didn't lose sight of it. Shadow liked to keep his visions simple, which he felt allowed himself to stay in harmony with the natural courses of life's events. To him, this was the bases of everything that led to his quality of life. Eventually, Raven sided up to Shadow as their travel continued. Shadow had noticed Raven keeping to himself more than usual. Raven had held up his end in the conflict, and Shadow knew for certain that he had killed.

"I hope we never have to do anything like that again," Raven began. "It's not the type of thing I want to be part of, if there is a choice."

"I hope not also, my son. That type of thing is too harsh to be repeated, but it was given to us without our seeking it out. I don't have any memory of such things as happening on our lands before, and we pray it won't ever again. Although in buffalo country, it is much more often that such occurrences as that could happen if you will continue going to that place. Beware, you could find yourself in another dire problem."

Raven felt he understood what his father had referred to, for he knew of the tales of unwarranted attacks on the Nimipu in that place. With that, he had more to consider for the time to come. Finally, they came within sight of their village. A couple previous early times, they had departed company from their Waptailmin companions. Now they were approaching home. The greeting came before they ever entered the camp. It was led by Wind, who came at a run upon a fine mature gelding and then pulled up abruptly in a skid, which brought a lot of exclamations from the returning warriors. He was closely followed by a line of well-wishers giving their welcome homes.

Before long, the parade of greeters, along with the triumphant home comers, made their way into the village. Once there, their mounts were taken into care by the children typically. The wives and parents gave them their special greetings, and it soon became a celebration. Some of the men who showed obvious wounds were fussed over with much pomp. Again, the drumming began, along with the dancing and feasting, which the returning fighters appreciated to the utmost. Shadow couldn't help but think that their Waptailmin friends were enjoying the same fanfare.

It wasn't long before life at the Palus band's camp began to return to some order of normality. The weather was as fine as anyone could want. Little Howling Wolf was growing rapidly and a source of great entertainment for any who found themselves in his presence. Shadow had come to see a distinct difference in his newest son and Wind when he was small. Wind was a finessing sort, it being a trait he showed at a young age, and he still operated the same way, smooth and precise. Shadow felt quite confidently that Howling Wolf was going to be a pressing forceful type. Raven presided somewhere in between. Shadow began to focus his attention on rearing Wind in this formative time in his life. He kept him close by in all his activities. He got him away from the camp life that wasn't conducive to manly behavior, as he did with Raven and as his father had done with him. He was spending a lot of time working with the herd and several ponies he had separated to be trained on different levels. He had time with the bow and arrow and was making tools and weapons. He exercised for toughness and stamina and learned to track game and to stay upwind of his intended prey. He was becoming practiced at the skills of gutting and skinning game after they had been taken. He knew how to survive on what could be readily found given the season and location. Shadow was trying to be firm with him but not so hard as to break his given spirit. It all seemed good and right to them both as the natural order of things was being followed.

Talon had settled in with Little Wing, very much enjoying one another's company, as it is with young lovers. Gray Wolf was appreciating his new life with his daughter and grandchildren.

The only one that felt unsettled was Raven. He was already coming under the spell of wanderlust, and it was very much pulling at him. So much so that he often found himself staring out at the horizons. He also was preoccupied with the tale he had heard his father tell on numerous occasions of his trek to Absaroka by way of the old Nimipu pass. He wasn't considering a journey of that magnitude, but he had inquired of a trail that would lead him to the entrance of that pass. He primarily wanted the knowledge of its location if he had need of it at some point in time. As it had been explained to him, he realized that it would take him, in going there, very near to the Upper Red Fish band's village where his good friend Cunning Fox lived. That intrigued him as well. He began to plan for a departure in the very near time. He brought this to Shadow and Gray Wolf's attention while conversing with them concerning ordinary matters. Both knew it wasn't their place to deny him. They wouldn't even consider it.

Gray Wolf kept silent while Shadow responded, "That would be a good trip with this fine weather for your travels. I hope for success in anything you attempt to do. We will look forward to your return."

Gray Wolf smiled at Raven, giving an agreeing nod to what had transpired.

As Raven made his departure, he was not aware of several young women who longed after him as he passed by. He had known them since childhood, but not being children any longer, their thoughts were on the most prospective of the young men in the village.

So Raven was on his first adventure of his own. He felt good, and his planned journey seemed right. He had prayed that the Great Spirit would watch over him and his spirit guide would stay close. What a beautiful lighttime it was. A refreshing breeze blew a fragrance of new grass in the air. All was well with his life. He was a lone venturer exuding a portrayal of dignified splendor. He was a fine figure of a man, astride his fine pony Ghost. He was dressed in an attire befitting a prince of these lands, with his medicine shield on display, along with another pony packed with all the traps befitting a proud nomad. Not a pride of conceit, but of someone who was blessed to have a fine mind and body and be born of a fine people, living in a fine land.

When Raven set his course, he headed primarily toward the land of the rising sun, with a slight inclination toward the land of the thorn plants. After several sleeps and just as many river crossings, he was coming near to the Upper Red Fish band's encampment. In his travels, he had come within close proximity to the Lower Red Fish band's village and was not opposed to stopping there to visit, but he decided he would look into that possibility on his return. When he gained sight of the village he sought, he was excited at being able to see his friends there again. Raven wandered into their camp uncontested, being a lone rider, although there definitely were those who took notice of the arrival of this outstanding Nimipu brave. After just a short while, there were some who recognized him as Cloud Shadow's son, which made him the winner of that highly competitive pony race between him and Cunning Fox. Yes, the people of this village remembered Raven.

Raven was directed to White Owl's lodge. There, he was greeted by White Owl, Bull Elk, and soon after Cunning Fox. He was warmly welcomed and even more well received by his close friend Cunning Fox. He also couldn't help but notice a tight little group of young women who appeared genuinely interested in his every move.

White Owl extended the offer. "Come rest and refresh yourself." He gestured toward his lodge. Raven entered the lodge, followed by his hosts, which included several other privileged men of their band. White Owl had heard a lot of tales of the previous buffalo hunt concerning the many facets of that journey—Shadow's ride upon the rampaging buffalo; of course, his grandson's fall of humility; and the elk hunt that could have ended the lives of many good men. He also was aware, as were the others, that Shadow, Raven, and the rest of Shadow's family continued in another direction upon the hunting party's leaving of that place. It was the time to get caught up on the rest of the story, but first they smoked and had small talk. They ate, and eventually the question was put to Raven. "Did it go well on your journey to the Place of Big Medicine?"

The Nimipu people loved a good story, and they could be very attentive listeners. It was only proper to give the teller respect and an open forum to articulate according to their manner. Raven had matured along these lines as well as others, and he began to expound freely and expertly captivate his audience. When he had finished, they all were thrilled that he had come to them with such an interesting tale.

They had never met Many Arrows, but hearing of his close relationship to Shadow and his death, they expressed their regret at the outcome.

White Owl was very intrigued with Raven's telling of his encounter with his spirit guide, knowing Black Eagle as his friend.

Raven continued with the story of his grandfather returning with him to live among the Palus band. Then he told of the revenge attack on the Kenistenoag, which caused the listeners to think it very odd to have to fight with those people so near to the Nimipu homeland.

Finally, he ended with the telling of the birth of Shadow's new son, Howling Wolf, bringing delight to them as well. By the time Raven had spoken of all that had taken place, the listeners were full with the story and were appreciative for it.

While Raven was spending time with his friends, he couldn't help noticing repeatedly a young woman who seemed to have general access to him, more so than any other women about the camp. At a point when she appeared in near proximity to him, his good friend Cunning Fox suddenly said, "I don't believe you have ever met my little sister, Vixen."

Raven was mildly surprised at the introduction. He also could vaguely recall seeing her when they were on their buffalo hunt. Of course, they were younger then and did not take interest in one another. "You're right. I have not. It is good to meet you, Vixen," he replied.

She did appear attractive to him. They both exchanged smiles, and then she dashed away.

Cunning Fox went on to say, "She has been pestering me to introduce her to you, and now it is done."

As some sleeps had passed since Raven's arrival, Cunning Fox brought up the question "What thing shall we do while we have this time to spend together?"

"When I set out to visit with you, I had been thinking to find the trail to the entrance of the old Nimipu pass that I have heard spoken of," responded Raven.

"Yes, I know a bit concerning that place. We shall go there. I have heard tell of another place that is within our lands, a place of medicine it is spoken of. I have been wanting to take that journey for my vision quest and would be honored to have you with me for such an important event," Cunning Fox added.

This all sounded very exciting to them both as Raven replied, "That would be a good thing for us. I am glad to accompany you on this quest."

When some of Cunning Fox's other friends heard him speak of it, they asked to accompany him also.

The idea of the quest was brought to Bull Elk's attention.

It came as no surprise to him, and then it was presented to White Owl, who was chief, as well as Cunning Fox's grandfather. Before long, the fellowship of young Nimipu braves found themselves sitting together with Bull Elk in White Owl's lodge, to be instructed in the ways to proceed.

The place that Cunning Fox had been referring to was known to the Nimipu people as the Beartooth Mountains. It was a name unfamiliar to Raven, although White Owl assured him that his grandfather was well aware of it, for it was where he and Big Cat had traveled to, seeking medicine, before arriving at the Upper Red Fish band's village at the time when White Owl had first met Black Eagle. That intrigued Raven beyond words, for he surely wanted to experience the Beartooth Mountains now.

CHAPTER 33

MORE VENTURE AND DANGER

The following lighttime, as the small group was preparing to leave, there gathered a throng of young women, apparently very interested in the proceedings. Some of the young braves had already struck up an affectionate relationship with certain of the throng and were paying particular attention to one another. Vixen was there among the well-wishers, with her doe eyes fixed on Raven, hoping to get some recognition from him.

After mounting his pony, Raven did look directly at her and gave her a distinct nod in acknowledgment.

It wasn't demonstrative in any way, but she felt sure it was for her to hold on to until the next time. Meanwhile, back at the Palus band camp, Howling Wolf was making every attempt to stand, and Wind was making every attempt to take horsemanship to its limits. All seemed well with the world for Shadow's immediate family. Shadow's thoughts wandered to his son Raven as he gave a short prayer for his well-being. He peered out in the direction he had taken in his departing.

Raven and Cunning Fox, along with the other braves, set off on their venture. They began their journey, moving along the trail and heading toward the land of the rising sun. Raven was determined to familiarize himself with the place of the old Nimipu pass. It was a place of importance yet still not known to him by personal experience. The other young men hadn't made the trip before either and were very much willing to see it and to incorporate it into their sphere of knowledge. So they proceeded with a true sense of purpose, feeling appreciative for the opportunity to get off on their own as men in their time and element. It was a time that all boys and adolescent males looked forward to and take pride in when that time arrived. This was that occasion they had longed for, and it was apparent to them as a whole. Their ponies were sensing the importance of the time as they frolicked along the way.

These men didn't portray the poise of a more mature party, as there was a more jovial atmosphere as they progressed in their travels, with the exception of Raven, who was experienced beyond his age. In a way, he felt responsible for their success or failure regarding the party's goals.

It was a fine lighttime with a slight breeze along with the sweet smell of the forest, also it's much varied plant life all about. Within a short time from their departure, they began to ascend to a higher elevation. Although as the lay of such places typically presents, they found themselves having to descend at times, only to find themselves climbing once again. The climbing took most of their time while moving in the general direction of the mountain pass. They pressed on with vigor, as it took considerable strength to make the journey under any conditions. After a long effort to gain an acceptable distance for their efforts, they stopped for that leg of their trip to hold up and refresh themselves, as well as the ponies. They had provisions for the time being and planned to hunt when needed. It wasn't long after their stopping that darkness began to envelope them.

They built fires to help keep the cougars at a manageable distance. The country they were in was heavily populated with the lions, so they felt it prudent to keep the fires well lit. Through the darktime, there was heard the screams and growls of the cats as they came within a relatively close range of one another, for they were always in dispute of hunting territory, the primary concern being their ponies. Raven awoke to the sounds periodically and would take notice of the stars in their multitude, as well as the obvious change in location of the moon on each observation. The wood they had collected before they retired would be applied whenever needed by whomever noticed the necessity, being careful not to let the fires diminish to any degree.

At first light, there was a bit of a mist all around, which obscured a view at any distance and added to the atmosphere of the deep forest experience. The party was eager to continue with their pursuit of the pass as they broke camp. Again, they pushed on and toughed out the grueling travel. The most satisfaction they obtained for their efforts that lighttime was to come to a landmark that White Owl had described to them. Near the landmark, they found a crossing trail that was considerably more well used than the one they had been following. This trail met the description as it was explained to them previously to lead them on to the pass.

It did seem at times that the knowledge of the location of this pass was not worth the effort that had been needed to obtain it. However, they understood that sometime, as individuals, they might need to lead a party there and as timely and efficiently as possible.

Again, they made camp to restore themselves and their hardworking ponies. The following lighttime, they felt confident they would reach the pass, which they did as the sun shone high above them. They were able to peer out on the distant horizon with a vista view into the direction of the path of the sun from its rising. They knew that they would not go any farther in that direction, but it stirred their wanderlust just to look out on a country yet untried by them. They remained there for some time then turned back to begin their journey to the Beartooth Mountains.

This they felt was where the adventure truly began for them.

"Now you receive the vision you seek and your spirit guide helper," Raven commented to Cunning Fox as they progressed through the heavily forested terrain. They had gone back in the way that they had come. At some point, they would move more in the direction of the land of the thorn plants. Old White Owl had given them good guidance for finding the pass. They had no reason to question his advice now.

"Yes, I believe that I will receive my medicine and vision at this place inhabited by much powerful medicine, for I have been seeking guidance from the Great Spirit on this matter," replied Cunning Fox as he rode along, facing backward on the back of his pony Lightning. He looked unconcerned about his precarious situation as if he were sitting at a story session at home.

"I hope we all get our medicine," said Young Old Man, who looked as if he had been thinking hard on their prospects. Young Old Man got his name from taking things more seriously than the other boys from the time that they were quite young. "If we honor our ancestors and follow the teachings of our elders, we should expect to receive our visions," Young Old Man stated. There was a consensual murmur among the party at that pronouncement.

"I know that I will be angry if I don't receive my vision after all the sacrifice I will have made," stated Bellowing Bull with a defined scowl on his brow. All the others ignored this obstinate intrusion into their positive anticipations, for it was well-known to be Bellowing Bull's general outlook on life. Cunning Fox and the others had tried to find a way to exclude him, but without success, for he wasn't one to be put off easily or with much difficulty, and so it was that he was along on their quest, to everyone's chagrin.

It was a long journey to the Beartooth Mountains from the Nimipu Pass. It took several sleeps and long sessions of travel. They brought down a few deer along the way and ate well. They weren't fearful of being discovered by any that they knew of and kept large fires in their camps whenever they stopped. They roasted fresh venison and gorged themselves before their time of fasting that they had planned on doing in the near coming time. They celebrated their coming of age as well as having good health in a great land. They gave thanks to the Life Giver for all that he had provided for the people. Bellowing Bull went along with a degree of sincerity.

Eventually, the time came when they began to gain sight of the Beartooth Mountains. As they drew closer the more the land became an area of extreme projections of high rock faces and snow-capped peaks. Off toward the land of the setting sun, it was apparent lay the Beartooth range, as it resembled a set of jagged teeth. Then toward the land of the rising sun was another range that had been told to them, the White Mountains. There was a stretch of open land between the ranges to travel on and make preparations for their seeking of some sign or vision to help guide them in the times and events that lie ahead for their individual lives. Raven had already purposed to prepare along with them and then to act as a help in any way that he could. Primarily, he was to guard over the camp and their belongings while tending to the ponies, watching for any possible troubles. It reminded him of the role he had already been doing for most of his life as a big brother.

He suggested they draw near to the Beartooth range so they could find a place where they might not be noticed by any who might be watching, for reasons they might have, that could be disruptive to the goals of their party.

As they came within a close proximity, they searched an alcove close to the base of the mountains. They found a suitable location, dismounted, and began to make themselves a camp in which to stay for a relatively extended period.

There had already been a discussion on the point of each person beginning a process of separation in their personal preparations of purging through meditation and prayer, as well as a cleansing of their bodies inside and out through bathing, fasting, and sweating. They were to separate in their association with one another for the purpose of drawing nearer in their relationship with the Great Spirit, as they sought guidance in their quest. The first thing they did, beside stop their intake of nutrition, was to build several small sweat lodges. They all understood through teachings since childhood that they could withdraw into their own personal spiritual quest without traveling any distance from one another at this beginning stage. They did, however, have little conversation to avoid distractions. As all this was done with seriousness, Raven had his reservations pertaining to Bellowing Bull's devotion, for he believed he had witnessed him eating something on more than just an occasion.

When the time came for the young men to ascend the mountainous terrain, it became needful for them to go their separate ways. The seekers all went off on foot, while Raven remained behind as was previously determined. Cunning Fox and Young Old Man began to climb in a somewhat close proximity, the others spreading out at farther distances before beginning their ascent. Raven watched as they slowly disappeared from his view, all the while he prayed for their well-being and success.

As Cunning Fox and Young Old Man continued along, they eventually came to a small alpine lake. Cunning Fox proceeded to a bank of the lake while Young Old Man took to an area on the lakeside across from him to spend his time supplicating before the Great Spirit for his help in obtaining the medicine he felt he needed for the power to have victory over the trials and tribulations that came against all living creatures. He would be giving thanks for his life and a desire to appreciate the majesty of creation more perfectly. Cunning Fox also sought in earnest, looking to the Life Giver for his favor. As the time passed, they both had profound spiritual experiences and were led away at first light to higher ground, apart from their initial places of outreach.

Bellowing Bull was happy to get off by himself to spend his time searching for edible things to try and satisfy the nagging hunger that would not be abated, convinced that the only things in these mountains were the obvious. He knew better than to voice such opinions openly, so he kept them to himself. He plodded along with his focus on searching for something for his belly only.

Raven, while in a state of continual prayer, tried also to keep a vigil lookout for any activity throughout the surrounding area. While tending to the ponies, he noticed them point their ears forward toward a particular direction. He immediately sought a view of the area in question. It wasn't plain as to the cause of the ponies' attention right away, but as he continued his observations, he began to notice there was a group of riders making their way past the location of the alcove, some distance from his position where he only just reared his head. As he followed their movement, he tried to deduce who these riders were and what they were up to. In his limited knowledge, he could not say for certain of what peoples they were. Whoever they were, it was disconcerting, and he did not feel good concerning their presence.

Back at the Palus band village, Shadow and Talon sat conversing on different matters, the beginning topic being about Little Wing's confiding of her being with child. When Talon spoke of it to Shadow, he responded with joy and positivity. "Good news, my brother. That is something that does my heart good to hear. I am sure this new one will be a fine member of our family, just as you and your woman are. I am glad for you both."

Just after Shadow made that statement, he felt a strong sense of perception concerning Raven. Talon noticed the change that came over him and inquired, "What is it that has distracted you, my brother?"

CHAPTER 34

VISIONS MADE CLEARER

Shadow told him, "I had a premonition concerning Raven, that he was facing some potential trouble. I will try to stay open to the matter if I am able." He once again became focused on Talon's questioning gaze.

At that, Shadow could no longer take interest in having any further conversation. He politely, as was his way, excused himself, conveying that he felt a need to get off by himself for a while. Talon understood and left Shadow to do what he felt he should, and within a relatively short period, he had come to a decision as to what he was going to do.

After leaving the alpine lake and some of the deepest ascent of his climb, Cunning Fox came to an even smaller lake. Unbeknownst to him, Young Old Man came into view of this same lake as well. Both of them, upon seeing it, reflected on the words of White Owl, who had spoken of a small lake that would still be partially frozen, near a pinnacle peak. He referred to it as Beartooth Lake.

There they both were peering at the lake seated at the base of this pinnacle peak, admiring the majestic scene before them, giving thanks in their hearts to be looking at this marvelous landscape. The sun was shining directly overhead, with the brightness of the glare being intense. Then something brought a sudden change to the vision before them. A cloud shadow seemed to come out of the blue and appeared across their immediate view. They looked up to see a cloud among an otherwise cloudless sky that was slowly passing before the sun. They also felt that they were receiving a conscious exhortation to trust in the leadership that had been provided for them. They both felt refreshed and clear minded after their experience, believing that their present leaders would be their spirit guides and to be content.

As Raven continued to look out in the direction that he had seen the riders travel in, he heard some commotion behind him. He turned to find Bellowing Bull blundering along toward the encampment. When Raven questioned him, he stated he was done with his quest and thought his experience adequate for now and felt it was time to break his fast. Before long, several others returned and also spoke of their interest in satisfying their hunger needs. They were talking among themselves, and someone made mention of a possible spiritual connection that had been made with a squirrel. Another believed that a porcupine had been trying to communicate with him, but he wasn't clear on what it was a about and would continue to pray about it.

Keeping his thoughts to himself, Bellowing Bull was angry that he didn't have any encounters of a spiritual kind and that he was being deprived as usual and had been wronged.

Before the darkness enveloped them, Cunning Fox and Young Old Man had made their way back to camp too. While everyone was conveying the events of their endeavors and filling their empty stomachs, Raven interjected with the mention of the passing riders, all sensing the silence that followed his account.

Young Old Man broke the silence after a short period of pondering the matter. "At first light, let's be prepared to depart to a better location for keeping watch as a precaution." They all concurred that it would be wise to do so.

While it was still shadowy in the not yet dawning of the early time, they began to move out. They had determined to cross over the open area toward the other range, being the White Mountains, hoping to gain some concealment before it became altogether light out. They moved along at a rather quick pace given the conditions they were traveling under.

They were making good headway and were within a relatively close proximity of the forested area at the base of the White Mountains. Cunning Fox glanced back to check on their state of secrecy concerning the ground they had just traversed.

"We've been found out," he loudly stated. Immediately, they all turned to look at what Cunning Fox was referring to, although they all had a good idea already.

When they looked behind them, not far off, they saw a small party of young Shoshone braves, the same in number as themselves. It was, at that point, a standoff, each group sizing up the other. It seemed to almost all who were among them that it might dissipate with each party regarding the other as irrelevant. Bellowing Bull was an exception. He was in a foul mood, which was not uncommon to him. Before anyone could think to say anything for or against it, he dismounted from his pony and then turned his backside to the Shoshone and bent over, lifting his loin skin and exposing his posterior. He shook his bared buttocks at the opposing party, a gesture that would be viewed as insulting behavior to any culture.

He not only succeeded in repulsing and shocking the Shoshone braves but his own traveling companions as well. But their disgust of Bellowing Bull was short-lived because right then, the Shoshone charged at them. Bellowing Bull's dismounting proved to be his undoing. As the Shoshone attacked, before they had gotten very close, they cast several spears from horseback at a fast run. One of these caught him directly in the spine as he had tried to mount his pony, inflicting a fatal wound which he instantaneously died from.

A Nimipu pack animal also received a fatal spear wound. The Shoshone were engaged and brought an aggressive battle forward, but the Nimipu had had their fury ignited as well. Within moments after the initial attack, there was an unleashing of arrows from both sides. A couple more Nimipu lost their lives, and several Shoshone succumbed to the volley of arrows cast into their rank.

Now they found themselves in the place of close combat conditions, and the clubs were out. All of them were young and inexperienced, all except Raven, and they were reluctant to engage. Raven, whose blood was heated, drove Ghost forward and dealt a deadly blow to a careless brave. Then he turned on another, seeking to do unto him in the same manner. This one was more aware and evaded him. Then he fled with his fellow companions in close pursuit.

The battle ended as quickly as it had begun, but they didn't know that the Shoshone had a camp not far from their present location. They were wise enough to make short the recovering of the bodies of their fallen companions and leaving the area, moving off in the direction of home. They also purposed to press on relentlessly without stops, not being overconfident of not being pursued. It was helpful, being the Shoshone camp had already received the news and were mounting an offensive. When the informed group of Shoshone warriors arrived at the place of the skirmish and found the bodies of their young men and the revelation that those responsible had fled the area, they left some to take care of the vanquished while they pursued the perpetrators, particularly Raven, who had been referred to as the bad one.

When the young men who had survived the encounter with the Nimipu returned to their camp telling of their tragic conflict of which they narrowly escaped, they spoke of the one on the gray pony with a red shield displaying the emblem of the black eagle, who fought like a mother grizzly defending her cubs.

As the Nimipu band pressed on toward home, Raven spoke his thoughts. "Someone should take the bodies of our slain brothers into camp as soon as they are able. The rest will try to lead any pursuers away from them. Any who get separated should meet at the pass."

The others listened, for he had gained a high level of respect from them on this trip, especially since the fight. When they came to a creek that took a general course in the direction of the Upper Red Fish village, Raven asked Cunning Fox to take the slain home while he and the others would make the attempt to divert any possible pursuers in another direction, away from the Nimipu camp.

Raven went on to say, "Head into the creek and stay with it for a lengthy distance to hide your trail. We will try to make a large circle back to the village. We hope to see you again on our return."

"I know it will be so, my friend. May the Great Spirit go with you in your efforts," replied Cunning Fox as he turned into the creek, leading the ponies with the dead secured to them. What they did not know at that point in time was that the Shoshone were not far behind them, with vengeance at their forethoughts.

Cunning Fox safely evaded the pursuers, but they stayed close on the trail of Raven, Young Old Man, and another brave, along with some additional ponies to help confuse their trail. They pressed on, not being certain of their own well-being or jeopardy. It became apparent, though, not long after the split with Cunning Fox, when several arrows came dangerously close to ending their concerns. Immediately, they broke rank and fled in separate directions. Raven and Ghost ran for their lives as if before a swarm of hornets. Raven was very much aware of a series of arrows cast toward him after the initial attack moments before. He caught a brief glimpse of what appeared to be a horde of pursuers, which did nothing toward slowing his flight.

Young Old Man knew that there were some who were devoted to his capture or death. He had had a brief sighting of a questionable number of some close behind him and had just escaped being taken out from arrows cast at him. It was forested terrain, with a limited line of sight for everyone, but for the hunted, it was no place to make a mistake. Don't stumble, don't fall, don't quit, and don't stop praying. Most of the time, Raven didn't know where he was, but he felt that he had gotten some space between himself and those that were after him. He sought to get some elevation in his travel on a gradual basis, which would help him come into proximity of the pass eventually, hoping to lead any pursuers away from the regions of the Nimipu homelands.

Unbeknownst to Young Old Man and Raven, their pursuers had fallen back and made camp, feeling somewhat satisfied that they had managed to slay one of those they were chasing. The Nimipu suspected that their pursuers were Shoshone, but the Shoshone were certain that the young braves they were after were Nimipu.

*****

Loud Swan was far from satisfied, for it was his son whom Raven had slain with his war club, and Loud Swan had been informed of that fact by witnesses of the deed. He personally had cast a couple of arrows at Raven during their pursuit. He was angry with himself for missing his target and was yet determined to avenge his son's death.

*****

Through much effort, Cunning Fox had managed to come within close proximity of the Upper Red Fish encampment when he was spotted by some of his fellow tribe members who hurried to his aid. Within a short time, word spread throughout the entire village of the ordeal that their young men had been involved with and was still not yet ended. Immediately, there were cries of mourning, as there also was a counsel called among the leading men to organize a measure of response.

After, a sufficient number of braves were gathered to go and attempt to protect and rescue their own from these adversaries. They left without delay, being led by Bull Elk.

Vixen went off from the camp to better survey her private worries. She had spent many long contemplative periods engaged in imaginings of a full and happy life as Raven's woman. Now it struck her as an affront to those happy thoughts to hear of his peril. While she was in her private place of near despair, she noticed some riders approaching the camp, of whom she was not certain of.

White Owl was present to greet Shadow, Talon, and Gray Wolf as they came near his lodge. Vixen also appeared in her curiosity and quickly deduced these visitors' relationship to the circumstances that were troubling all of them.

Shortly after White Owl invited the new arrivals into his lodge, Cunning Fox was summoned. He was already aware of why, having been informed by his sister of the new development.

When Cunning Fox entered the lodge, Shadow and his fellow travelers had already heard some of the story, as told to them by White Owl. Cunning Fox respectfully acknowledged his elders, with some of that respect being prompted by his recent vision experience.

It caused him a stirring of emotions and thoughts to hear that Cloud Shadow had suddenly appeared in their village and that he was to be so soon in his presence. Although it made perfect sense that he would want to hear from one who was involved with this situation concerning his son.

White Owl spoke. "My grandson, your telling of the encounter with this warring group of braves is requested by our honored guests."

Cunning Fox went on to tell of the circumstances leading up to the time that he had departed company from his companions and had returned to the village. He ended by saying that he wished to be among those who were looking for them, to try and help in any way that was needed. He added that his father and grandfather had felt that he was too exhausted at the time the searchers were leaving, but he felt he had recovered sufficiently to be of assistance to their efforts.

Shadow spoke, saying, "It is good to see that you have come out of this difficult situation. Your involvement will be very helpful. You will be an appreciated companion to have along with us. We are glad to have you, and we will be leaving very soon."

Cunning Fox let his elders know that he would be ready right away. When he left the lodge, Vixen hurried after him, inquiring of what was said. Her brother gave her a quick summary as he busied himself with his preparations to leave. Vixen didn't reply, but she withdrew herself once again to her seclusive worrying spot. She felt better knowing that there were more forces being mounted on Raven's behalf.

CHAPTER 35

TO VIXEN'S JOY

The small party left from the Upper Red Fish band's village bound for the Nimipu pass as Raven had spoken of, that the separated should try to come together there, being a location away from the Nimipu homelands yet familiar to them all.

The Shoshone party was becoming disheartened concerning their hopes of overtaking the remnants of the Nimipu that had been their objective. After a heated debate over continuing the hunt or calling it off, those in favor of calling it off won.

Loud Swan purposed to continue, alone at all cost, which he did. It wasn't long after Loud Swan had moved on in the trailing of Raven that Bull Elk's search party came across the Shoshone on their return to their camp. A forward scout, after a relatively close observation, reported that there was no sign of any Nimipu captives with the Shoshone. Bull Elk decided not to pursue them as they moved away from the vicinity that he considered their territory, not knowing if they were associated with the previous troubles.

It wasn't until the following early time that they found the body of the young Nimipu brave who had been badly treated following his death. His pony also died of serious wounds. Then they were left to be consumed by the scavengers. At that point, Bull Elk knew without question that the band of Shoshone they had encountered were clearly associated with this atrocious act. Although it wasn't apparent that there were any still pursuing the remaining evaders.

At that point, he sent several very capable braves to seek out the Shoshone camp and report back of its location. He pressed on, trying to unravel the whereabouts of Young Old Man and Raven. He also was given the information concerning the pass and was moving that way.

Raven had managed to reach the proximity of the pass already and had found a spot where he felt that he and Ghost were safely concealed. Young Old Man, unbeknownst to either of them, was just a short distance from Raven, while both watched for any signs of enemies about.

Shadow and his group were drawing nearer, not far behind Bull Elk's search and rescue party. There was also another who was undetected, someone who had vowed to take the life of Raven, as long as either still had the breath of life. Loud Swan was in close range of the young Nimipu braves.

Raven was picking up signals from the forest that he wasn't the only human in the near vicinity. He put out the cry of the hawk then waited for a return response. He soon heard the caw of a crow. He repeated the cry. Again, the caw. Still he waited, then again the cry, followed by the caw. He waited and watched. Not long after, he saw Young Old Man come into the open. He then mounted Ghost and rode out to meet him. Then at that moment, Young Old Man took an arrow in his side, which caused him to fall from his pony and lay writhing on the ground in agony. Raven stopped, trying to make a decision about the predicament. But before he came to any conclusion, Loud Swan leaped from atop a large boulder and landed on him, driving him to the ground. Loud Swan had his club ready to deal Raven his end. He drew back to swing as Raven was sprawled out in a helpless position.

Cloud Shadow had already nocked his arrow and had drawn his bow, the bow Many Arrows's son had given him, of which he never carried with him, except on this trip. They had gained the lead over Bull Elk. Shadow felt a sense of dire urgency to do so. He had already prayed to the Great Spirit to guide his arrow true, along with thanks to his old friend for this fine weapon. He released the arrow just as Loud Swan had positioned himself to deliver the killing blow.

It was a miracle cast, given the timing that was needed, and that it cleared every bit of foliage in its path of trajectory, at a distance not seen by any there in their memory, driving deep into Loud Swan's chest, stopping his heart on contact. He collapsed over Raven's splayed out body.

As quickly as anyone could, they saw to Young Old Man's dreadful situation. He wasn't in as much pain now as he was at the initial strike from the arrow. It was Gray Wolf who managed to dislodge the arrow from his side, stating that he believed that he could recover from the wound after some time with proper care and determination, still being young and strong.

Bull Elk, along with the other searchers, came up to where all the excitement had just occurred. Cunning Fox proclaimed to all, "As long as I live, I will never forget the bow shot I witnessed that saved Raven's life." He then told of the events that resulted in the satisfying conclusion.

It took Raven a bit of time to gather his senses after his near-death experience. He was certain of the fact that he was glad to be alive. He spoke with Young Old Man, telling him that he felt in his heart that he would be well again. He went on to thank his father for always being there when he needed him.

"The time will surely come that I will no longer be here for anyone, but I also am thankful that I could be here at this time for you," replied Shadow as he and Talon and Gray Wolf stood around Raven with their concern and affection.

Bull Elk and Cunning Fox were also close by with their respect for the family of Black Eagle and Cloud Shadow. They had come to feel that it was an honor to know them and to be able to call them close friends.

They took their time as they began the journey toward the homeland. Not far along on their return, the scouts met up with them to report that they had found the location of the Shoshone camp, and that it was somewhat large.

Bull Elk appeared to be giving thought to the news then stated, "We will visit their camp in the not-too-distant time from now."

With that, they proceeded with the knowledge of the leaving behind of the body of Loud Swan to be devoured by scavengers.

In time, they made their return, with the body of one and the lives of Young Old Man and Raven. There was mourning along with celebration throughout the village.

When Cunning Fox and Raven were in a moment of privacy, Cunning Fox told him, "My sister wishes to speak with you, Raven."

"I would like that also," he replied.

"She asks that you meet with her over by that group of trees," Cunning Fox continued, pointing at a stand of trees in the near distance.

"Now?" asked Raven.

"Yes," responded Cunning Fox, nodding to emphasize the point.

Raven really did want to speak with Vixen and wasted no time to meet with her. As soon as he got there, she wrapped her arms around him, placed her head on his chest, and said, "I have prayed for your safe return and have worried that I would never be able to hold you close to me."

Raven was enjoying their closeness as well, for he also held on to her, placing his head on hers, saying, "It is good to have this time with you in this way. I am glad for your caring so much for my return."

With that, Vixen led him to a secluded place where they made love and remained for a considerable amount of time, continuing in their enjoyment of one another's company.

Raven spoke to his father and hers of his love for Vixen, and that he would tarry there with them for some time and take her to be his woman, if there were no objections. This information was not a surprise, for they had already been told of his daughter's amorous desires for Raven. So while Shadow still remained with Bull Elk and Raven, Bull Elk replied, "I will be honored to have your family and ours to be one. You have my full approval to have my daughter in marriage and become my son as well."

This information spread through the camp and was immediately deemed an occasion for a celebration. Anyone observing the new couple would have to say that they were the absolute portrayal of happiness. The smiles and the laughter were infectious as everyone enjoyed themselves more than any time in recent memory. There were games and feasting and dancing, along with the laughter and joyful shouts of the children. Shadow, Talon, and Gray Wolf were treated as honored guests with much pomp. The following early time, they gave their farewells, with a hope to be united again in the not too distant coming time.

There in the Upper Red Fish village, within a relatively short while, White Owl's family had constructed a fine tipi lodge for the new couple for their privacy and habitation. Then after staying among Vixen's people for some time, Raven informed her that they would be leaving soon to live with the people of the Palus. He had enjoyed his time there and felt certain that he would continue to enjoy his time with his woman, who satisfied him in every way that a man would want from a woman companion.

The time came to leave, and he said his goodbyes and farewells all around. The same affection was shown to him by everyone. Vixen, with tears, also gave her departing words and wishes to all. They had their new lodge and other possessions secured on the pack ponies as they proceeded on their way. Some feelings of sadness prevailed, but mostly of joy and happiness, for their new love and the lives they looked forward to living together. Even Young Old Man was on his feet to see his good friend off, with promises of seeing one another again.

Back at the Palus camp, the news had come to them with the return of Shadow, Talon, and Gray Wolf of the marriage of Raven to Bull Elk's daughter. There was an anticipation for their coming home.

The time arrived when Wind came racing into camp, proclaiming that Raven and his woman were on there way, then he raced off to meet with his older brother again.

Vixen was warmly received by all the women in Raven's family. Running Wild, Rain, Little Wing, along with Flower and Butterfly, met her affectionately, all having a recollection of her from the buffalo hunt. Vixen was very grateful for their kindness and making her feel so welcome.

Raven was also greeted by little Howling Wolf as a perpetual force of activity anywhere he went, combined with a lot of varied vocalizations, mostly on the loud side. There could be no being unaware of his presence.

"He has a couple speeds only, awake and asleep," stated Running Wild as she chased after him to check his loin skin.

He was home and looked around at his friends and family, along with the land he was born and raised on. After his confrontation with being on the brink of death, now everything seemed new to Raven and so much more meaningful. Before he allowed their tipi lodge to be erected, he insisted on painting a depiction of the black eagle near the entryway. He felt it to be of utmost importance.

It was a time of abundance for all the Nimipu. Their not-too-distant forests were teeming with game. The rivers were filled with easily accessible fish, along with waterfowl. There were roots and berries for the taking when they wanted. The pony herds flourished on the rich grass lands, with plenty of freshwater for all with all the streams and creeks and rivers. The children laughed and played. The women sang while they worked. The men enjoyed the camaraderie while they attended to their work of fishing, hunting, and herd tending, along with tool and weapon repair and replacement. It was good to be alive. They were a free people in their own land, conducting their own business as was necessary, no more, no less. They had the companionship of their fellow tribe members to help share in the burdens as well as the abundance. Then there were the wonderful ponies that brought such a significant change to their lives for the positive, to also share in their burdens as well as the good times. They did not fail to give their thanks to the Great Spirit for such blessings.

CHAPTER 36

STRANGE TALES FROM A DISTANT PLACE

Shadow turned to look in the direction of a sudden commotion to see Wild Wind and some of his friends racing by on their distinctly colored and patterned ponies. On seeing it, the thought came to his mind that it was time to give Wind a more spirited animal of his choosing. The following lighttime, Shadow stopped Wind as he was heading out to play.

"My son, I enjoy seeing your riding skills progress. You have become a good horseman yet being very young."

"Thank you, Father. I do love working with the ponies. It is my greatest fun," Wind responded.

"Later this lighttime, come and find me, and we will go together to pick out a more spirited pony for you of your choice," he continued.

"That will be wonderful. I am so happy to hear it. I will come to look for you, Father. Thank you," Wind responded as he hurried off to tell his friends the exciting news. Wind already had a pony in mind, and he knew that it was going to be somewhat a touchy issue to obtain him because it belonged to his uncle, Talon. Bright Star had sired a colt with another Appaloosa filly that was of the premier linage of Sun Dancer. He was about a full cycle of the seasons old.

Talon already knew of Wind's fascination with the colt from the time it was born, and he didn't have any objections with him having it. He did, however, feel that it was up to his brother to determine when or if he should have such a pony.

After Wind spent some time with his peers in deep imaginative discussions about the limitless possibilities of a life on horseback, he decided it was time to go see his father.

Wind located Shadow, who had been busy with his many routine dealings. "Father, I have come to seek out a new pony, as you had mentioned I should," Wind concluded in an inquiring kind of way.

"That's good. I was expecting you," Shadow stated. "Are you ready to make your decision?"

"I already know which pony I would like to have, although I am not so sure if I may have it," Wind replied.

At hearing that, Shadow's interest was raised. "Well, let me hear of which pony this is that you have in mind, my son," he asked as he stood, looking down at Wild Wind's not yet full stature.

Wind hesitated a bit, with not quite the confidence to just blurt it out. "Well, there is a colt that I have taken an interest in since it was born, and now it is almost full grown, and I think that it is a very fine animal, and I was wondering if you could get it for me."

"Get it? Why couldn't I get it? Doesn't it belong to me?" inquired Shadow, even more curious now.

"No, Father. It belongs to Uncle. It is Bright Star's colt," answered Wind, still not certain of the response he was going to receive.

Shadow's first thought was that this most likely was a fine colt and that he would see what could be done to obtain it for his son. "Let us go and talk with your uncle of this matter. Come. We will see."

Talon's lodge was nearby, and when they arrived there, Little Wing was serving him a meal out in front of their tipi. Talon gestured that they sit with him when they arrived.

"What brings you to my lodge at this time?" asked Talon as he then took some from his bowl with a utensil and placed it in his mouth, along with a questioning look on his face.

Wind looked very serious, which was somewhat perplexing as Shadow looked humored and not concerned in particular. Shadow then said, "My brother, there is a thing that your nephew would ask of you."

Wind was taken by surprise that his father was leaving the asking up to him. After all, he was just a boy. "Yes, I was wondering if maybe you might consider…well, if you thought it might be… I mean, do you think that maybe I could…well, I wish I could have Bright Star's colt."

Shadow tried to keep a straight face as he watched Wind watching Talon to see what he was going to say or do. Then Talon, taking the opportunity to have a little fun with his beloved nephew, looked at Wind with the look of disturbed concern, saying, "You would take that colt from me?"

Wind sat with a look of puzzlement on his face. Talon continued to look into his eyes for a long moment as Wind began to feel uncomfortable.

Then he smiled real wide and said, "I would be glad for you to have that colt. I was wondering if you would ever ask me to have it."

Then Wind laughed, and then Shadow laughed, and then Talon laughed. Little Wing began to laugh too, even though she didn't know why. But it didn't matter. They were just enjoying the opportunity of having a good laugh together. Wind was filled with happiness. Shadow was glad for his son. Talon was proud to be able to do something so big for his nephew. And Little Wing was caught up in the pleasant atmosphere.

"Wait for me to finish my meal, and we'll go get that colt so you can begin to be together," Talon stated as he resumed his eating.

Before long, they were out among Talon's herd, searching for the colt of Wind's desire. Wind spotted him and dismounted, carrying a length of braided hide with a noose on one end to bring the colt along, providing he could get it onto the colt's neck. He kept the cord low as he slowly walked up to the pony and rubbed his muzzle and then his neck while slowly lifting the noose into position, then slowly slipping it over the colt's head. Talon and Shadow just watched with pride in this up-and-coming horseman, of which they were an important influence.

Wind led the colt near enough for him to mount the pony he was riding, and they all proceeded to return to the encampment. When they arrived there, Wind staked the hide cord to the ground outside Shadow's lodge. With the colt tethered, he then, with humility and sincerity, thanked his uncle for the gift of his fine present. He also thanked his father for the opportunity to obtain this spirited animal at this time in his young life.

"I hope he serves you well, my nephew, and enjoy him for all he is able to do," Talon nobly responded.

"Work with him until he becomes part of you, and then he will learn to respond with you and will know what you want of him when you need him most," expounded Shadow with a tone of seriousness.

"I will, Father. He and I will be as if we belonged together in purpose," Wind replied while he continually kept the colt under his touch.

"I know anyone could see that what you say is so, and I also am sure that you will enjoy him as your uncle wants you to," Shadow concluded, having the contentment of seeing Wind with the pony he most wanted.

Within a relatively short time after the cold time began to make its coming known once again, Vixen made it known that she was with child. Beautiful Flower had become amorously involved in a relationship with a respected brave of the Palus band whose name was Leaping Buck, also causing much excitement.

Leaping Buck appeared before Cloud Shadow to ask that Flower would be his woman, bringing gifts for her father and family. Shadow knew that Flower wanted Leaping Buck as her man, and that was all that mattered to him. But the young man insisted that they have the gifts, and so they were not refused but accepted graciously.

"I am happy for my daughter and yourself to have your lives together. You have my consent and my hopes for a long and happy life with one another," Shadow pronounced to the young man, with his daughter in hearing distance. Now there would be a celebration of the marriage of his oldest daughter, with a grandchild on the way. Life was full and good for Cloud Shadow's family.

On an occasion, soon after Flower's marriage to her love Leaping Buck, a visitor came to the Palus village. Red Dreamer had come to counsel with his old friend Cloud Shadow. When he appeared at his lodge, Shadow invited him into his tipi for rest and to refresh himself there.

After some time of smoking, not a staunch ritual with Shadow and small talk, they had a meal and sipped broth of venison. Dreamer certainly appreciated his friendship with Shadow, as Shadow did likewise. After some more time passed between them, Dreamer began to tell of why he had come at this time.

"My friend, I'm sure you recall my telling of my vision of the coming of a white race to our country and that it would lead to the end of our lives as we have known it."

Shadow replied, "Yes, I remember well your telling to me of this thing. I could not forget something such as that."

"There is more I have come to say about this matter," he began again, with Shadow transfixed in attention. "There were some of my tribe members who met up with several members of the Chinook tribe, who do trade with the Clatsop tribe along the big water, who told of seeing white men who came on the big water in giant canoes," Dreamer told Shadow as they both looked into one another's eyes with an amazed yet stressed gaze.

"I am surprised to hear such a thing. My heart says it is not true, but my mind wonders at this talk," Shadow responded after an extended moment.

"That is the way I received it also, my friend, with disbelief. After thinking on it, I thought to come here and tell you," Dreamer continued. Again, there was a pause, with both men not sure where to go with their thoughts while stumbling over this information.

"This is very strange to know. How are they here? Where are they from? What do they want? Do they talk?" Shadow spoke absentmindedly as if to no one in particular. He remembered his father telling of men with hairy faces and shining clothes and headdresses, who it was said had many ponies from the direction of the land of the thorn plants. There were also tales of giant canoes. Were they the same peoples? And what about Dreamer's vision? Black Eagle had found it all too hard to believe. It was so very, very curious. All these things raced through Shadow's thoughts.

CHAPTER 37

Deep Snow Trials

Red Dreamer let Shadow know that he would be leaving soon because he was concerned that it was going to begin snowing anytime, and he did not want to get caught in a blizzard.

Soon after, they had their parting words, with Shadow adding, "I thank you for coming to us with this information, and I will come to you when the warming takes place to counsel more concerning this matter."

At this Dreamer, left for home, feeling better for having shared the news with Shadow.

With Dreamer's departing, Shadow seemed a bit preoccupied with his thoughts and somewhat withdrawn to all those who spent their time near him. Right away, his family began to inquire as to why he would be this way. Shadow told them that he was well enough and that he just needed to be able to have some time to ponder a matter that Dreamer had brought to his attention.

Not long after this time, he summoned Talon, Raven, and Gray Wolf to his lodge for counsel. They all welcomed the invitation, for they were all concerned with his behavior of late.

They came to his lodge collectively and entered. The covering was opened, signaling welcome. They made themselves comfortable although feeling somewhat apprehensive over what this was going to concern.

Shadow began, "When I first met Red Dreamer many winters past, he let my father and I know that he was a person who had received big medicine. Visions had been given to him about a race of white men coming to our land that when they came, our way of life would be no more. I thought it a very strange thing and have been troubled by it since. When Dreamer visited me a short time ago, he came with another most troubling tale concerning this white race."

By this time, his guests were engrossed in what they were being told. Shadow continued the telling as it had been told to him, having been brought a long traveling from the shore of the big water to their home of the Palus band by others, and now to their ears as well. When Shadow had told all he had heard concerning the white men in a giant canoe then ended his speaking on the matter, there was silence. It was a strange silence that these men were not accustomed to when the group of them were gathered together.

Gray Wolf spoke first. "It is hard for me to believe what I have been hearing. I think that maybe I do not understand what you said. I am confused."

"I did not want to confuse anyone, but this is a hard thing to know. When you have seen me acting as another and not myself, you can maybe understand that surely this is a hard thing to know," Shadow responded to the perplexed appearances on the faces of his family.

They all gave their affirmations to what Shadow had conveyed. "We will counsel on this again soon. Now we will just think some more concerning the matter." Shadow ended their meeting with that.

One could not know how far across the land this story had already traveled, but it was apparent that it had traveled through the village like water passing through a coarse basket. Everywhere anyone went, it was being talked about.

Shadow, being the individual he was, could not keep from the idea that a Nimipu needed to go to this place where it was being said that these white men were being seen.

As the course of things were known to happen, the cold time set in in a type of siege that a person could not always do the things they wanted or even sometimes needed to do.

Everyone took it in stride. It was just the way of it.

On a cold time dusk, Leaping Buck and Flower were visiting with Raven and Vixen in the couple's lodge. They had become in close association with many commonalities.

The subject of snowshoes came up after discussions on the difficulties of traversing areas just outside their village boundaries. None of them had any personal experience with them but had seen them used by some who were industrious enough to construct them. Shadow, Running Wild, and Rain were among that category.

Raven, having his curiosity aroused, purposed to ask of them concerning he and Leaping Buck being given access to the snowshoes so that they could experience their capabilities for themselves. All of them together began to become excited with the idea. Things had slowed down along the lines of entertainment, so it became easier to get excited over small things.

On the following early time, Raven paid a visit to his parents' lodge and made an inquiry about the snowshoes. Shadow let him know that he believed them to still be around, but he wasn't sure where.

Rain interjected by saying, "I remember them to be in the big basket that we keep in Gray Wolf's lodge. Let us go and look."

Everyone was a little bored, so they all made their way to Gray Wolf's lodge.

Wind and Howling Wolf were already there visiting with him. Howling Wolf had followed Wind as he often tried to keep up with his doings. Gray Wolf was happy to have them. He was also glad for the arrival of Rain, Raven, Running Wild, and Shadow.

Rain went over to a basket out of several and lifted some hides and pulled out a snowshoe, and then she proceeded to pull out some more until she had those that had been made by herself and Running Wild and Shadow, so that there was a pair from each of them.

Wind was intrigued. Raven looked pleased as well with the prospect of having them to try out.

Flower and Vixen and Leaping Buck were nearby, keeping an eye on Raven's progress at obtaining these snowshoes. They discussed their previous idea when they saw Raven and Wind carrying them out. There was a bit of a commotion with their anticipation.

After Wind understood that Raven and Leaping Buck were going to put them on and go out into the deep snow accumulations, he asked to as well.

"Of course, you are welcome to join in, little brother," replied Raven as they sought for a good place to put them on.

All the snowfall within the boundaries of their village had been tramped down to where walking about wasn't with much difficulty. Maybe they would slip onto their backside on occasion, but generally, it wasn't of much consequence. They took the snowshoes near to where the snow became deep before putting them on.

Once they had secured them to their feet, they headed toward the open land before them. Right away they were delighted at the ability they had to remain on the very surface of the deep snow. After moving about for a while, Leaping Buck tried hurrying on them and found he could almost run. Before long, they were racing each other from one point to another.

After a long while of playing on fine snow, they had come back to where the rest of the family had been watching and enjoying their antics. Then different ones took their turns, working with the wonderful snowshoes.

At this time the fun was coming to an end, Wind prodded his parents into allowing him to hang on to a pair of the snowshoes for the time being, to enjoy when he got the opportunity.

Not long after their initial snowshoe playtime, there came a heavy continual snowfall, along with very cold temperatures that created a lot of fine deep snow. There was talk that there might be another time of losing many ponies to starvation.

Before the snow got too bad, most of the ponies that were considered too important to lose were herded into much closer proximity, where the snow could be removed so they could access the plant life for them to feed on. There was a lot of work involved, and Wind did his share. Also, there was a certain colt that he made sure got his share of the available grazing.

Early after waking, Wind made his way to check on his pony. As he approached the location where he felt he would find him, he came upon a pack of large, seemingly desperate coyotes stocking his pony. The pony was kicking and even trying to stomp them. Wind ran at the coyotes, causing them to scatter. But when they backed off from their attack, the pony bolted, running for more open area with the coyotes in close pursuit.

As Wind watched in dreadful frustration, he soon saw the pony plunge into an area of deep snow that he could hardly move through, although the coyotes weren't making any better headway.

Immediately, he turned and ran to his parents' lodge. And without saying a word to anyone, he grabbed the snowshoes, a bow, and a quiver full of arrows. Then he ran back to where his pony was still struggling to flee from the hunger-crazed predators.

As quickly as he could, he secured the snowshoes to his feet and headed toward the fray. With bow in hand and quiver on his back, he nocked an arrow. He was able to move much faster than the coyotes. It wasn't long before he was able to cast an arrow, then another, and another.

He killed several of the coyotes, and the others stopped their pursuit and did their utmost best effort to get away with their lives.

His poor pony was in a bad way from the strain of its ordeal. It understood that the threat had ended, but it was not doing well under the conditions.

It wasn't long after the running off of the coyotes that Shadow and Talon had made their way to the pony's side as well, using the other snowshoes. Talon thought to bring a length of hide cord to help lead the pony in the direction they needed it to go.

After a lot of effort, they managed to get the pony to shallow snow, where they worked to massage it and got it to take some water while slowly walking it about. After some time, it appeared to be doing better.

CHAPTER 38

Looking for Guidance

"That was fast thinking and good work to save your pony, my nephew," Talon commented as he watched Wind still massaging the colt.

"I just couldn't lose him, Uncle," Wind replied. "He means so much to me. I have a name for him now after seeing him deep in the snow with only his head sticking out."

"What name would that to be, my son?" Shadow asked, listening to their conversation.

"Snowman," Wind answered, having a look about him of pride and satisfaction.

It was a long cold time, but as it always happens, eventually there began to be signs of change in the weather. At a time of a significant change, Little Wing stated that she was very close to giving birth. Running Wild and Rain were called to look after her needs. She was helped to the lodge of birthing and menstruating females. The child was reluctant to come into the world, and when he finally did, it was with a shrieking sound that demanded attention.

Talon was informed of his son's birth and that mother and child were doing well. He could hear his son testing his lungs with varied high-pitch sounds, which caused him to think of his uncle Big Cat. He spoke out at that time, saying, "The boy's name will be Screaming Panther." He felt confident that he would grow into the name.

Talon, Little Wing, and their new baby were the center of attention around their village for some time thereafter. Although Howling Wolf would not let himself be overlooked. Also, Raven and Vixen just had to glance at her belly to be reminded their time was not far off.

The times grew warmer, and the village became more active. They had lost a lot of ponies to starvation, but the majority of the herds came through and would make a strong comeback to regain their state of health.

Sometime soon after the weather had changed to first showing of new grass, the village received some visitors.

It was Cunning Fox and Young Old Man, wanting to visit the Palus band for personal reasons and also bearing grievous news. Bull Elk was dead.

Raven, at first seeing his close friends, was ecstatic. But upon hearing the news of her father's untimely death, Vixen, in her delicate state, took a hard turn.

Shadow had also taken the news hard, remembering how it was Bull Elk who had rescued him from the back of the buffalo during that dramatic episode, probably saving his life.

The story came out concerning the tragic event. It happened as a result of Bull Elk and Cunning Fox organizing a retaliation on the Shoshone camp of interlopers who had caused so much misery for so many.

He and his followers made their way to the Shoshone encampment. There they attacked some of the Shoshone that were found outside the boundaries of the main part of their camp. It was just meant to be a hit-and-run raid to harass them and add insult to injury.

While Bull Elk rampaged through their ranks, a young brave picked up a freshly cut lodgepole and impaled him with it, causing a terrible wound within his intestinal area.

Cunning Fox went on to tell how his father had stayed mounted, remaining with the retreating riders for some distance before succumbing to his injuries.

It was a very sad tale, and all were upset at its telling. Although it was worse for Vixen, who had taken ill from the hearing of it and was unable to recover while her brother tried to console her, as did Raven, along with all the women of the family.

Cunning Fox had been miserable over his father's death, and now he was extremely upset by his sister's reaction to the news, as well being near term in her pregnancy.

Cunning Fox and Young Old Man let Raven and the others in the family know that they wished to stay with the Palus band to be of any assistance to Raven and Vixen.

Raven nodded in agreement but felt that his own troubles were directly related to Vixen and the child she carried, and until that improved, he would not.

Cunning Fox and Young Old Man stayed nearby where a lodge had been constructed for them. Vixen didn't improve as the women of the family waited on her continually, making sure that she always had nourishing broth to sustain her, keeping her clean, and being present for any assistance that might be needed.

Raven felt he had to go off from the village to pray and meditate, to seek his medicine in this time of need. When he brought this up to his father, Shadow replied, "Go to Tahoma, my son, and seek the Great Spirit there. He can be better found in the clarity of that place."

The following first light, Raven came to Vixen's side and placed his face to hers. "I go to seek your healing, my woman. I will return as soon as possible."

Vixen opened her eyes slightly in a very weakened state. It was so hard for him to see her in that way. He turned away and left with a determination to do all that could be done through supplication.

He rode out of camp shortly thereafter alone. He and Ghost would go to the Waptailmin village, where he could leave his pony and continue on foot to the higher ground of Tahoma.

Cunning Fox and Young Old Man had never had an opportunity to relate to Shadow the experience they both had on the Beartooth Lake vision quest.

They both discussed it with one another, remembering all so well the cloud shadow that appeared so supernaturally, being previously undetected. It was followed by the strong impression to trust in the leadership that had been already provided for them.

They requested of Shadow that they could counsel with him in private. He agreed without reservation, considering the hardships that they had been faced with, not even wondering what the purpose might be.

After they had seated themselves within the lodge and all formalities had been observed with respect, Cunning Fox began. "We are honored to be here with you, Cloud Shadow, and want to convey the tale of our vision quest, seeking your opinion concerning the outcome of it."

"I have to believe that you feel that I might be able to give some interpretation of your experience," Shadow stated with a questioning look on his face.

"Yes, as well as possibly some reasoning to help us come to a concluding understanding," Young Old Man replied.

"Well," Shadow responded, "let me hear this tale, and we'll try to determine from there."

Young Old Man began the story with their preparation and then the journey to the higher ground. Occasionally, Cunning Fox would take over from his perspective, and they together did an accurate job with the telling, leaving off with a questioning look of their own.

Shadow was searching his own thoughts for a serious and responsible response. His first reaction was that this was not at all what he expected. He thought it would be connected to the death of Bull Elk or Vixen's condition. Now his mind was trying to decipher this puzzling story.

"So you believe these events pertain to me somehow?"

"Yes," Young Old responded. "It was right after this experience that you showed up at our village and then became the one who saved Raven and I from the Shoshone in such a miraculous manner."

"I will have to pray and seek after the Great Spirit for the wisdom to say more. That is all," Shadow concluded.

In time, Raven came to the Waptailmin village. There he sought out Red Dreamer to ask him to take care of his pony while he was away. He informed him of his intention to make a journey to Tahoma, seeking healing for his wife. He told him the story and how his father had told him to come to Tahoma for what he sought.

"Your father is wise and knows of the power that inhabits that mountain. The Great Spirit can be found there more readily." Dreamer spoke, for the most part, the words of Shadow.

"I will follow the instructions I have received to show me the path I should travel, praying for guidance for the time to come," Raven expounded in the manner of a true heart.

Dreamer bid him a safe and successful trip before he departed.

Vixen continued as she had been when Raven last saw her.

Her brother visited with her regularly, and she was able to give him recognition, but that was all. The Palus camp women tended to her every need with skill and concern.

These times were to Shadow some of the most trying he had ever known. The sighting of white men, the death of Bull Elk, and its effect on everyone. This recent development of it being suggested that he held some position of power among his people. Shadow went to the only place he knew for solace. He prayed and meditated, seeking understanding and wisdom from the source he had the most confidence in—the Great Spirit, the Life Giver, the Creator.

Meanwhile, Raven climbed onward and upward the mountain, being farther than it appeared in its great size.

He had never been to this exact area, but he felt like he was coming home. He had been very troubled of late, but with every effort toward Tahoma, he received more and more of a peace that refreshed his heart and mind. He was feeling assured that the need was going to be met. He stopped for darkness, not being able to see any longer. At first light, he continued. Tahoma loomed larger and larger. The meadows were teeming with flowers, the musical sounds of the brooks, the birds and butterflies fluttering about. He stopped and filled his lungs with the pure air of this altitude.

When he reached the crags near the base of the mountain's abrupt incline, being a clear day, he stood in place and tried to block out all thought except the majesty of it all and his desire to receive what he felt he needed to enforce his belief in the power of the Life Giver. Time passed by, but Raven didn't take any notice of how long he stood and waited, meditating upon his quest. Then he thought he detected motion on his strong arm side over his shoulder. He then noticed a large mountain goat standing on a ledge, which appeared to be looking at him. He immediately thought of his father. Then a shadow was cast over him. Then looking up, he saw a cloud passing in front of the sun. As he continued looking upward, he saw an eagle fly across his field of vision. It was somewhat distant, but as it drew nearer and cried out, Raven spoke to himself, "It's black."

Cloud Shadow had been seeking a sign of the Great Spirit's intentions for him, if he could be a help for the needs that were pressing those he cared for.

The signs that Raven was witnessing were taking place while Cloud Shadow was entreating the Life Giver most earnestly with all his heart.

As Raven watched, the cloud seemed to dissipate, the eagle had vanished, and the goat was no longer there. Cloud Shadow was given the strongest assurance he had yet received, as his beseeching was culminated. He was given the clear conscious impression that the powers of wisdom and healing would be his, given to him by the Life Giver.

Also, that he would be a man of great medicine for his people till the end of his time.

In the lodge where Vixen lay in her state of weakness, as her brother and friend Young Old Man sat by her side, the entry opened, and Cloud Shadow appeared. The young men made way for Shadow to approach her there.

He reached out and placed his strong hand on her forehead and began to pray for her and his grandchild. After a short while, Vixen began to stir. Then her eyes opened wide, and she looked about at the faces of those who loved her, and she smiled.

An extended moment later, she sat up as tears rolled down her face.

"I'm sad for my father, but I am glad to be alive," she stated as Shadow helped her to her feet.

CHAPTER 39

BIG WATER LOOMS LARGER

Cunning Fox and Young Old Man looked at each other and grinned. Shadow placed a hand on each of their shoulders and said, "I am a man of medicine. Whoever you meet, tell them what you have seen and heard here."

By the time Raven returned, Vixen was going about her activities like nothing had happened. The story of her miraculous healing was on everyone's lips.

Raven met with his father shortly after his return. "The story that I have heard from Cunning Fox and Young Old Man and my wife, is it so?"

"Yes, my son. The Life Giver has given me a power to help others," Shadow replied. "I am a medicine man, as you know Black Eagle had great medicine before me."

"I know what you say is true. I was shown that truth on my quest with wonder. Now it has been made clear to me that you are a prominent leader for our people, and I am so thankful for my wife's healing, my father," Raven concluded.

"You have received what you asked for, my son, and I look forward to hearing of your quest. We are all thankful for your safe return." Shadow put a hand of assurance on his son's arm as they ended their speaking.

Vixen gave birth to a healthy girl they named Rainbow, honoring Raven's mother and adding something that everyone considered beautiful. Howling Wolf, around the same time, was running everywhere he went, just as well as he pleased, and speaking quite clearly. Screaming Panther was crawling about, seeking attention from the nearest source. Shadow was busier than ever before with the people's affairs, as well as family and friends. He also could not shake that something which would continually come to his thoughts, causing an uneasiness deep within. White men were sighted around the Big Water.

Although he had a hard time with his imaginings of just what all the Big Water entailed, he understood that it was not all so far away.

Shadow took some time to go and visit the Waptailmin tribe and his friend Red Dreamer. While he was there, he and Dreamer conversed on many subjects, including Raven's recent quest and the healing of Vixen and the birth of Rainbow. Finally, the topic of the issue revolving around these white men, firstly coming in a vision, then in the flesh, was told by multiple witnesses.

"I will go to the Big Water myself," said Shadow, "to see of this thing. I feel I must."

"My friend, I will go also to help with the trials of such a journey," replied Dreamer.

"No, I ask that you don't," Shadow responded. "I believe I need to go alone in meditation and prayer."

Dreamer nodded in agreement to his request. "I understand and will also pray for your safety and success, my good and wise friend."

When Shadow returned to his village, he summoned Talon, Raven, Gray Wolf, and Leaping Buck. They entered Shadow's lodge, and he spoke to them of his decision to go to the big Water to seek understanding and evidence concerning these white men. He went on to tell them his plans for crafting a dugout canoe to be readied for when the weather would permit him to make the trip.

There was some disagreement on his family's part that he should travel alone, but Shadow was adamant as to needing the solitude for his communing for spiritual guidance. They reluctantly agreed, and their meeting ended.

The weather was beginning to turn, and colder times followed. Shadow and Raven went in search of a suitable tree for a proper canoe. After some consideration, they chose the one they decided was best suited to the need. It wasn't an overly large tree because his dugout needed to be something he could manage by himself.

They were able to secure it with much difficulty, having to drag it a considerable distance with the help of several additional ponies.

Although Shadow knew that he could not conceive everything that he would encounter, he did know that there would be areas that would be unnavigable, and he would have to portage. He understood that he didn't want the dugout to be any larger than it needed to be.

There was an atmosphere of concern in regard to Shadow's up-and-coming quest by all who were privy to his intent. And as the story was becoming more well-known throughout the tribe, the accuracy of its retelling was an unknown as it was passed along. Although, even with this general concern, the people carried on as well as possible. Wild Wind spent most of his time working with Snowman and didn't feel much concern for his father taking a long trip to an unfamiliar place. As far as he knew, his father could do anything without any need for worry. Little brother Howling Wolf didn't appear particularly concerned either. However, with Raven, Running Wild, and Rain, it was another matter. They were well aware of the danger this venture presented. One obvious point was that the Chinooks along the river were known for their unpredictability when confronting outsiders, along with many other perils he surely would be facing.

Even so, their routine events of the camp kept them busy. There was always something that needed their attention, working as a distraction from idle thoughts. Life was full, and it was good to be alive. There were, however, unpleasant events that were told of as news travels, one being a story of Yellow Jacket being killed in the buffalo country by Siksika in their overzealous protection of their hunting grounds. Another was the death of Rising Moon of the Lower Red Fish band. He was thrown off his pony after it had tripped in a hole at a full gallop.

These tragic accidents were not so uncommon with their constant use of the ponies. Things happened, and no one was excluded from the possibility of a deadly incident. Shadow, among other things, spent time creating his canoe. First, he chopped a groove the length of his log, and then he began burning out the core with white-hot coals.

After the area from the core was removed sufficiently, he began shaping the exterior in a painstakingly careful manner. He was determined to be successful on his first attempt, not wanting to have to create another, believing that time wouldn't allow for it.

Not long after Shadow had completed the dugout, the weather took a convincing turn toward the cold time. He elevated the canoe onto the remaining log ends and then covered it with branch framing and hides. He then maintained a smoky fire under it, working at slowly drying it, doing all he could to prevent it from cracking.

Once again, the cold time set in, and it was back to their mode of persistent endeavor to overcome the obstacles of snow, ice, wind, and bone-chilling cold.

Not long after this, there came an occasion when Wind and Snowman went out hunting for small game on the open ground that surrounded their village. The snow hadn't yet gotten very deep, allowing them free travel. Wind had managed to take down a pheasant with an arrow. They had also added a rabbit to their success. As the snow began to fall heavily, they headed back for home.

The village was straight ahead some distance yet and still in sight. As they plodded on, the snow grew very heavy, with the wind blowing at a sharp slant. Within a relatively short time, Wind could no longer see the village. He began to imagine that he might not be going in line with the village any longer and the conditions of the weather had become a snowstorm with the temperatures dropping as well.

After travelling a considerable distance, which should have gotten him close to the encampment, he still could not see the village. He was worried now. He wasn't of the type that felt fear, but it was always based on what he could see. This was different, being of a sort that was beyond his abilities to bring any of his powers to bear. He did hold on, however, to hope—hope that he would reach shelter on time. Even at his young age, he was aware that this was turning into a life-threatening situation. He began to pray with earnest.

Back in the village, Shadow had become aware that Wind was out in the storm. But just where, there was no certainty.

Shadow felt helpless to aid him, knowing that he would be searching in vain out in the blizzard.

The thing that Shadow and Wind were both counting on were the rivers. If Wind could come across the Palus or the Winding Rivers, he would have a line of travel that would lead him to the camp, providing he didn't lose all sense of direction. He also had to hold up to the biting and possibly paralyzing cold, frozen limbs being a certainty before one succumbed altogether.

Wind thought he could make out some dark objects in the near proximity. Yes, they were ponies hunkering from the storm. He was very much encouraged as he pushed on. Then he believed he could make out what appeared to be a river. He continued traveling in the way he felt he needed to reach the camp.

By the time Wind reached the village, he was almost all in. Snowman wasn't so well off either. Some in the camp helped him to the lodge where his family anxiously hoped for his return. When he finally arrived, they were elated over seeing him alive.

CHAPTER 40

A Float Downstream

Eventually, Wind, as well as Snowman, regained all their strength, and the entire incident was given over to a lesson learned. The unexpected could be your undoing.

The time passed as it always does, and Shadow looked forward to his coming journey. The tension that began to emanate from his wives as the time drew near was difficult for him and them.

"Pray for me if you want to help me to return safely," he exhorted them. They promised that they would, of which he had no reason to doubt.

It came to pass that the warming time began to show its signs of coming. Shadow had managed to dry his dugout with a low continual heat for weight reduction and buoyancy. Once the weather conditions reached a certain degree of favorableness, he uncovered his canoe. He then made an adequate supply of black paint from charcoal and bear oil. Then he painted his small vessel inside and out with it. After his initial painting had dried, he then made up a white paint from clay and pitch that he used to draw a large pair of eyes on the sleek bow of his watercraft. To Shadow, the eyes represented the all-seeing guide that he was counting on for his success in overcoming the many obstacles that lie ahead.

He was feeling pressed to be on his way, knowing that there would be considerable time involved with completing this trek.

He had gotten Running Wild to make a large hide pouch to place his loose belongings into. He planned on securing the pouch by a length of corded hide that had been sewn into the pouch opening, to then be attached to a piece of deer antler that he had bored into the top edge of his craft, leaving a V-shaped section protruding out to tie it to.

The items he was taking were his bow and quiver of arrows and a long with hatchet and knife. He also had a fire-making kit, a buffalo robe, extra moccasins, leggings, and a long sleeve shirt. If all his clothes got wet, he could possibly stay wet for a long while until he could get them dried by sun or fire or wind or a combination of those sources. Rain also added a bundle containing a good supply of pemmican and dried quamash root, ground into a meal.

The time came when he was ready to put his canoe into the water and actually depart. The Palus River was in the near vicinity of his lodge, which would take him shortly thereafter into the Winding River, which in time would merge into the Mother River. This, Shadow felt, would be one of the major challenges of his lifetime. He was unsettled concerning the vastness of his undertaking, but at the same time, he had a compelling notion that would not let him do otherwise.

Shadow's family knew that the time had come for his leaving, and they were gathered together. Without a doubt, there was sadness over the occasion. Shadow felt it also.

He managed his dugout into the water well enough. Then he held onto the rest of the length of the cord that was already tied to the antler and secured to his travel pouch. He eased himself into the vessel. Then with a paddle, he pushed off.

He looked to his family and now a throng of villagers as well and waved his goodbye. Many with their grave concerns waved farewells to him in turn.

Shadow moved along with the current almost effortlessly, periodically steering with a slight movement of the paddle. Waterfowl took flight as smaller birds fluttered about along the water's edge. It was fast becoming nice weather, giving the feeling of relaxation and contentment. It was seeming so much the opposite of his feelings just a relatively short time before. Just awhile later, the craft entered the Winding River as it took its course heading in the direction of the land of the setting sun.

After he entered the Winding River, it became a very fast run, shooting the rapids of swelling, boiling, and whirling waters all about him. He heard himself let out a cry from the mixture of excitement and fear that could not be suppressed. It wasn't the type of fear that would cause him to turn back, but rather of a sort that bursts forth at the moment of being severely startled while still rushing onward at times with amazing speed.

As the light began to lessen to the point that it was becoming limited visibility, he stopped his travel by picking out a stretch of shore that was free of rocks or potential damaging debris.

Even though the distance he had traveled on the Winding River was not all fast current—for as it was with almost all rivers, there were stretches of fairly calm waters—he felt it had been a trial of his wits to the extreme that had carried him this far.

He slipped his craft up on shore and collapsed into a much-needed state of recovery, mentally and physically. At first light, he left again, feeling somewhat weary and a bit unnerved. The rapids were still treacherous, but he actually felt he was handling it with more skill, being fully aware of the difficulties involved and more prepared for it as it presented itself.

Onward he went, thinking at times that he was enjoying the challenge. Not long after he had begun his travels again, he came to the spot where the Winding River flowed into the Mother River. The accomplishment of making it to this part of his journey gave him encouragement.

He proceeded along, as was his intent, to take all opportunity to progress whenever possible, only excluding his periods of rest, which he had planned would almost always take place when visibility became the deciding factor. Not long after he had entered the Mother River, he began to encounter people whom he assumed were of the Chinook tribe. On occasion, he chanced to give them a wave of recognition. At times, he would receive a wave in return. He tried to focus on the many difficult areas along the river course as opposed to outside potential problems. Given that outlook on his situation, he worked at that which he had some immediate control.

He covered a good bit of distance before the approaching dusk gave him the inclination to hold over again for his rest and safety.

While he slept an uncomfortable and intermittent sleep, he was suddenly awakened by several pairs of strong hands seizing his arms and dragging him up the riverbank. Shadow didn't put up too much struggle against this out-of-his-control situation. Within a short time after his apprehension, he was secured to a sturdy upright post. He was bound with a series of wraps and a thin leather strap around his neck, holding his head tight to the post, which prevented him from moving from that spot in any way.

The reasoning by the Chinook for this particular method of holding him fast was to allow for hand sign talk by their captive when the time came. Although, after he was bound, he was left alone until light would come again.

The Chinook who had taken him captive had only one primary motive—to extract a price from him for his passing on what they considered their domain. To them he was of no more consequence than any other person.

The following early time, he found himself confronted by several Chinook men. While he looked at these men, he noticed their necklaces were made from human fingers. All in all, it did pose an intimidating circumstance.

These men spoke with an old man who did not appear to be of the Chinook tribe. Then the old man began to do sign talk with Shadow, letting him know that a price was being demanded of him.

Shadow signed that he was on a journey to see about a sighting of white men by the Clatsop tribe, and he was a Nimipu medicine man on a mission under the protection of the Great Spirit. He had nothing of much value with him.

The old man spoke to the Chinook relating Shadow's reply. At that, they began a discussion among themselves.

As time went on, there began to develop a gathering of certain members of this tribe just out of curiosity. It wasn't unfamiliar to them to see an outsider taken captive for a toll. The thing that was almost always in question was the outcome of such a situation. The Chinook were not an overly unreasonable people. They just clearly felt that they had the right to take from any who used their waterway.

The old man once again was approached by the Chinook men and was spoken to briefly. Afterward, he signed to Shadow, questioning him as to the name he was called by.

"Cloud Shadow," he signed as he spoke in reply.

The old man related the reply, although they understood the response, for they had heard of that name. Once again, they entered a discussion. There was obvious disagreement between them that went on for some time. Then the most fierce-looking of the group broke from the others and approached Shadow, drawing a knife then cutting his bindings. This caused him to fall to his knees, gasping for an adequate measure of air. The fierce one spoke something loudly to Shadow, who looked up at old man, who gave him the sign to go. He managed to get to his feet and make his way back to his dugout. All his belongings remained as he had left them.

He continued in his efforts for leaving right away.

He got the canoe in the river, slipped in, then pushed off. After just a short time, he was far beyond the location where he had been seized. He thanked the Great Spirit and sighed with a relief from a terrible tension that had suddenly given way.

CHAPTER 41

Another Dream

As he continued on the river course, there were numerous occasions when he needed to make portage due to impassable areas of extremely fast and treacherous currents and falls. He had to pull the dugout and his other belongings along, covering difficult distances.

He was on the river after another period of pulling all his things overland, feeling grateful to be able to let the river do the work once again. Suddenly, he dropped over an unexpected short waterfall and was pitched forward out the craft. His head was struck on a fairly large protruding stone, immediately rendering him unconscious.

*****

Talon awoke in the early time with a nagging need to do some hunting for certain large animals to replenish their supply of meat. After getting himself readied, he went in search of Raven. He found him with Wind, making arrows. Wind was being shown what to do and what not to do, that the arrow was to be a missile that could be counted on when put to service.

"My nephews, how does it go for you?" Talon asked.

"Good," they replied.

"How is it for you, Uncle?" Raven inquired.

"I am well but hungry for meat of the kind of which we have none," he responded.

Raven and Wind nodded in agreement, for they understood what he was implying.

"Would you join me on a hunt for what we can take down from the not-too-distant mountain forests?" he asked of Raven.

"I will. It is a good time for a hunt, and all would be glad for fresh meat, I know," Raven replied.

"I will come as well," Wind interjected. Wind hadn't gone on the hunt yet in his young life, and both Talon and Raven took his response in stride, nodding to him in compliance.

"It is time that you did, my nephew," Talon stated as he held an arrow that Raven had finished, inspecting the work.

"We'll leave at first light," he concluded.

*****

Shadow floated on his back in shallow water, unconscious and deep in a dream state. He was listening to someone talking to him.

"Cloud Shadow, the white men you seek are flesh and blood as you are. They have many languages, and the time will come that the Nimipu will speak the language of the white men. It will be a very different life for your people, and the life that you have come to know will be no more. You are in the plan of the Life Giver. He will protect you, and it will be well with you and your people for these times." Then he had a sensation of total darkness come over him. Then it was light.

Shadow awoke looking at a passing cloud, then all blue sky. He began to sink into the water's depth and had to get his legs beneath him to stabilize himself. He was able to stand with most of his upper body being out of the moving water that surrounded him.

He shook his head, still trying to put together what had happened to him. He slowly began to recall being pitched from his craft. Then he panicked as he looked around for his things.

He soon realized that his quiver and arrows were still on his back. Other than that, he had no idea.

He knew that if there was a chance of retrieving them, he would have to follow the river's flow. So with all his resolve, he began walking.

He walked for a long while until there was no longer enough light to see. And then he waited in place till dawn. It had been a long cold dark time, being still somewhat wet with no fire to warm himself.

At first light, he was on the move again. He began to have doubts as to the reasons he had come. He was deep in thought when he spotted something ahead near the water's edge.

It was his dugout, neatly tucked into a cluster of downed brush, intact, with his pouch and bow still tied to the antler. He had a renewed confidence for his continuing.

*****

Talon, Raven, and Wind, along with their ponies Bright Star, Ghost, and Snowman, as well as an additional pack pony for each hunter's bounty, left in search for game to once again supply the family and others in their band with fresh meat. It was something that was always eagerly received whenever it was available.

Wind was elated with this time imagined, and now he was on an actual hunting trip, accompanying his uncle and big brother, a pair of accomplished and experienced hunters who would teach him to also become an accomplished predator.

Primarily, they would be hunting deer, elk, or bear.

If Wind proved himself on this hunt, he would allow himself to think on a possible buffalo hunt in the not-too-distant time.

*****

Shadow pulled his canoe onto shore and fetched his pouch, removing his fire-starting kit. After selecting a suitable location alongside a large boulder that would block the wind, he built a fire. He placed the fire to where it would also heat the stone as well. He intended to generate enough heat to get rid of the chill that had stayed with him since his extended time in the cold waters of the river.

He was planning on holding up for a while before leaving again. He got his change of shirt, leggings, and moccasins to wear and stripped off his still damp skins. After his changing, he set up a drying rack to help with removing all the moisture from them.

He created a soft mat consisting of pine needles and other forest debris with some elasticity. Then he laid out his buffalo robe, turning the hairs to the inside. He was bundled between the boulder and a deep bed of coals.

Later, he awoke from a good sleep then took his time about the campsite, reinvigorating the fire and relaxing.

He did exert himself enough to catch a few fish to bake, and then some more relaxing.

He began to ponder the creditable story of the white men once again, followed by recalling his vivid dream concerning them too. The Nimipu speaking white man language seemed all too unbelievable to be true.

*****

After a stop over and a sleep, Wind and his notable companions were approaching the forest's edge, where they would make their base camp, of which they would use as a location to skin and butcher their intended prey.

Wind hadn't had any experience in the deep forest, having been raised on the wide-open grasslands. He was looking forward to it with a real passion. The following early time, they were already well awake and left out on foot, prepared to take down any prospective animal that would serve their need.

Wind was no novice with his bow and arrows. Like all the young males among the Nimipu, they practiced diligently for the mastery. Some certainly did better than others. As with most things, Wind had accomplished proficiency.

Talon whispered, "Split up and converge again farther up ahead."

"Look up in the trees as you move about. A lot of times, the bears will tree up at their first detection of the presence of men," Raven instructed Wind just as they began to separate from one another.

They proceeded along as stealthily as they were able when suddenly, a buck bolted from the brush. Talon immediately drew on him, but Raven had already released an arrow, only to see Wind's arrow strike the buck first. Raven's arrow also found its mark, whereas Talon hadn't even cast his.

He shook his head and gave a laugh. "Outdone by both my nephews." He laughed again and was joined by Raven and Wind with their shared humor.

It was a good effort from the hunters on their first attempt. They took several deer and a bear. They then managed to bring up the pack ponies to take the game back to their base camp.

The following lighttime, Talon volunteered to stay at camp and finish the skinning and butchering while at the same time also keeping a watch over their bounty to see that it didn't get molested by scavengers.

Wind and Raven left together, looking to take more meat for their efforts. Raven made an arrangement with Wind to hold up in an open area, with Wind on one side and himself on the other, trying to stay out of sight. They continued there for a while, waiting for some unwary animal to happen along.

Raven was about to move out of his place of relative concealment when he thought he heard a commotion. He peered in the direction of the sound. There came a large buck bursting through the open area between them.

The brothers locked onto him with drawn bows. Just before Wind released, he saw out of the corner of his eye another movement. It was a large lion at a full-on charge. As the deer fell with Raven's arrow buried deep with a fatal blow, Wind cast his shot at his fast-moving target, his arrow passing through the panther's neck. It wasn't the location he had hoped for, but it was sufficient to stop the cat in its tracks.

"A mountain lion on your first hunt. That is a good sign, my brother."

Wind felt that it was a gift to him, to have a lion pelt of his own. What an honor that the Great Spirit had given him, he believed.

*****

Shadow was feeling refreshed, having had adequate nourishment and rest. He planned to leave again at first light.

He awoke thinking of his family and his village, then the dream of the white men's language. It was a lot to think on, and he sincerely wanted not to spend a lot of his time sitting in place and dwelling on them.

He missed his family and felt he would rather be with them than be where he was right then. Although he also knew that he would not be turning back before reaching the destination he had set out for. It wasn't in him to do so. He made ready and departed, glad once again for the dugout that had served him so well thus far.

There began to be long periods of much rainfall, causing poor visibility. He would have to stop just because of the weather conditions. The closer he got to the Big Water, the worse the conditions became.

Many sleeps came and went, and progress was slow. Eventually, there came a time when he believed he could smell what he thought to be an odor coming from the Big Water, although he had never experienced the odor before.

After much hardship and effort, Shadow made it to what he believed to be the shore of the Big Water. He could hear the surf rolling in. But from where he stood, he could see nothing. Between the fog and rain and gray clouded sky, lighttime or darktime, it was impossible to see any distance. Again, he felt somewhat disheartened.

Was this what he had come all this way for?

Chapter 42

Is a Symbol a Sign?

Back at the Palus camp, there were festivities and a celebratory atmosphere over the return of the small hunting party. Talon had pledged to share the deer and bear meat they had gotten with the entire village in honoring their successful hunt and Wind's taking of the stalking lion. Even though it wasn't stalking him, the fact that the lion was killed by the hunter while it was in pursuit of prey was significant.

Little Howling Wolf was still a small child, but he was aware enough to know that the jubilance was due to something his brother Wind had accomplished. Therefore, he was excited for him as he ran about, shouting and laughing, being caught up in the occasion along with everyone else.

Not long after Raven had dismounted on their return and was greeting as well as being greeted, he felt a tug at his leggings. Then, looking down, he saw Rainbow grinning up at him.

"There's my little girl!" he exclaimed, which excited her even more than she had been already. Vixen stood by, beaming at her man on his return. Raven gave her a big and loving smile. It was good to be alive within their sphere.

*****

Shadow pulled back off the beach to wait out the unfavorable weather conditions. He constructed his camp and waited and waited and waited. One darktime, while pondering his predicament, it occurred to him that this was very much a trial of his patience, well aware that he had gone through his share of trials, but this was of another kind. He awoke the following early time and purposely lingered in his sleeping robe, not feeling in a hurry to do anything in particular. There was something that made a noticeable impression. It was brighter out than he had experienced at any time previously since he had arrived there. He got himself up and ate some pemmican and drank some water that he had collected from the rain. After a short time of picking up, he walked down to the beach.

He became very excited at his first actual viewing of the Big Water. It was a sight that staggered his mind. The immenseness was unimaginable.

He stared long at the oddity he beheld, with his thoughts moving across this horizon of infinity, but then he had to pause. It wasn't infinity.

What did he see at a far distance coming into view from some alien shore? A giant canoe with wings. His heart raced. White men, maybe, possibly. Could it be them?

He continued staring. Although after a period of uncertain duration, he concluded that the vessel was getting smaller and harder to see. It was beginning to disappear, and then it was gone.

Had he really seen what he thought he had? It all seemed to be more than he could grasp. The abnormality of it all, along with this sighting of the giant canoe, and it did have wings. He felt he had to reevaluate the whole situation.

The next thought he had was *How would others receive this story?*

He then left from that spot and walked most of that lighttime in the direction that was more in line with where the strange sighting had been. Finally, he came to a stop, thinking he had gone far enough. By this time, he had concluded that he had confirmed his goal. He had clearly seen the Big Water and understood how vast it was. He had also seen a craft that was not of his kind.

He turned for his camp when he noticed something shining on the coarse beach before him. He stopped to pick up a small flat object, metallic and having a number of distinct conforming edges, along with certain symbols marked upon it. It also had a raised area in the center with a pair of holes bored through it.

It was a thing of great curiosity to Shadow, for he felt sure that it was not a thing of local origin. It seemed very important yet terrible, seeming to make this mystery so much more real to him.

*****

Running Wild looked over at Rain and spoke, saying, "We need our husband home with us, my sister."

"Yes, it is past time for him to come back to us. We beseech the Life Giver for his soon return," Rain concluded as she gazed off into the direction of the setting sun, for the cold time had already come and gone.

Wild Wind had matured much since his father's departure. He began to think of a venture that he could take part in, something daring and bold. Something that would provide him with the self-satisfaction that was acquired with a passing through the rite of manhood. He felt he was still lacking in that regard, and it made him anxious to achieve it.

His family had been aware of his moodiness and dissatisfaction with his current status from his own perspective.

Raven and Talon had had discussions with Wind concerning the matter and had consoled him with the prospect of a trip to the buffalo country.

Something that kept Talon from committing to the trip at that time was the hope for the return of Shadow, rather than making that decision in his absence.

Although with the uncertainty of the time of his return, if ever, and the narrow window of opportunity for such a journey, he began to feel pressed to make his decision soon.

*****

After finding the shiny metallic object, Shadow had purposed to begin a homeward trek as soon as condition would allow. He still had a desire that he might yet make a sighting of these said white men.

*****

Talon sought Raven out not long after their talks of going on an extended hunt for the buffalo. "I believe that it is now time that we should go on our buffalo hunt, my nephew. It will fill an important need for our band," Talon told him.

Raven didn't feel as confident as Talon concerning the matter but conceded understanding that his uncle was more mature and experienced. So he agreed to support the effort with all his ability. Although in his heart he had reservations, but he purposed to keep them to himself. He answered his uncle, "That certainly would be a help to the band to have a new supply of that strength-giving meat. Whatever I can do to help achieve our success, I will do uncle."

*****

Shadow decided that on the following lighttime, he would move along the shoreline in the direction of Cold Wind Grandfather to see what he might find out in doing so.

The following early time, he broke camp for some more exploration of this all so unfamiliar region. The weather was once again agreeable and allowed him to take in many amazing sights of which he would never have imagined, like the rising and lowering of the water's edge and the varied shells scattered along the beach. He had seen shelled necklaces but never actually understood where they had been collected from. He saw a fur-bearing animal that inhabited the large rocks just offshore of which he could not name, being beyond his description. He did not have the words for such things.

As he made his way along the Big Water's edge, he saw a sight in the distance that held his curiosity. At a point, he had to believe that he was looking at a skeleton of an animal of enormous size. With an unwavering gaze, he approached it. When he arrived at its location, he again stared for a long time with a questioning mind. It certainly appeared to be fishlike, yet the rib cage stood as tall as he did. After an extended time, he managed to break himself away and proceed along the shore farther yet.

After he continued awhile, there was some activity at the water's edge that caught his attention. He stopped and got down low as he continued to study the sight ahead.

He looked on while several large canoes that were highly decorated and high sided and heavily manned were drawing near to shore. He very much wanted to approach them but was apprehensive to do so. He assumed them to be Clatsop and had decided that he was not going to reveal himself to them, remembering his ordeal with the Chinook previously.

He watched, not being able to turn his eyes away. The men were large and elaborately dressed and adorned from the waist up and naked from the waist down. They had on headdresses of furs and feathers, along with large necklaces of shells and bone. Their vessels were intricately carved with faces and designs of skilled craftsmanship. Again, Shadow found himself entranced at the sight before him. After some time in his observations, he felt compelled to be leaving that location, being concerned at them finding him there. He took care to remain out of their line of view as he made his way back in the direction he had come.

On his return, he came to the great skeleton again. He stopped there and managed to dislodge a rib bone that he wanted to take back with him to his homeland.

CHAPTER 43

SEEKING A TALISMAN

Shadow had spent his last passing periods with little expectations of an encounter with these outsiders, whom he now felt confident of their existence.

The weather had been rainy and foggy for a while now, but his waiting had come to its point of ending, and he was already organized to depart.

By coincidence, Shadow set out on his return trip at the same time that his brother and oldest sons departed with the hunting party toward buffalo country.

Red Bone sat outside his tipi lodge, crafting his sacred red stone pipe. He had been, and still was, recuperating from a serious leg wound that he had received in a violent confrontation with the Mandan not so long time past.

He belonged to a highly respected group within the Lakota Society known as those who do not retreat. While making a stand against an onslaught by a retaliating war party of Mandan, he was lanced by a mounted warrior as he held his ground against their assault. The Mandan were repelled, but not without a high price of wounded and dead.

Red Bone had suffered with his wound but felt confident that he was recovering and would yet be able to go on and do all the things that a mature Lakota warrior would need to do with his life.

He had been pondering what he would most want to do once he was again physically able and had been fondly embracing the thought of a trip toward the setting sun and gaze upon the shining mountains again.

*****

Shadow was once more using the Mother River as his course back to the lands of the Nimipu. Paddling against the current, for him, was doable, but he found himself having to resort to portages more often than his initial effort going with the current. The travel was most certainly slower, although he was making progress.

*****

Wind felt ever so strongly that this was his time to accomplish all the valiant things he had been imagining for himself. He was elated, riding along with the other hunters. As for Raven, he was reserved with a stable workman-like outlook. Talon was proceeding as one who had matured into a very able headman. They continued along with the utmost determined efficiency.

*****

Red Bone took immense pride in the pipe he was making, having taken the journey to the red stone quarry himself in his younger time then returning to his village with a personal stash of the stone to last him all the time that could be left to him in his life.

The pipe that he had always kept near had been destroyed by the same spearing that had inflicted the wound to his leg. He truly believed that the deflection that took place due to the stone pipe also being in the line of trajectory of the lance caused his injury to be considerably less than had it not been there.

That pipe had been given to him by a medicine man, who also happened to be his uncle, who was now deceased. It had been told to Red Bone by his uncle, and always unquestioned, that the pipe itself held strong medicine. Therefore, it was of no wonder to him that the pipe had provided him with that protection.

His focus now was that the pipe he was now crafting could be made to possess that same quality and ability as its predecessor, which was a question. Always feeling the need to get some affirmation that would give him the confidence, that what he hoped would be so.

The first order of business for him as his recovery would allow was to return to the place of his vision quest with the new pipe upon its completion. He would seek the blessing of his spirit guide in granting the power that he sought for this his newly created, hoped-to-be talisman. It would be somewhat of a journey to the Black Hills of medicine, although it was not all so far that it could not be done within a few sleeps from where the Lakota village was located at the present.

*****

Beautiful Flower's husband, Leaping Buck, had also come along on the hunt. He and Raven had become close companions, spending a lot of time together in work and play.

"Your youngest brother seemed angry not to be coming along with us," Leaping Buck remarked as he rode alongside of Raven.

"Yes, Howling Wolf doesn't accept that he is still too young for such a venture," responded Raven.

"He already has the heart of a hunter, warrior," Leaping Buck continued.

"He will be a force to contend with when he is of age," Raven replied as they drew ever closer to the hunting grounds they were destined toward.

Back at the Palus band encampment, Running Wild went searching for Howling Wolf, who had been off exploring along the Palus River. He met his mother on his return to their village.

"You are not old enough to stay gone for such a long time," she scolded him. "You make me worry. I have enough things to concern me without having to come see where you have been for so long."

"You have to learn not to worry about me, Mother. I am fine," Howling Wolf plainly spoke. "Save your worry for others," he continued as he made his way past her, anxious to have a meal, for he was hungry from much exertion.

*****

Shadow made his slow methodical progression back toward his homeland, with a longing to be among his family again.

*****

Red Bone had made all his preparations for his trek to the Black Hills to seek the powerful medicine he believed he needed. He felt well healed and determined. He had spoken at length with his warrior cult brothers on a meeting place and time for an adventure hunt as they pursued the land of the setting sun together once again, but first to the Black Hills.

*****

Talon was somewhat perplexed at the eventual uncovering of the fact that there wasn't any recent sign of buffalo anywhere to be seen since they had come onto the plains of their intention. All he could think to do was to continue in the direction of the rising sun. Among those along for this hunt, none had ever gone farther in that direction than they had already come. They were all more than willing to do so. It was only that there was never a need to do it before now.

Wind simply accepted the idea that it was necessary to accomplish their objective. So onward they went in pursuit of that which they had come for—a substantial herd of buffalo.

*****

When Red Bone reached the Black Hills, he had already been spending his time in prayer and meditation, trying to convey his respect and sincerity in his belief and purpose in coming to this place of medicine to petition his spirit guide. Knowing there was the source to be had, of which he sought, if it would only be granted to him.

He returned to the outcropping of stone that he had waited upon for the fulfillment of his vision quest in earlier times, of which he had received his convincing vision.

So now he climbed the stone heights and then removed his pipe from its protective hide sleeve. He then placed it on a rock shelf he had chosen and left it there, climbing back down to the forested area below.

Then he settled in for more meditation and prayer, giving the location the reverence of his time and patience. After a couple of sleeps, there came a significant change in the weather with a strong wind prevailing. It then began to pour down rain. He then noticed some far-off lightning strikes, followed by booming thunder. It all was an apparent display of power. As he beheld and pondered the occurrences, a nearby lightning strike sent some rock debris through the air. It startled him yet intrigued him as well.

Not long after the weather disturbance took place, it ended. The following early time, he climbed back to the location where he had placed his pipe. It was obvious to him that the lightning strike had occurred within a short distance of his pipe. Encouraged greatly, he lifted his medicine pipe, feeling its newly acquired weight of power, of which he now had confidence.

Not much time after recovering his valued pipe and securing his belongings, he left to meet up with his friends and fellow warriors, very much looking forward to whatever the trail held in store.

CHAPTER 44

A Captive Wind

Red Bone caught up with the party of his peers the lighttime after his leaving from the Black Hills. They were a close-knit group and could read the look of a successful endeavor in Red Bone's countenance. They immediately shared in his feelings of elation and satisfaction, with the exception of Bloody Knife, who showed little emotion.

*****

It certainly seemed an odd circumstance to them, as the Nimipu hunting party continued their search, having been several sleeps already and still no recent sign of buffalo.

Being the strong, brave, and determined hunters that they were, they pressed on.

Finally, one lighttime, there came words of inspiration. Raven and Leaping Buck returned to the band after a forward scouting, telling of seeing definite recent sign of a passing large herd of buffalo. It caused excitement as well as relief among them as they quickened their pace at Raven's direction.

After some time, they came to the place where the herd had passed and went into pursuit.

The following early time, they came into view of what was indeed a very large herd. By this time, they had traveled farther away from the homeland than they had ever heard tell of by any of their people.

Wind felt proud that on his first trip to buffalo country, he would be part of such an undertaking.

The party was anxious to begin the slaughtering of their prey. Talon gave some basic instructions, telling Wild Wind to follow behind him and enter the killing when he felt the opportunity came about.

They approached the herd by way of a dry creek bed, which provided them cover. When the time came that they were certain when they rose up to the plain again, they would be in position to begin their taking of the beasts.

Then up they went, being able to spread out on the perimeter of the herd. Wind was overwhelmed with the anticipation of his heart's desire drawing near, yet he had the wherewithal to bring himself into focus.

Raven led out, prodding Ghost into a run. They all followed in suit. Soon the arrows began to find their intended marks. Bison began to drop along the course of the hunters' assaults.

Not long into their pursuit, Wind unleashed his skills as a young man well trained in the craft of a bowman.

All the Nimipu, well mounted on the finest ponies in the land, put on a splendid display of how it should be done.

Even Red Bone and his colleagues were impressed as they lay prone on the top of a nearby hill, taking in the action going on before them.

The Lakota were in full agreement that these hunters were not of a sort of any they had come across in their previous encounters. Also, the Appaloosas that they rode stood out with distinction.

That late time, the Lakota began to make plans to show themselves the masters of this domain by killing and perhaps capturing one of these intruders, as well as taking their ponies for their own.

Red Bone proposed that they take their captive before they set out to kill the remaining hunters, if it were possible. Within a short time after he had spoken of it, it was agreed on.

In the Nimipu camp, the atmosphere was jubilant after having such a successful first hunt of these buffalo.

"Well, my brother, how are you feeling after such an eventful time as we have just had?" Raven inquired of Wind as they roasted ribs over the coals from the burning of dung that glowed in the darkness.

"I feel like a man of purpose, my brother, and I am very thankful for this chance to fulfill the dreams of my youth," Wind replied with genuine gladness.

"It is good that this hunt has given you an opportunity to become an experienced hunter of the buffalo. It took more distance of travel, but it has proven worth it," Talon went on to say. And then he also added, "In the early time, I want Wind along with a few others to come with me to hunt again. Raven and Leaping Buck will need help to continue preparing the meat and hides."

All were willing to do what was needed for the success of their undertaking, and they all nodded in agreement.

That following lighttime, Talon and Wind, along with some of the other hunters, left to take down more bison.

The remaining members of the party started with the butchering that still needed tending to.

Red Bone and his fellow Lakota had anticipated the hunters' return to their pursuit of more buffalo and kept watch over them from their first movements on leaving camp.

They had devised a plan to isolate a hunter enough to capture him if an opportunity presented itself. It would take a close observation of the Nimipu without being seen too early. There were sufficient low-lying hills and vales to be used for the purpose of observation, along with concealment.

It wasn't long after the hunted had departed from their camp that their view was lost to those remaining behind.

As the hunters moved toward the herd of buffalo, they again began to spread apart before rushing their prey. Talon gave Wind the lead position to begin the assault. Wind left when he felt the time was right, charging forward toward a nearby cow with bow drawn. The rest of the hunters followed his lead as the hunt was underway.

The usual course of events soon began to take place, with bison falling in the line of their slaughter. And as it often happened, there began to develop a divide of some distance between the hunters as they set about their work.

When Red Bone felt the situation was to their advantage, he gave the signal, and they went about implementing their plan.

He and another brave left to capture Wind, if possible.

The other Lakota warriors set out to kill the remaining Nimipu hunters, with the intent of stealing their ponies.

Talon was the first to spot the attackers as they appeared from their cover. His initial focus was on Red Bone and the other brave moving in his nephew's direction. Immediately, he headed toward the trouble he saw developing, but before he went very far, battle cries drew his attention to a closer proximity, of which he was in.

He went down with an arrow lodged in his shoulder. His pony, Bright Star, having made a sharp turning motion then making an abrupt halt, left Talon lying on the ground on his side as he watched the Lakota warriors attacking the individual Nimipu hunters.

Meanwhile, Wind became aware of the commotion taking place not so far from where he was. After briefly surveying the mayhem and at the same time realizing that he, too, was under attack, he attempted to bolt out of harm's way. As he was fleeing from his pursuers, he managed to turn his torso in a manner that allowed him to take a bowshot, hitting one of them and inflicting a grievous wound and stopping him then and there.

Red Bone couldn't help but notice the great skill that had been used to take out his companion and was once again impressed with this outsider.

Wind, encouraged at this reduction of his opposition, turned to face Red Bone as he continued to come at him. By the time he himself turned to face the attack, it was too late.

Red Bone knew that it was to his advantage to press full speed ahead to meet this enemy as he came around and was ready with his club. He had the ideal opportunity to kill Wind but chose to use his experience to apply just enough force to knock him unconscious.

It worked just as he planned, and Wind went down after being struck along the side of his head.

Red Bone then quickly draped Wind's limp body over the back of Snowman, securing him there and then led him away from the immediate area.

The fight waxed hot between the Lakota and the Nimipu, but the Lakota prevailed, largely due to their surprise tactics. Eventually, the Nimipu hunters succumbed to their onslaught.

The only Lakota that lost his life was the one that Wind had unleashed his arrow upon. The victors collected their slain companion and departed.

Chapter 45

The Shadow's Back

As the sun began to wane, Raven became increasingly concerned. He asked Leaping Buck to come with him to see what was keeping the others from returning.

*****

The warriors of the Lakota reunited with Red Bone and his captive at a predetermined location, with their Nimipu ponies in tow. They were ecstatic in their defeat of the outsiders as they waved the scalps of the vanquished about them.

*****

What Raven and Leaping Buck found when they arrived at the site of carnage was almost too hard to witness. They didn't want to see what was before their eyes, but they knew they must.

All had been scalped and left for the carrion eaters to dispense with. The hardest thing for them to take was the finding of Talon's body. Such a force of a man rendered lifeless was almost too bitter to face. It scarred their senses in a manner that was never to be undone.

Then the thoughts that dominated their minds became *Who did this, and where is Wild Wind?*

*****

Shadow had accomplished making it back within the near vicinity of his village and felt confident that he would be home soon.

Back at the Palus band village, Talon's woman, Little Wing, played with their son while she hoped for her husband's safe return.

*****

Some of the Lakota warriors wanted to set a trap for the remaining Nimipu party. Bloody Knife, being the most adamant, said, "We have only begun what we started out to do. There are yet more scalps and ponies to claim for our own."

Red Bone, along with others, disagreed, stating that they should be leaving the area now to increase their chances of keeping all that they had already obtained. The rest conceded, and they came to the agreement to leave for their own country right away. Bloody Knife reluctantly went along.

After a burial for their fallen companions, Raven and the remaining party set out following the sign that the Lakota had left in their departure. It had been very difficult to keep from leaving out after them right away, but they knew that they had to tend to their dead before they could do anything else. Respect had to be observed, first and foremost.

As for the knowledge of Wind's circumstances, they could only wonder.

After following their sign for a couple of sleeps, they came to a river where, after an exhaustive search, they had lost the trail. With much frustration and reluctance, they made the decision to head home with nothing more than heartache and bad news.

*****

When Shadow got to the location of where the Chinook had taken him prisoner for a short spell, he was hailed by some along the shore who recognized him. He gave them a wave in response but thought better of stopping there.

After embarking once again from another stop over, he soon came to a location where he could see the place where the Winding River flowed into the Mother River, which was a point of much encouragement, believing that by the following early time, he could finally be home.

After another sleep, he approached the place of the merging of the Palus River with the Winding River, and there at that same place he was looking upon a large encampment, and he knew that it was the village of his people who would use that location as one of their primary camp spots during these times. He felt a flood of emotion come over him, having been gone all the seasons and even longer yet.

As he came up to their adjoining shore, he was immediately spotted and recognized. Within a short time, he was surrounded by his fellow band members. Soon after his entering the village, his wives and daughters and youngest son appeared and led him to their particular lodge locations.

His arrival came as a surprise to some, who didn't expect him to return at all, having been gone so long. He once again proved his resiliency. He himself attributed it all to the protection granted him from the Great Spirit.

All of Shadow's family and friends who were present, as well as the majority of the Palus band, were relieved to have him back among them.

When he learned of the departing of his brother and sons, along with his son by marriage to his oldest daughter, he was disappointed that they were not there to be embraced and to share in the joy of being together again. What he got was not just as he hoped, but he was appreciative with the circumstances as they were, which were more than adequate to him.

They celebrated for some time over his return. Even Gray Wolf found himself feeling glad concerning his arrival.

*****

Wind first became aware of his captivity when the other Lakota warriors had arrived in their noisy jubilance. He began to gain consciousness, vaguely taking notice of the flailing of the scalps before losing consciousness again. Then not too much later, he again awoke to his dismay in finding his sorry predicament confirmed.

Before the Lakota departed, one of the braves slapped Wind on his head wound as he stood before him. After doing so, Red Bone stepped in front of the brave and gave him a reprimand, leading Wind to think that he was interested in his well-being to some degree.

When the Lakota left for their homeland, they secured Wind once again to Snowman, this time in a sitting position.

Lighttime after lighttime, the Lakota party continued their travel farther and farther into the land of the rising sun. They had passed through country that was beyond Wind's imagination up till now.

There were a number of things that Red Bone found engaging about Wind. One obvious consideration he gave him was his youth. It impressed him that even with his lack of experience, he showed tremendous skill and courage. Then there was the horsemanship he had witnessed, which he also accredited to the fine ponies they rode. It added to the mutual lingering question between both parties: *Who are these people?*

Red Bone hoped to gain more understanding concerning his captive, and so he intended to take care that he fared well so that obtaining this information would be more forthcoming.

*****

When word reached Dreamer that Cloud Shadow had returned, he then wasted no time in going to visit his old friend. When Red

Dreamer appeared at the village, Shadow was very happy to receive his Waptailmin friend.

After some casual conversation, Shadow began to tell of his journey to the Big Water. He told of being held and released by the Chinook and his vision of speaking a white man language in the coming times, then at the edge of the Big Water, spotting the giant canoe with wings and the finding of the metallic object. After which, he reached into the tiny pouch he had made to contain it. He then removed it from its pouch and handed it to Dreamer.

The concentration on Dreamer's face when he peered at the object of such interest and curiosity was absolute. He moved it about in his bands and fingertips, moving it closer to his eyes then farther away. Finally, he handed it back to Shadow.

Dreamer was mesmerized at his friend's tale. "My friend, I believe that these things continue to build a more convincing bearing out of the vision I told you of all that time ago," he stated.

"I believe the same, my friend. It becomes more troubling the more I know about it," Shadow responded as he replaced the metallic object back in its pouch. Of course, the rib bone from the giant fish was another of Shadow's showpieces that he liked to bring out for entertainment. It was something more to marvel at.

Dreamer returned home, again having very much enjoyed his visit with the Palus people. He was enriched with the time spent among them.

CHAPTER 46

STRANGER IN THEIR MIDST

Wind's captors arrived at their village, a village that was larger than any Wind had ever heard tell of. Red Bone took him to his lodge, fending off all inquiries with a wave of his hand as that of a feared and well-respected warrior. He arrived at his tipi, and a woman greeted him with a show of affection. Red Bone said a few words to her, and she began to prepare for a meal.

The lodge was spacious and comfortable with many supple furs strewn about. It was a lodge of an individual of substance and position of hierarchy among his people. When the meal was served, Red Bone motioned to Wind to partake. As Wind gorged himself on the nourishment offered, Red Bone studied him with interest and respect.

While Wind's time was being spent among the Lakota, he was treated well enough and encouraged to get involved with the activities of the village whenever he cared to. Red Bone worked with him to develop their sign talk, with hopes of a comprehendible communication between them to enrich their collection of knowledge, which also added to their growing bond.

*****

At the Palus band camp, there was a stir when it was reported that Raven was approaching the perimeter of the village. Within a short time thereafter, Raven and Leaping Buck, along with the remaining braves of their party, trotted into the central area of the encampment.

With the news of the tragic events concerning the buffalo hunt, there came a grieving along with wailing the likes of which were not known by any there up to that time. The death of Talon and the disappearance of Wild Wind was devastating to Shadow and his family.

Shadow wanted so badly to leave immediately to search and avenge, but it was an obvious fact that with the cold time once again approaching, it would be impossible. For Raven, finding that Shadow had returned was a great relief for his emotional state.

There was, as well, a deep appreciation of having those back among them who were able to return.

Little Wing could not be consoled, but even she was glad for the return of the other men, providing the account of their harrowing story, which, in a far less than ideal way, brought a relief of sorts to all the families concerned.

Beautiful Flower and Vixen felt so grateful for the return of their men.

Raven had an extremely hard time recounting the details to his father. Shadow made him repeat them several times. He couldn't help himself. He had become obsessed.

It was a long cold time for the Palus band, along with the longing for permissible weather, so an avenging search party could be mounted for a return trip to buffalo country, yet there was still more waiting.

When the time finally came that a departure could be made, they began their preparations.

Not long after their readying was completed, they left. The women of the village were distraught with fear for their sons and husbands. The terrible things to be imagined were almost without limit.

Gray Wolf could not be kept from this journey, although no one tried to do so. He felt that this terrible thing had happened in the land of his people, the Siksika. It was important for him to go and try to muster support from Big Sun's band, to find out who was responsible, being those who had returned were at a loss on that point.

Among the braves who did not have a direct connection with those who had lost their lives, it was required that they draw lengths of grass for the right to come along. For it was essential that a certain number of men remained behind.

So as soon as it had been possible, they proceeded onto the trail of dire intent, with Shadow at the lead.

*****

While Wind was staying in Red Bone's lodge, it became common for them to smoke together. Red Bone began to try to relate the story of the red stone quarry to Wind through sign talk as he spoke. He also conveyed the incident of how his pipe had protected him from a more serious wound during an enemy attack. He told him of his creation of a new pipe after the destruction of the former. He also told of the receiving of power he had been granted for that pipe, of which they were now enjoying.

Red Bone let Wind know that he still had plenty of the red stone left and that he would give him some if he wanted it.

As time went by, with their continued conversing, Wind made the comment that he would like to experience the red stone quarry himself. Red Bone responded by saying, "I would be glad to show you the way to that place of such medicine. We will plan for a journey there." All the time he spoke, he continued to follow his speech with sign talk.

Wind was learning the Lakota tongue and was also becoming more skilled in the sign talk. He tried to relate as much as he could to Red Bone concerning the Nimipu homeland and their beliefs and cultural practices, along with the story of the beginning of the Appaloosa breed as it was told to him by his father, Cloud Shadow.

Wind felt in his mind that he should be hateful toward the Lakota for what they had done, yet the kindness that had been shown to him since his abduction allowed him to feel a friendship toward them. There was very little that had been told to him concerning his fellow hunters. He had asked Red Bone about it once and was told that he himself hadn't harmed any of them, but he told no more of the matter. Wind remembered seeing the scalps. He knew they had some of the Nimipu ponies and that one of them was his uncle's. He tried not to dwell on the matter. It confused and troubled him.

As more time passed, Wind was taken along on a hunt with Red Bone and some of his warrior cult associates. They came across a small herd of bison, and they as a group took down a sufficient number of them. The downed beasts were to be set upon by an approaching group of women to be butchered by them.

The one called Bloody Knife rode Talon's pony, Bright Star. Wind was troubled emotionally every time he laid eyes on him. It not only was his uncle's favorite mount, but he was also Snowman's sire. They had dismounted in the midst of their kill, and some of the hunters were removing choice parts from selected animals.

Wind stood near Bloody Knife as he cut into a young cow, seeking her liver for some refreshing nourishment, and blurted out, "How is it that you ride the stallion my uncle called his?"

At hearing that, Bloody Knife stopped his process of retrieving the organ from the cow and instead sliced a small area of the fur from off the top of the bison's head. He then turned and squared himself before Wind and said, "I took your uncle's life. Then I took his scalp. Then I took his pony."

Wind stared into Bloody Knife's eyes that were cold as a snake's. Bloody Knife tossed the bison scalp at Wind's feet then went back to cutting into the beast he was disemboweling.

Wind made up his mind right at that time. He was going to kill Bloody Knife. There was no way he was going to allow any man to stand before him and admit to such a thing and then go ahead and accept it. It was all he could do to hold himself from acting on it under the present circumstances, but he held back. He was of a lineage of those that were able to keep themselves composed until they could do that which was warranted. When the occasion presented itself, at that right time and place, he would act.

*****

Raven took up the rear of the revenge search party. He was as determined as anyone could be to get some satisfaction out of there effort. Ever since the events of that dreadful encounter, he felt responsible for the outcome. Even though every time he rehearsed it in his thoughts, he could not think of how he could have prevented it, except to have stood against their ever going on the hunt at all. He carried his shield with him. It hadn't initially been intended to be a war shield, but he decided to designate it to be so. He was beginning to think of it as the standard for the Palus avengers. He had prayed over it, asking the Great Spirit to respect this article of war as a symbol of their intent with authority. On this quest, his and his companions' intent was that the perpetrators of the murders and kidnapping would pay with their own lives and that the Great Spirit would direct their efforts. All the while, the black eagle, embossed over a red background, peered out at the trail of these stouthearted warriors as they relentlessly pressed on.

CHAPTER 47

HELP FOR WIND'S RESCUE

When there was some time between activities, Red Bone spoke to Wind about a ritual that was going to be taking place the following lighttime near to the council lodge.

Wind pictured the council lodge as he spoke. It was the largest structure in the village. It somewhat looked like a not so small hill that was reinforced with slender trees and large branches.

He went on to explain that the ritual was the culmination of the sun dance. The celebration had been going on for some time already. Wind had been fully aware of the festive activities, even being involved in some, not understanding that it was all leading up to a concluding ceremony.

This ceremony, he told him, would involve certain young men in the tribe making what they called a vow to the sun. He continued by stating that the whole affair would hopefully help the tribe have more open contact with the spirit world for a renewing of the different life-sustaining aspects of their environment, to keep the buffalo plentiful, to bring victory in battle, to heal the sick, all being dependent on their acceptance by the sun deity through the fulfilling of their vows.

After Red Bone had finished teaching Wind on these beliefs, Wind, without hesitation, reminded himself that a ritual of this kind was certainly nothing he would allow himself to follow after. He had been taught differently. There was only the one deity he acknowledged—the Great Spirit. He also believed in other powers, and he accepted those he knew to be subject to the one. Although the sun was important, it was another subject to the Life Giver, as was the rest of creation.

The following lighttime, the inhabitants of the Lakota village began to gather in the center of the camp, in the location of the council lodge. There, in an open area, stood a very tall pole with a number of hide cords hanging down from the top of it, sprawled about the ground around the base of it.

Wind was there, along with Red Bone, among the other villagers. Not long after the people had congregated, there were certain young men brought forward before the tribe. When Wind first looked upon them, his initial thought was, *These men are the same number of winters as me.*

There were older men presiding over the event and preparations for it. Red Bone explained that they were medicine men and shamans. Some were known as healers, others as spiritual mediators, some claiming the abilities of both. After a period of oration and extensive forms of chanting, along with dancing to rhythmic drumming, the presiding figures began to place pointed skewers under the skin and thin layer of the pectoral muscles, leaving the ends of the skewers exposed. They then attached the hide cords to these ends in a manner that could be used to place tension between the skewers and the pole.

After the tension began to be created for each participant in full view of all, the young men slowly proceeded to lean back to increase the tension. The drumming and chanting and dancing continued as these willing participants performed their sacrificial vows, placing more and more of their weight at the point of the connected skewers as they leaned farther backward yet.

The stress came to the level that their flesh could no longer sustain, with some of the skewers torn lose from their place. With others, they lingered on, having a greater reward for their added suffering, they believed.

Eventually, all were torn loose, whatever degree of tension was needed to break free of their torment. So the sun dance ended, and the expected benefits could once again be enjoyed by the Lakota tribe. Wind felt distressed for having witnessed it.

*****

As the party of avengers drew closer, Gray Wolf began to petition for the involvement of the Siksika in achieving their goal. At first, Shadow made an adamant stand against it, eventually yielding after Raven interceded on behalf of his grandfather's plan.

"It is not certain that the Siksika will have any interest in getting involved," Gray Wolf stated, having become fluent in the Nimipu language. "Although they may have much to add to our cause," he added.

The farther the party went along, the more appealing the idea became.

Eventually, they came into the vicinity of what they considered to be the stronghold of the Siksika nation. At that point, Gray Wolf asked that the party hold up while he and Raven went to find Big Sun's village to inquire of their interest in the matter. Once they became informed of their thoughts, they would return so the party could act accordingly. Shadow reluctantly agreed, and so Gray Wolf and Raven left to seek possible assistance.

After a sleep and yet some more travel, they came onto the Siksika camp they were seeking. When they entered, there wasn't a lot of recognition given to them initially. It was a large encampment, without fears of outsiders causing them any problems.

Not long after their arrival at the village, someone spoke out in a loud voice, "Gray Wolf has returned. That is Gray Wolf. I am certain of it!"

At hearing that, Gray Wolf looked over at the man who had spoken out and asked, "Is Big Sun among you?"

Immediately, he was informed that his tipi would be found in the center of the village.

By this time, there was a large group of inhabitants that were following toward the central area of their camp.

When they arrived at Big Sun's lodge, the chief was already standing, there awaiting his company.

"Greetings, my old friend," Big Sun responded at the recognition of Gray Wolf. "It has been too long since we have been together. I see you have come with your fine grandson. It does my heart good to see it," he added.

"I, too, am glad in my heart to find you standing here before me, my friend," replied Gray Wolf.

"Come, rest and refresh yourselves," Big Sun invited. There was much to talk about between them without even getting to the reason they had come. By the time the subject of their visit came around, they had already been there for some time, but in its own time, they got to the point concerning the trouble they had come to deal with.

After relating the details of the event in question, Big Sun told them he didn't have any personal account for them, but he had heard of some of their braves witnessing some occurrences that might be connected to these sad events that they spoke of.

At that, they asked these braves to be summoned to tell what they knew concerning the matter, if anything. When the men arrived, they felt that they did have some information about the subject that had been asked of them. They told of several of their tribe seeing Lakota come into the area in question. Raven watched his grandfather's reaction to this news. Gray Wolf's eyebrows raised, and then he leaned in closer, as if he didn't want to miss a word of this report.

They told of others of the tribe who told of seeing a Nimipu hunting party in the same general vicinity. Then there were others who said they had come across dead men in that same location and immediately left from that place, not knowing who was responsible for the killings. Not until sometime later, hearing the discussions within the camp, did some come to believe that the dead were the Nimipu hunters, and the killers were the larger group of Lakota that had been seen in the proximity.

After hearing these things, Big Sun said, "the Lakota have come this way in times past, it sounds as if we have learned who is responsible for your losses."

Raven was filled with a new vigor, having received actual information on who had committed the unforgivable deeds.

Then Big Sun excused those who had been summoned, thanking them for their help.

"We have come to get revenge for what was done and to find Raven's brother Wild Wind. Is there any among you who are willing to assist us in our purpose?" Gray Wolf asked of Big Sun.

"We will talk more of this matter," Big Sun told him. "I will let you know what we are willing to do for you when the sun rises again."

When it was explained to Raven in detail what was conveyed to his grandfather, he had to conclude that these Siksika had seen the dead Nimipu before they had found them themselves.

CHAPTER 48

Cultural Heritage

Red Bone and Wind made preparations for an extensive journey to the red stone quarry. Red Bone had given Wind an idea of the location of the quarry. It was obvious to him that they would be traveling even farther in the direction of the rising sun.

The time came when their preparations were complete, and Red Bone made his departing gestures to his woman. They then began their journey and passed through the village. It felt good to go on the trail again. They mutually agreed.

They genuinely liked each other and enjoyed each other's company, even though their being on the trail together involved a strange bit of circumstances.

Once the lighttime began to fade, they made their camp, having already traveled a good distance.

When they traveled and while they camped, Red Bone spoke of strong medicine and spirit guides and even reflected on his own vision quest.

Wind was fascinated with such things, having listened to his father and older brother relate their tales of their experiences with similar events as those Red Bone spoke of.

The following lighttime, as they proceeded toward the quarry, Wind spoke of his views concerning a vision quest. "I have been looking to the time for my own experience that would make me feel like I had secured a bond with my spirit guide. I have prayed about it and meditated concerning the matter. I haven't yet though felt compelled to go toward a certain place to seek the medicine that I believe I need for my life."

Red Bone felt he understood and replied, "Keep yourself open to the chance of that certain place and time to meet up with you. Your spirit guide knows you already and may be calling you. We can be mistaken when we think we are always the ones who seek encounter when it could be your spirit guide drawing you along to that place where you shall meet, so be ready if that should happen to you."

Wind was encouraged by these words and believed that it could very well be that way for him. "Thank you for those words. I feel that they are truly meant for me."

*****

Big Sun summoned Gray Wolf and Raven at the time of which he had stipulated. When they arrived, he told them, "After counselling with other elders of the tribe, I have words for you on your purpose here. We have come to learn that a large party of our warriors are willing to join with you to come against the Lakota concerning this offense against your, as well as our, people. We also believe that the best chance for our plan is to be led separately from the Nimipu, with Gray Wolf at their lead. Then when the Nimipu come within a certain distance of the Lakota encampment, they should be certain to make themselves obvious so to draw out the Lakota. At that time, our warriors will enter the fight to help avenge this unjust act that was committed within our domain. This, I believe, will give you a good chance to succeed in your goal."

Gray Wolf and Raven thanked Big Sun and complimented him and the other elders on their wise and bold strategy. Raven and his grandfather talked at length about how they would keep within a reasonable proximity between the parties. After their discussions were concluded, Raven left to return to the Nimipu camp and give his father the good news.

*****

Wind and Red Bone were drawing closer to their destination. It was all country that was new and unfamiliar to Wind. As they journeyed along, there began to develop some severe weather changes. Red Bone made the attempt to prepare Wind for the possibility of some dangerous conditions. Wind couldn't get a grasp on what these sorts of conditions would be. It all sounded so different. He was unable to imagine it.

Just after that, there began to be a deep darkening of the sky, along with lightning and thunder, which didn't seem unusual to Wind. Although there was a sticky wet sensation in the air that did seem much different than any prior experiences that he had ever had.

Red Bone pointed to a stand of very large stones and motioned for them to head for them. Not long before they arrived at the stones, Red Bone again directed Wind's attention toward the direction of the oncoming winds that were becoming very strong.

Wind scanned the horizon and spotted something that he definitely had never seen before. He had to stare for some time, not even sure if what he saw was making any sense in his mind. At first, he thought it looked like a massive black snake wiggling across the plains on the tip of its tail. As he continued to watch, he saw that it was spinning, and everywhere it went, it was tearing up the ground beneath it. It looked like it was as tall as a mountain. Fear gripped his thoughts, and he cried out, "What is it?"

Red Bone answered, "It is the spirit wind, and we cannot know where it will go, so we must wait here in the shelter of these stones until it passes."

Just before they slipped into an opening between a couple of very substantial rock outcroppings, Wind could see that the spirit wind was coming their way.

They dismounted and secured the ponies to themselves to attempt to keep them from bolting in a panic. Now it was hold on and pray, as the power of the wind began to scream around them. Along with flashes of lightning and booms from the thunder, the atmosphere was all together intimidating.

When the tornado came to within a very close distance, Snowman swung into Wind with a strong push that threw him against the rock, totally taking his breath away. It caused him to lose consciousness and collapse to the ground.

Afterward, Red Bone told Wind that he only lay there a short time. Although to Wind, it seemed to last much longer than that.

While he lay their unconscious, a phenomenal thing occurred concerning him. He believed with certainty that a voice spoke to him, saying, "I am your spirit guide. I ride the wind. I was present at your birth. You have not sought me because I have always been close by you. Continue on your journey with a true heart, and you will prevail in all you attempt to do."

When he regained his consciousness, he didn't speak to Red Bone of his experience. Even though he considered him a friend, he had a very strong premonition come to him. Because he was Nimipu and not Lakota, he needed to avenge the wrongs that had been perpetrated against his people, and that he should be more guarded about his thoughts and intents.

After a short rest, he and Red Bone resumed their journey with the weather, making a miraculous turn for the better.

*****

When Raven made it back to the camp where his father and companions waited, he began to tell of the occurrences at Big Sun's village.

Shadow responded by saying, "When at first I saw that you returned alone, I wondered what had come of your grandfather. Now I understand what has prevented his return. It is good, the news you bring. I do have hope that all will be settled before this journey is through."

The following early time, the Nimipu broke camp, as was predetermined between Gray Wolf and Raven. They struck out toward the rising sun.

After a couple sleeps journey, Raven said, "I believe that the next lighttime, we will be coming near to the Lakota lands, according to what I was told at Big Sun's village. Gray Wolf is scouting our location as we move along. We will continue until the Lakota come out against us."

*****

Red Bone pointed to a high ridge of rock in the distance and commented, "Up there is the quarry we seek."

Wind was looking forward to being able to partake of this place of strong medicine after all he had heard tell concerning it.

Red Bone had told of how it was a place of truce between any tribe who might come in contact with each other within the boundaries of the quarry. He spoke of all the totems that had been carved within the stone by so many over great periods. He also took an interest in what was said concerning a column that stood alone at a distance that can be surmounted by a very brave man by leaping onto its formidable top. He said that some had accomplished it and, in doing so, brought much renown to themselves by any who gave witness. He also added, "But if you fail, you face certain death on the crags below."

After considerable effort, they climbed to the top of the ridge. They looked along the face of the ridge as they peered inward at the quarry. It appeared to gleam like ice in the sunlight.

CHAPTER 49

The Witness of Strength and Valor

Red Bone explained that on the level area, at the base, under the soil, lay the red stone.

As Wind got a closer look at the ridge wall, he could see that the gleaming substance was highly polished quartz. He felt that the Great Spirit must have polished it for his own viewing pleasure, for he truly felt his presence in this place.

Red Bone pointed out the column that he called the leaping rock.

It was agreed that the following lighttime, they would accumulate some of the red stone, for Wind had let it be known his desire to possess some for this own.

The next early time, they began to dig for the pipe stone. While they were occupied with their efforts, unbeknownst to them, a party of Mandan had entered the quarry. Being highly keen in their senses, they became aware of the Mandan soon enough. Red Bone assured Wild Wind that they need not worry, saying with confidence that they wouldn't attempt to harm them. They then continued their digging.

Wind couldn't keep from glancing in the direction of the Mandan as they moved across the quarry. After getting a fairly good look at them, he noticed that some of the braves had a pale skin like none he had ever seen before. The Mandan also surely found Wild Wind's pony a thing of great interest, but they passed by without making any threatening gestures whatsoever.

Eventually, he and Red Bone managed to uncover the pipe stone and remove a quantity that was sufficient.

The following lighttime, Red Bone showed Wind the location where totems were engraved, as he looked on the many different symbols before him. He decided to carve in a depiction of the spirit wind. After creating the funnel tower, he made a depiction of the destructive force as it tore at the ground beneath it.

After he had finished his engraving, he let Red Bone know he wanted to go near the leaping rock.

They made their way over to a place where it was plain to see the distance that needed to be covered to reach the flat surface at the top of the column. Wild Wind dismounted, and as he stood there, he could also see a few assorted arrows that had been placed there at the top of the column. Red Bone went on to tell how the arrows belonged to the few who had successfully made the daring attempt. While they stood there looking at the leaping rock, they had drawn the attention of the Mandan, who had taken to their own digging location.

It was apparent that they believed they were going to witness an attempt at clearing that distance that separated the doers from the talkers. Wind was aware of their peering at him, but it didn't mean a thing to him, because he had already determined to make the jump without any prodding from onlookers.

When he returned to Snowman and removed an arrow from his quiver, Red Bone stepped into his path, saying, "My friend, I hope you are not planning on taking this challenge. It is a very difficult thing to accomplish."

"I hope that you will not try to stop me. Do not stand in my way, my friend, because I do plan on getting to that place of distinction," Wind replied.

Red Bone had no intention of allowing Wind to leap to his death, but intention or not, he stood aside, not even sure why he did so.

At that, Wind positioned himself and then ran at that open space between himself and a safe landing with all the speed and strength he was capable of. And he let fly toward his goal. The Mandan looked on as he flew to that perch with authority. When he landed there unscathed, he became another man in Red Bone's eyes. He was elevated to a status that few others had obtained in his life's memories.

The Mandan also made gestures of admiration, glad to have witnessed such a feat of bravery.

Now all he had to do was to make it back. His onlookers continued to watch with apprehension. He asked Red Bone to assist him on his leap back to the safety of the ridge. Red Bone attached a hide cord around Snowman's neck and threw the rest of it to Wind. Wind wrapped it around his hand then placed his arrow on top of the others that laid in a slightly hollowed out place, which helped them to remain there. He then went to his farthest point possible and ran to make his return leap.

It was good that Red Bone stood by because as Wind landed at the ledge, he was able to reach out to him so that he and Red Bone locked arms, allowing Wind to get his footing and finally a stable stance.

At that, the Mandan returned to their digging.

*****

Shadow had a gut feeling that they had crossed over into what the Lakota considered their lands. The Nimipu continued resolutely with no reservations. It was do-or-die for them.

Raven felt confident of the commitment of his grandfather's people. When the time came for their support, Gray Wolf and the Siksika would be there.

Shadow's attention was drawn to some smoke on a hill up ahead that was broken in its consistency, rising in puffs. Before long, the same thing was seen on another distant hill somewhat farther away. It reminded him of a story told to him by his friend Many Arrows about smoke being used for signaling by some tribes. He began to believe that this was what he was witnessing. He brought it to the attention of the others, with an emphasis on the possibility of a confrontation coming their way sooner rather than later.

There was also another movement that caught their attention. It was what appeared to be a large black eagle soaring overhead. More than once, it flew off toward the rising sun, only to return to soar above them once again.

It was taken as a sign for strong encouragement by Raven and Shadow, but it also heightened their sense of an attack to take place at any moment.

They continued their advance, feeling the pressure of their anticipation. Shadow had been hoping that by showing a relatively small force of opposition, they would draw a force that could be dealt with on a more even bases. He considered it was also the same idea that the Siksika elders had in mind from the conception of their plan.

Not long after the smoke signals had been seen, there appeared a substantial war party of Lakota spread out before the approaching Nimipu. It was meant as a show of intimidation, and it had its desired effect. *So much for hoping for a lesser force*, Shadow thought. *We're here now, come what may.*

The Lakota showed many war bonnets along with many lances that were to be used for thrusting at these mounted invaders. Shadow made himself heard to the Nimipu warriors, "Look to the Great Spirit for his strength and direction, and the courage that is needed will be ours. The black eagle awaits the battle."

The Lakota felt confident of the outcome, based on what they perceived to be their opposition.

They sent a couple riders forward just as a display of ceremony. The riders came to within a fairly close distance. Then one of them hollered out to the Nimipu.

"I am Bloody Knife. Come and receive your deaths as your countrymen before you."

Shadow didn't understand the language but got the idea given the body gestures. In response, he yelled across to them, "We have come to avenge our people and to spill the blood of those responsible. This lighttime, there will be mourning among the Lakota for their own."

At that, Raven cast an arrow just over their heads, making them turn and bolt for a safer distance.

When the remaining Lakota saw what had happened, they rushed forward in a charge. Before they covered the ground to reach the Nimipu, a horde of Siksika poured down from a hill that previously had had smoke signals coming off it, with Gray Wolf at their lead. Before the Lakota could make any changes, the Siksika entered the fray.

Bloody Knife, although cruel, was also brave. His first reaction to the Siksika charge was to drive toward the onslaught, which consequently resulted in him knocking Gray Wolf to the ground on contact. Before Gray Wolf could sufficiently recover, he drove a lance into his heart, ending his life.

The fight waxed fierce and unrelenting for an extended period. None were willing to concede to the other. When it finally ended, only a small group of Lakota escaped with their lives. Bloody Knife being one, but only after he had brought death to a number of his adversaries. If Raven would have realized that the escaping Bloody Knife had killed Gray Wolf, he would have pursued him, but he wasn't yet aware of the death of his grandfather.

The Nimipu and Siksika had won a great victory over the Lakota. Yet they knew they couldn't linger, for the Lakota would soon reorganize to retaliate.

When Raven's attention was brought to the death of his grandfather, he knelt beside his body and wept. He wasn't even aware of anyone else's presence. He was going through a spontaneous reaction based completely on emotion.

However, he didn't allow himself to go on that way for long. Gaining his composure, he stood and got someone to assist him to place Gray Wolf's body on to his pony to be buried in a place of their own choosing. Shadow sat in a posture of solemn respect for this fallen warrior as he looked on from the back of his pony.

They then hastened to leave from that place.

CHAPTER 50

An Escape for the Avenger

When Bloody Knife got back to the Lakota village with the news of the rout, there immediately ensued a state of confusion. Instead of being able to organize a retaliation, he was met with astonishment and fear and a stubborn reluctance. Also, he was getting questions of how it was possible that they had suffered this loss. Then there began the wailing for those who had not returned.

While the Lakota delayed their decision to mount another attack, the Nimipu and Siksika took every advantage to cover as much territory as possible before they did any slowing at all.

Red Bone and Wind were on their return toward the Lakota village. As they drew ever nearer, they came upon some Lakota who passed on a not yet confirmed story that their village had suffered a devastating loss in a battle with some intruders. The information they received was so vague that neither of them could make any personal connection to what they had been told.

When they arrived at the village, there was still an element of disarray. After a short time from their arrival, they were confronted by Bloody Knife and some others of influence within the tribe.

Bloody Knife spoke. "This outsider friend of yours is not welcome here any longer."

Red Bone replied, "He will stay for as long as I say he will."

Having anticipated this reaction, a number of braves that had gathered there held Red Bone and Wind. Red Bone was taken to the council lodge, and Wind was bound and placed in confinement.

After being reprimanded for his behavior, Red Bone, realizing that he could not fight against the will of the elders, conceded by agreeing to relinquish all interest in Wind's life.

However, that darktime, he succeeded in getting Wind's guards to leave him unattended for a brief time, allowing him to release Wind from his bonds.

Wind thanked Red Bone, and they embraced. He had not been able to retrieve Snowman for him, given the haste of his efforts to free him. Red Bone cautioned Wind to stay covered until he could get to the outskirts of the village, and there he should be able to secure a pony to escape with. He then presented him with a buffalo robe for a covering and wished him well. Again, they embraced, and Wind departed. However, he knew where Bloody Knife's lodge was, and he wasn't quite ready to leave the Lakota village behind him as yet.

After making his way near the tipi of his hated foe, he tried not to appear conspicuous while looking for a chance to encounter him. Within a short time, Bloody Knife stepped out of his lodge along with another brave. Soon the visitor departed, and the foe he sought reentered his tipi. Right away, Wind went to the tipi and also entered, being covered in his robe. When he first stepped into the dwelling, Bloody Knife was bent over an article of his possessions. He sensed someone had entered his lodge. Looking up, he was met with a length of deer antler going directly into his throat. Wind quickly reached around the back of Bloody Knife's head, drawing him farther up the natural dagger. His foe gasped as his hands pulled at the hand that held the antler. As his strength began to fail him, he managed some sounds, but mostly what came out of his mouth was blood.

He lived long enough to recognize his killer as Wind uttered, "I took his life, then his scalp, then his pony."

After removing Bloody Knife's scalp with his own knife, he slipped out of the tipi, and there staked nearby was Bright Star. Wind untied him and leaped onto his back, only slowing to gather the cord that secured Snowman as the Great Spirited directed him, he was certain. How else could he have accomplished such a satisfying victory as he and the Appaloosa stallions raced away from their Lakota captors?

As the course of events continued to unfold, Wind was able to track the avengers to Big Sun's village, having been informed by Red Bone that it was Nimipu and Siksika that had fought the victorious battle against the Lakota of that very recent time.

When Wild Wind came riding into the Siksika village, being directed to the location of his father and brother, it set off a joyous reunion, joined by all who were participants of the effort.

Eventually, the focus returned to those who had paid the ultimate price in the fight. The Siksika and the Nimipu mourned their losses. The loss of Gray Wolf was particularly hard for Raven and Big Sun. He had died a warrior's death, which was a bitter consolation.

Raven couldn't help but still be troubled by the thoughts of having failed at keeping an eye on his grandfather. Despite the fact that he hadn't even known of his death until after the battle was over, it still took its toll on his emotions. First his uncle, then his grandfather. It was all so hard to accept.

Big Sun couldn't keep from feeling that it was his agreeing to allow his warriors to be a part of the conflict that led to his friend's demise, along with others of his tribe who didn't survive, sadly being a cost of leadership at such a time as this.

However, the return of Wild Wind to their camp did a lot to alleviate the sorrow that they were experiencing. Shadow was so uplifted by his return that he could hardly maintain his composure. Considering from the time that he had first heard of his son's disappearance, along with the account of his brother's death, he had been inconsolable, but now he felt a great weight had been lifted from his heart and mind.

Wind was also understandably relieved at his successful escape. Even though at times he had had his doubts of the outcome against the many obstacles that presented themselves.

All in all, the coming times were still filled with potential for more fulfilment in every aspect of their lives. With that outlook at their forefront, the Nimipu departed from Big Sun's camp, having made it known that they were sincerely grateful for all the Siksika had done for them.

Also, there had been another lingering development while they continued there. The subject of Raven being led by a black eagle spirit guide had once again come to the surface. It began to create an uneasiness, as it had a number of winters past leading to his and Gray Wolf's quick departure from that place. This time, there had begun to arise some insinuation that it might have contributed to some of their losses during this latest fighting they had undertaken.

It helped prompt their decision to leave right away. So it had been discussed and agreed to that they would proceed onto Spotted Feather's village and spend the cold time with the Salish people there before they would yet be able to go home.

After a few sleeps, they were close to arriving at the Salish encampment.

When they had come close to the village, they were met by a large host of Salish braves who had come to try them, not being certain of their intent. It was resolved quickly and without incident upon recognition of who the party was made up of.

Before long, an emotional welcoming was taking place. Spotted Feather was startled at how overcome he was with joy at this surprise visit by Shadow, Raven, and Wind.

When they had managed to get settled in and the time allowed for some detailed conversing, again Spotted Feather was near overwhelmed by all that was told to him by his guests. When it was put in the order of occurrences, it came out first with Shadow being away on a journey to the Big Water. Next, they told of the trip made by Talon, Raven, and Wind with a hunting party to the buffalo country. Then the tale of the attack by the Lakota, resulting in the death of Talon as well as the capturing of Wind. All these things Spotted Feather listened to in a near state of disbelief while he looked from one member of Shadow's family to another as the story unfolded. Raven spoke of his failure to find out who was responsible and to be able to answer the question of what had become of his brother. Then making their trek back home to have to tell of the tragic events that had befallen them since they had been away.

Shadow, being present, having already returned from his time away, to hear of these things yet not being able to act on it at that time do to the approaching cold time. Then finally, the avenging party being able to make their way back to do all that could be done to settle the matter.

Then the story of the success they had with the aid of the Siksika, not withholding the account of the death of Gray Wolf.

Then Wind gave his own personal tale of his time in captivity and then of his escape, which included the part of his revenge on Bloody Knife for the death of his uncle. Also unbeknownst to any of them, for Gray Wolf's as well.

Then he was united again with his father and brother. It was all a most dramatic chain of events.

CHAPTER 51

A Returning Wind

Back at the Palus band, Running Wild and Rain could not help but wonder of their departed loved ones' well-being. Although they both had every confidence in the one to who their hopes and prayers were directed, the Life Giver.

Howling Wolf conveyed his outlook, saying, "I believe we will see them here before the next cold time." He rode off from them upon a pony he had broken and trained on his own in the absence of his father and older brothers.

The time passed, and the weather conditions improved, and so the Nimipu inhabiting the Salish camp began to make preparations to leave.

During the many discourses that took place between Shadow and Spotted Feather, the dissatisfaction of the Salish not being included with the avenging for the attack by the Lakota came out on more than one occasion. Although he had to agree in time that it was not at all convenient for them to seek his people out, given the circumstances.

When the time did come to leave, as always there was plenty of heartfelt emotion. "Goodbye once again, my very good friend. Give my love to your wonderful wives," Spotted Feather said with utmost sincerity.

"I have enjoyed being able to spend this time with you again, my brother of the trail of many adventures. You will always be in my thoughts and prayers as well as all your fine people," Shadow spoke in his final farewell as he mounted his pony and led off with a wave of his arm to all the Salish people present, as did all of the departing Nimipu on their leaving from the village.

The elation of the homebound party was powerful with the realization that they were finally on the move once again, in the direction of home.

Shadow was exceedingly pleased with the man Wild Wind had become. There was a time when he had told himself that he wouldn't hold his expectations for his other sons in comparison to Raven, who he felt was exceptional in his manly qualities. Although, now even though no comparisons were necessary, he could see that Wind had developed into a man who also was without peers in his own right. He also felt, and rightly so, that Wind looked a lot like himself when he was that many winters. Even so, he couldn't deny there were unmistakable attributes of his mother evident, which could only be said a good thing by any who knew Running Wild.

After Wind had recounted his time with the Lakota, telling of all that had transpired during the time spent while apart from his people, he had received a degree of respect from all who had come to know of it that could not and would not be disputed.

They were hardy travelers everyone. Still, the trip, as always, was long and not without its many challenging obstacles. Eventually, they came to the location of the Kooskia band, being once again within their own country. They held up there out of respect for their brethren but did not linger long. The following lighttime, they left again.

As their persistence would have it, after another sleep, they reached the outskirts of the Palus territory, feeling jubilant at the thought of being with their families soon.

After a while, riders appeared moving in their direction, and as they drew near, it was heard from their lead rider to holler out, "I knew you would return at this time. My father and brothers are here. They have come home!" This was followed by much shouting and obvious sounds of jubilance. Howling Wolf and Screaming Panther and the other young men that were with them rejoiced.

When they entered the camp and the commotion that was taking place, it was late into the lighttime, with the smoke from the cooking fires adrift between the lodges, the barking curs, the cries of small children, and the ecstatic voices of the people hailing the returning heroes.

The young men who had met them previously had hurried ahead, telling the news of Wild Wind being recovered, and they were all being celebrated as victorious conquerors, the people having not heard anything more.

Running Wild and Rain, who were as attentive as any could be, noticed the absence of Gray Wolf immediately. It was a difficult matter emotionally, given the overall exuberance seeing Wind back among them, along with Shadow and Raven, as well as the other men.

It took some sleeps for things to settle down with the Palus band. All of the story eventually came out, which did make for an extraordinary tale. There was so much involved, resulting in the evident outcome.

There was also an extensive mourning to pay their respects to those that were lost in the ordeal.

Wind's recounting fascinated all who came to know the details of his captivity and escape. He also became one of the most desired young men by the young women of the band. He sometimes caused them to lose their composure when he was near them. Almost all of them were powerless in his presence, but there was one who was not at all.

She was a very confident young woman who believed that she could attract Wind's attention and hold it. She was called Songbird, for she sang the songs of the people, as well as composing her own.

At one of the feasts that were held, not all so long after the avengers had returned, she asked to be able to sing for the people at their gathering. Those who were in a position to grant her the opportunity were glad to do so, being already appreciative of her past contributions in such a way.

When the time came for Songbird to present her song, those who were there gave her their attention. She seemed to be a gift given by favor of the Life Giver. She was attractive and skilled with an ability to adorn herself in attire that enhanced her physical appeal. Then, as all were in agreement, her voice was her finest attribute. She was still young and did not yet know her future potential. As she began to sing, there emerged a splendid love song that was envied by the women and captivating to the men, especially the younger ones who felt that possibly the song could be intended for them. All this was not lost on Wild Wind, who was also very much taken in by the sweetness of the lyrics and melody from this lovely songstress. She was modest enough not to be blatant toward Wind. Although shortly afterward, she approached Beautiful Flower, asking her to let Wind know that she had meant that song for him. She wanted to give her chance to be his woman the utmost possibility to come to fruition rather than waiting on her hopes and prayers, yet all were about to come to be.

When he received the message that Songbird intended it for him, it caused him to feel glad. He was glad to hear that the song of love that he had heard was for him, and he was surprised at the effect that it had on him, which was refreshing and uplifting in a way that he had never known before. He had another feeling come racing forward. He suddenly believed that he was in love with her, which also came as a surprise.

After experiencing these innermost thoughts and feelings, he came out of his musings and gazed out at his surroundings before him to see Songbird there in his line of sight, looking directly at him. He didn't hesitate and walked to her, smitten with this thing that had so rapidly taken the position of that which was foremost in his thoughts.

From that moment on, they were together in purpose, doing all things for each other's well-being, not making light of the pleasure they enjoyed at being in love.

The rest of Shadow's family were also glad at the development of their relationship. It all added to the happiness and contentment of being a united family again.

Talon's woman, Little Wing, had become part of Shadow's household, with all the rights of a wife of his. Her and Talon's child,

Screaming Panther, who was fast developing into a young man, was treated like a son. It was a relatively smooth transition.

Not long after the avenging party's return, the cold time began to assert itself on the band once again. Making ready for it took precedence over all else until they believed they had accomplished their preparations.

Songbird's family provided her and Wind with a lodge for their wedding present.

Raven and Vixen, along with their daughter Rainbow, were all so happy to be together again. They were enjoying their time as much as humanly possible.

There had been too much separation for too long for a lot of the men of the village to consider taking any extended travels. Several winters past with the band's focus being on their needs that were based on what means they had within the surrounding area.

CHAPTER 52

SEEKING THE HAVEN OF ABUNDANCE

Red Dreamer had come to visit the Palus band a couple times since the return of the avenging party. On a fine warm lighttime, he made his way into their camp once again.

Always glad to see his old friend, Shadow bid him welcome. "Come, rest and refresh yourself," he invited.

Dreamer dismounted and entered the lodge with Shadow, as they had already begun to take pleasure in one another's company, conversing on all their shared points of interest.

After a short period on various subjects, Dreamer blurted out, "You have been tied to your home here long enough. I think that you and your family should come with me and my family to a place that you have not been, a place that we Waptailmin are very fond of. It is certain that the Nimipu have visited there, but having become well informed by you of your travels, this would be a different place to you. It is cooler during the hot time, with an abundance of good things to be had to meet our needs while we stay there. What are your thoughts on such an idea?"

"I will seriously think on it while you are here among us and give you an answer before you depart, my friend," Shadow responded. "Tell me, where is this place of which you speak?" he asked, unable to withhold his curiosity.

"It is near to our neighbor mountain we call Pahpo. We would travel a trail that my people know very well, back into the high country of some forests and streams and lakes and rivers, a haven for the tribes. You will enjoy it should you choose to go," he answered Cloud Shadow.

"You do know me well, my friend, and what I would enjoy. It sounds to be something that we need to experience, and I thank you for this offer," Shadow replied.

Shadow made time to present the invitation to his family during their friend's visit. Before Dreamer returned to the Waptailmin village, Shadow let him know that he and his family would be coming on the trek that he had proposed.

"We will come to your village not many sleeps from now. Please be watching for our coming, because we will be wanting to be able to get to our final point of travel as soon as we can without being pressed all so much on this trip, having time yet still for a return while the season is still favorable for us."

With the agreement being made, the preparations began. Shadow's wives were excited to be taking a lengthy trip. All his sons and daughters wanted to go along with their mates and children. It certainly was turning into a family affair.

When the time came to depart, there were others also of their band who had decided to come along. It was a rather large party that left that lighttime, bound for a place that none of them were familiar. Although the fact that Shadow and Dreamer were the minds behind the idea made it a venture that they entered with confidence. Howling Wolf and Screaming Panther were soaring with expectation and excitement. This trip held so much potential for adventure for them. It defied their imaginations. Raven and Wind made sure that they were well mounted so they could get the most out of the expedition.

As the Nimipu party made their way across the extensive distance, Howling Wolf and Screaming Panther made forays upon the land, seeking plunder on the grounds for whatever they could prevail over—marmots, rabbits, grouse, pheasants. They managed to trample some, strike some with sticks, and on occasion hit them with an arrow. They were proud of any contributions that they were able to make to the party as they all drew nearer to the Waptailmin village.

Within the time allotted, they were safe and secure at the village of Red Dreamer's people.

After a short stay in their camp, all that were going on the trip to the haven of the tribes departed with an abundance of camaraderie among them.

Dreamer led the procession, following the Waptailmin Narrow River toward the place where it joined with the Mother River on her trip to the Big Water. Before they had gotten to that place of joining, they made a sharp turn toward the place of Cold Wind Grandfather, now facing the not-too-distant mountain Pahpo, where they stopped to rest and sleep over before continuing on to their destination.

Before they were to reach the high forests that were enticingly evident ahead of them, there was an extensive stretch of a dry desolate terrain that they yet needed to traverse.

Eventually, they began to ascend into the periodic areas of forest that they had been looking forward to and all the wonders that were to be found along the way. Over to their strong side, they could begin to see the nearby mountain and its glaciers feeding all the lands below it with streams and creeks and rivers.

As they continued this trek into this dramatic change of environment, one of the many noticeable sensations that they experienced was the plentiful varied fragrances of the plant life that was all about them in these initial stages of the mountains. It was being enjoyed by the first-time visitors as well as the frequenters of this place. It was something that appealed to their senses as sure as the sweetness of fine weather.

It didn't end there but rather was just the beginning of an extended period of a most enjoyable time in this place that was known as a haven for all the tribes of the area from both sides of the mountain range. Although it was purely seasonal, as the cold time would cause all who enjoyed this area to seek shelter from the elements, returning once again to the lower elevations from which they had come.

These wayfarers, being led by Dreamer, had planned their visit accordingly to get the most out of the time that was convenient to this place of splendor and tranquility.

The young duo of Howling Wolf and Screaming Panther were seen everywhere as if there were several pairs of them ranging about the area, seeming to explore all that the party passed through.

As usual, they hunted for any game as a rule, being relatively successful. But more importantly, they were gaining experience each time the attempt was made. Some of their experience was based on using teamwork to accomplish their objective. They found that if they separated to a certain distance, either one could take advantage of any flushed animal that the other had stirred from their concealment. It had proven very useful as their attempts continued. After a period of travel, it was stated by Dreamer and others of his family that they were drawing near to the area known as a haven.

Having arrived there through a gradual climb, they came to this place with extensive clusters of forest and areas of open grasslands as well. Periodically, there were very abrupt outcroppings of stone that, in some instances, stood very high above the lay of the land.

The following lighttime, after being informed they were close to their destination, they came to that place that was known to the repeating visitors as the fields of berries, which was in proximity to a group of towering rock crags they referred to as the Mountain of Sharp Teeth.

When the first-time visitors surveyed the surroundings, they were very pleased with the prospects of staying in this location for the time of the hot weather. Dreamer and his family went on to assure them that there were other fine aspects to their nearby surroundings.

As their time passed, besides the abundance of sustenance they enjoyed, they all appreciated the relief from the all so well-known sweltering heat that was being experienced in the lowlands of home.

While they stayed in the haven, the Waptailmin hosts took their Nimipu guests to many delightful places. There were lots of small lakes and creeks and streams, along with a river that provided a series of waterfalls originating from the neighboring mountain Pahpo. One of these falls that they referred to was the Crescent Moons. It was particularly beautiful and pleasant. It was also a place of great fishing. It yielded bountifully to any who fished that place. As the season progressed, the huckleberries began to come into their time of ripening. The berries found throughout the mountain range were particularly plentiful in this place that was a haven for the peoples of the surrounding lands.

    They dried fish and berries by the baskets. They would seek to do these things wheresoever they were at during this time, but this place was a very fine alternative from their usual settings.

CHAPTER 53

HOWLING WOLF FINDS GUIDANCE

While in the haven vicinity, the Nimipu and Waptailmin encountered peoples from other tribes. As it happened, some men entered a discourse with Shadow and Dreamer with a combination of sign and verbal, with various subjects discussed. At a point, the subject of the white men entered their talks. Dreamer brought up his vision of the coming of the white men into their lands many winters ago. Then Shadow spoke of his trek to the Big Water and what he encountered there. Then they both got a startling surprise when they were informed that there had been so many recent sightings of white men along the area of the Big Water that it had become common occurrence. After this had been conveyed and questioned as to if what they had heard tell was correct, they, for a while afterward, carried a look of concern and apprehension, convinced that it was.

Previously, Howling Wolf had voiced that he was giving serious consideration to going on a spirit guide vision quest while being in the area of the haven. He took it upon himself to spend time fasting and praying for direction on the matter. One early time, he informed his family that he was going up the river from Pahpo in search of help concerning his destiny.

He was told by the party that not many sleeps hence, they would need to depart, although no one questioned his right to go on the quest. He set out on foot with the promise of not staying away for an overly extended time.

As he followed the river, he was able to become one with his surroundings. So sublime was the experience that he knew he would never forget it.

The time passed as he drew nearer to the base of Pahpo. While seeking life's path and meditating on his prospects, he obtained a view through an unobstructed opening in the landscape, yet still being concealed by the forested area himself. There within his clear line of sight, he saw a creature he was unfamiliar with attack a full-grown antlered buck, latching onto its upper foreleg and pulling it to the ground. It then managed to get a fixed bite onto the stag's throat. Then it placed another crushing bite that ended its life. While Wolf stood transfixed watching this drama unfold, the wolverine turned its head, staring into his eyes. Then it returned its attention back to its meal. He stayed and watched as the beast devoured an amazing amount of its kill while expending deep growling sounds. He continued there, waiting and watching until the wolverine eventually had had enough, and then it dragged the remains into the tree line.

Wolf then continued to the base of the mountain where he stopped on account of the approaching darkness. That late time, he fell into a deep sleep that included a stark dream in which he was confronted by a wolf, a panther, and a bear in unison, attempting to surround him and overtake him. He felt helpless, being alone in his struggle. He began to call on the Great Spirit for help. As the dream went on, he felt the presence of the Life Giver come to him, saying, "I send you help in your time of need. Trust in him to show you the way."

Then as he waited on the promise, and feeling very much overwhelmed, there came a ferocious growling sound that dominated those of his opponents. It was followed by the wolverine he had seen along the way. Then with amazing speed, it leaped into the middle of the developing onslaught with a dominance that could hardly be imagined by this creature, which was not all so large in stature and bulk. It brought retribution on the perpetrators, scattering them in every direction.

Afterward, the wolverine turned its attention on Howling Wolf, speaking to him plainly, "I am your guide. Believe in the abilities that have been given to me, for I have come to you for this purpose." Then Wolf awoke as if startled from a fall.

He then spent some time trying to digest all that he had experienced. After a while, he gathered himself enough to head back to where he had left out from.

He took his time and was absorbed in thought. Yet he was keeping a well-honed guard over his position at all times while staying with the river as his course. He made his way. When he arrived at the Crescent Moons falls, he lingered there in its tranquility and beauty. He was not alone there, for typically others were present during this time of season, taking in the benefits that were found at this place of solace. Some continued to reap the harvest of the redfish that made their way to this location during this time. Others were still collecting the abundance of huckleberries, while some swam and bathed in the deep side of the river located at the base of a crescent of slower falling water, creating a large pool. The entire falls had a considerable expanse consisting of several crescent-shaped falls in a parallel line. It was a place one was reluctant to depart from, having the cares of life washed away by the clear blue waters that flowed by.

After staying there through the darktime, he left at first light, feeling extremely good about the outcome from his undertaking, believing in the experience and the architect of creation.

When Wolf returned to the encampment of their party, he was met with jubilation by his family and his Waptailmin friends. Panther had so many questions for him that he had to ask him to give him some time, and he would tell him all that took place.

As was becoming the usual occurrence, Shadow was once again altogether impressed with this experience that his youngest son had had. He also was very happy for him, for it was obvious to all that he was extremely satisfied with the quest.

Howling Wolf had matured considerably in mind, body, and spirit since his coming on this trip. He had gone from one who was looking for his life's course to one who believed he had entered onto the path to his place in this life, whatever that might entail.

Not long after Wolf's return, the party departed toward their homelands, with their ponies laden with dried fish and berries, along with venison and bear. All things considered, it had been a fine diversion from their normal experiences around home.

They gave themselves a sufficient amount of time to make the trip back without real danger of severe weather. However, the cold time was showing its presence at intervals along the way, having had numerous camps in wet and windy conditions.

Their departure from the Waptailmin people when the time came was an emotional one, for their bonds once again had been reinforced. Having said their farewells, they proceeded onward, longing for the comforts of their own village once again.

As before, Wolf and Panther ranged here and there, seeming to be everywhere about the rolling hills they passed through without regard for the weather.

Raven and Wind would join them at times, being interested in the lay of the land for information's sake, all being travelers without rival.

Once they had all returned safely, besides the joy of being back home from a successful excursion, it was brought to everyone's attention that Songbird was with child, which heightened their exuberance.

Of course, there was none happier at the news than Wild Wind, who had received it firsthand before any of the others.

The cold time gripped the land again, and again the Nimipu people lived closer to their encampments. When the weather began to improve, visitors began to arrive periodically just to see Cloud Shadow, for his position of renown had not faded among the people. They believed that he had a medicine power that could be very helpful in its use for their tribe. It was an expectation he felt that was not always adequately met. Nevertheless, they came, and he always tried to be respectful and to do what he could for them.

Word began to arrive by different ones who came there that White Owl had died. The first person to bring the news was Cunning Fox. He relayed the event to his sister, Vixen, before he made it known to the others, although White Owl had many friends among the Palus band. Shadow was grieved to hear tell of it, the old chief holding a special place in his heart. Yet he knew that there would come a time when such news would be told pertaining to him as well.

CHAPTER 54

VIXEN'S RETURN

Raven and Vixen began to prepare for a trip to the village of the Upper Red Fish river band. When Howling Wolf learned of their plans, he asked to come along, as did Screaming Panther. When the time came for their departing, the traveling party was made up of Raven and Vixen, along with little Rainbow, as well as Cunning Fox, Wolf, and Panther.

Howling Wolf brought up his desire to visit the Wallowa band, of whom he had heard much but had seen little. He had met some Wallowa visitors yet had never been to the lands of the Wallowa people. Although to him, growing up, it had always been a place of importance just through the varied stories he had heard told. The traveling party consented to his interests, with their own personal desires to visit there.

Before they had left, Wild Wind had become a father. Songbird had given birth to a fine baby boy they named Sweet Breeze. She told everyone that she was certain there was a comforting breeze blowing the entire time she was giving birth. Wind made it known that he had been asking his spirit guide to aid Songbird in her time of need. Thus, Sweet Breeze was born, and to a very happy mother and father as well as a loving and caring extended family. Wolf and Panther, as was their nature, were very excited at the possibilities of this trek to these areas of intrigue.

Also, before they had departed, Wind had presented Panther with a stallion sired by Snowman, being of the lineage of Bright Star. He had intended to do so all along and felt it was the appropriate time. It was a pleasing sight to see the look of the importance to him of the gesture that had been made. Now he rode along, looking proud and poised on his great stallion. It also stirred his thoughts of his father, Talon.

Wolf had been given a stallion of that prized lineage too, both being of their beloved Appaloosa stock. The travelers made their way in the direction of the Small mountains that stood before the Wallowa band's territory. They camped when they cared to, but they were hardy and disciplined travelers that typically covered long distances whenever they set out to reach a destination. As they moved through the areas along their way, Wolf and Panther were appreciating their surroundings. The weather was fine, the views were inspiring, and all was new to them. Such a wonderful country that the creator had endowed the Nimipu with. The feeling of thankfulness swept over them throughout the journey.

Eventually, their course brought them to the lands of the Wallowa band, a place that encompassed all the attributes of abundant life. The sights all about them caused their hearts to swell with pride and soar with delight. Raven led the party to the Wallowa band's central camp, where they were greeted warmly by their fellow tribe members.

Cunning Fox, having already gone on ahead of them toward his home with obligations to uphold that waited for him there. The Wallowa band enjoyed the relative safety of their location, being on the outer fringe of hostile neighbors, as did the Palus band as well. So their camps were rarely on any type of high alert, making them openly accessible to all who came there.

The Wallowa people were very much acquainted with the family of Cloud Shadow, if not personally then at least by the stories that they had regularly heard throughout the band. Raven was quite aware of these facts, but Wolf and Panther were just beginning to become introduced to this aspect that had become part of their heritage.

While they visited and conversed, they were being familiarized with members of the band who had blood ties to Shadow's mother's family, Fawn, being born of the Wallowa band.

Some were young men and women whom they had not known through any prior contact. A couple of these introductions were a brother and sister who were Wolf and Panther's number in winters. The young man's name was Mountain Thunder, and his sister was Smiles A Lot.

The young man immediately befriended the Palus wayfarers. He let them know that he wanted to continue with them onto their destination to visit with the Upper Red Fish river band and to give the condolences on behalf of the Wallowa people in regard to the death of White Owl. Smiles A Lot was taken with Vixen's baby daughter, spending much of the time giving attention to her. Mountain Thunder blended in well with Wolf and Panther, and the trio bonded tightly in a short period. Of course, no one raised any objection to him coming along.

The party stayed on with the Wallowa band for a period of sleeps while enjoying their hospitality.

The time came when they knew that it was needful for them to proceed with their intentions to go on to the band of Vixen's family. Smiles A Lot, having befriended Vixen and Rainbow, also asked to come along with them when they left.

Back at the Palus encampment, there was a development that had been brought to Cloud Shadow's attention and to everyone else as well in time. Little Wing was expecting another child.

It came as no surprise to Running Wild and Rain, for they were well aware of Shadow's propensity toward the manner of such behavior. She had lived as his third wife for a while, and so it was that he was to become a father once again.

The wayfaring party made their way to the tribes crossing place on the Winding River that snaked its way throughout the region. The crossing was difficult, but they managed without incident.

Leaving the Wallowa band had been an emotional trial, with Mountain Thunder and Smiles A Lot's family being somewhat reluctant to see them leave on their journey. Although there were plenty of assurances that all would be well. After the party had made the successful crossing, it was only another sleep before they were on the outskirts of their fellow tribe's territory. Vixen was becoming more excited with every bit of progress that they made now. She hadn't been home for too long, it seemed. She thought back on the news of the death of her father and the ordeal of her pregnancy following that news. It was all becoming more important to her to be home at this time the closer they got. Smiles A Lot was sensing her emotions, having heard tell of those events, and was sharing her excitement.

Finally, they came into view of the location of their village. Unlike the villages of the Palus and Wallowa bands, they were immediately met by readied braves to greet or confront any who came to their habitation. For these lands had begun to be known to have roving parties of Shoshones and Piautes, who were opportunists of an insatiable degree.

Right away, after their recognition, a festive reunion erupted. It had been common knowledge within the band that Cunning Fox had traveled to the Palus band's village to tell Vixen of White Owl's passing. When Cunning Fox had returned with the news that she was coming home, along with Raven and their new daughter, there had been an atmosphere of expectation along with excitement there. Now that their arrival had occurred, it was being well received.

Young Old Man made sure that he would be one of the first to greet them. He, along with his family, came forward to meet Raven and his family.

"Young Old Man, you're beginning to look more the old man. Maybe it's time to change your name, my good friend!" Raven exclaimed.

"Yes, I am just glad that I am around still to give not to serious thought to what you say, my brother of the trails," he responded. "Come and rest and refresh yourselves. We are very glad to have you here with us."

Once they were all dismounted, they were waited on as honored guests. As their customs are, their conversations led to storytelling, which began to bring out events concerning Black Eagle and Big Cat's relationship with White Owl. They also came to Bull Elk, Cunning

Fox, and Young Old Man's interactions with Cloud Shadow and Raven, along with others of the Nimipu. After some time involved with these tales, Wolf and Panther and Mountain Thunder began to gain a better understanding of the bonds among them.

The women of the band absorbed Vixen and Smiles A Lot, along with little Rainbow, into their activities.

Many of the young men began to take part in competitions on different levels. It was all going well enough, being a sufficient pastime for all the participants. Although there came a point when there seemed to be a lull in their enthusiasm. Several of them seemed to be pondering the matter when, as if by order, some other Nimipu braves arrived. They came with word of a raid on their hunting camp by Paiutes, causing a quick stirring among the band for retribution.

CHAPTER 55

Paiute Problems

The hunters told how when they had returned to their hunting camp, they found that all they had left there that was useful had been stolen from them, even the hides off their shelters.

There was an inciting fervor that began to rise with the young braves when they heard the tale of trespass that was being told by the hunters.

Before long, word reached Cunning Fox and Young Old Man, with Raven in attendance. Right away, the discussion of how to go about retrieving their property and rendering the penalty for such a grievous wrongdoing was in full swing.

Within a short time, they had a mounted party of braves on their way in search of the culprits.

After a full lighttime of travel, with their forward scouts keeping the party on point, they tracked the pillagers. It was reported to Cunning Fox that they had found the Paiutes held up not so far away from where the search party was at that time.

The violators were weighed down with more than they could carry, and it had been slow going for them. Although their greed and foolish defiant confidence would not allow them to abandon their spoils but rather were spending their time in celebration.

The Nimipu decided to make their move against the pillagers' camp at first light, as they held up in a vale just within the vicinity, for darkness was closing in.

Long before light began to make its appearance, they began to position themselves closer to their objective.

Raven and Cunning Fox had come near to the Paiutes' campsite even before their celebrating had ceased for the time. As they watched from the dark fringes of the firelight, they made the observations that could be helpful for their assault. As they continued to peer in, they could view the offenders going about their activities of jubilance, being unaffected from the possibilities of retaliation by them.

They were no small number for a marauding party, being close to equal with the Nimipu who had come to face them. It was no surprise to Cunning Fox, for the scouts had already surmised as much. He would have preferred to overpower them and have them flee for their lives, but he realized that this was going to be an all-out fight, and all went to the victor. He knew that the braves who had come on the search were more than ready to test their skill and strength, as well as bravery. He decided that all the choice they had was to try and take any advantage that was available to them, which was an unexpected attack being their best chance for the desired outcome.

After Raven and Cunning Fox left from making their observations, Cunning Fox consulted with Raven concerning his thoughts on what they had witnessed from the Paiute camp.

"My brother, what do you say about all you have seen and heard, on what to do with these thieves?"

"I think that once we enter ourselves into this encounter, we cannot just hope that they will run in panic, but we must attack, because our hoped-for outcome will only come through our fighting them. We will leave them away out, for some will flee. Then we can try to push them toward an escape but must not suppose that they will not stand and fight," Raven replied as they moved back toward the awaiting party, not liking the potential for lives being lost and inevitable wounded.

When they arrived at the location where the Nimipu braves were gathered, they told of what they had seen and what they were going to need to do in regard to accomplishing the needed outcome.

Raven was troubled at the presence of Wolf and Panther, as well as Mountain Thunder. They, on the other hand, were ecstatic at this opportunity to rise in stature within the tribe. Being young and naive concerning these matters, they only allowed themselves to imagine a victorious outcome for their effort.

Raven separated them to say, "You must stay to the rear of the attack and learn from what you see. I don't want any of you being injured in this fight." Although he knew that all he could do was hope for the best results. They all agreed that they would hold back as well as the situation would allow.

None of those among them had any idea of the fighting abilities of these Paiute invaders, yet with the full understanding that any cornered creature could be dangerous. Cunning Fox and Young Old Man decided that it was time to begin to move toward the camp of these raiders. They wanted to be well situated when the dawn began to break.

Once in place, while looking over their camp, all seemed peaceful and calm. Raven looked over the positioned Nimipu, all poised for an attack. He felt that any moment, one of the ponies would be giving their presence away. The light was revealing more each passing moment when he saw a dark form come to perch in a tall nearby pine tree. It struck his curiosity keenly, because he was sure it was an eagle, a black one. His next thought was *This is going to be a fight in which some are going to die.*

It appeared the Paiutes were strewn about the camp, laid up under their robes. A moment later, one of them got up to make water. Cunning Fox took it as a sign for the attack and led off into their camp with a cry for battle, along with the others following his example.

Their plan was to come in with the shape of an inverted hoofprint, leaving the rear area open for escape for any of their adversary who chose to do so. When they reached their campsite, something wasn't right. The individual who had gotten up had run into the surrounding forest. Then as they came to a stop and looked about, another source of pitched screaming was heard as riders came rushing from the woods about the area, brandishing their weapons with their fierce painted faces in a grimace. It was a trap.

Arrows flew. Nimipu fell to the ground. Some Nimipu got off some arrows as well. Within moments, it was kill or be killed, with clubs being swung, different ones leaping off their ponies onto their opponents, then continuing the battle on foot or rolling across the ground, locked in deadly combat. Their foe was in an all-out aggressive assault for the glory of dominion over these Nimipu braves.

Their leader was a fearless man who demanded the same from any who followed his trait of plundering. He was Crazy Bear, and he had his focus on Raven as he bore down on him. Raven was occupied with an assault from another direction. Just before the attacking Paiute reached him, Panther's pony made a quick backing retreat from some attackers lunging at them. He ended up between Raven and Crazy Bear and received the club end that was being swung, and he was knocked off his mount. Raven felt the commotion and turned in time to catch Crazy Bear's flying body coming in a head-on dive at him, causing a backward fall to the ground with his assailant landing on top of him. When Crazy Bear landed on Raven, it pushed all the air from his lungs, and he went unconscious. Crazy Bear raised his club to take Raven's life when Howling Wolf reached him, driving an arrow he held in his hands down the side of his collarbone and into his heart, killing him instantly.

The battle raged on, but with the death of Crazy Bear, the Paiutes began to seek every opportunity to flee the fight until finally the Nimipu were victorious.

Right around the conclusion of the battle, Raven came back to his senses, taking some moments to gain his bearings. When he was able to grasp the situation, he made out Howling Wolf kneeling over Screaming Panther's still body. When Raven was able to take an assessment of the outcome, he was glad to find Mountain Thunder was fine with some cuts and bruises, but he would recover. Cunning Fox had done well, but Young Old Man had not survived, along with a significant number of others who had lost their lives.

Those who had fought their way through the entire conflict had high praise for Howling Wolf, telling of how he fought like a ferocious beast, and none could stand before him as he dealt out a deadly destruction. It was brought to Raven's attention that it was he who had saved him from the war club of the big Paiute who sought to slay him. Although he couldn't help from recalling the presence of his spirit guide as well.

The losses that had been sustained had not been reasonably contemplated. It was a very hard lesson learned by the survivors. The sadness was so painful, it proved to be beyond their capability to contain their feelings, with the grief showing on their countenances, one and all.

They were able to gather the dead and injured onto ponies and travois and move on toward their village. They had reclaimed their possessions, but not without a high price. Howling Wolf had the prized stallion in tow, with the body of Screaming Panther draped over its back. There was also a single scalp tied to Panther's wrist. It previously belonged to Crazy Bear.

CHAPTER 56

COYOTE AND THE BUTTERFLY

Mountain Thunder tried to be a diversion for Howling Wolf and succeeded for short periods, but there was no consoling Wolf during this time. Even though the bond between them was growing into a close-knit one.

They were all looking forward to getting back to the village, but at the same time they were also dreading it. With so many dead and wounded, it would be more sadness heaped upon the gloom they were already carrying with them. Even so, eventually they arrived back at the Upper Red Fish river band's encampment.

When they began to appear to their tribe members, the first reaction was of jubilation, which quickly turned to cries of anguish.

There was much to do concerning the losses that had taken place from this excursion—the preparations, the burials, the mourning, along with the ceremonies based around their ritualistic observances. It all took time to follow through in a proper respectful manner.

As it turned out, they buried Screaming Panther there as well. Not that they had a choice, although the fact that he could not be returned to the Palus band was another unpleasant aspect of his demise. It was somewhat common, however, that a tribe member would lose their life a long distance from home. So it was a fact it could be a very real possibility in one's existence. Traveling as much as they did, it was an occurrence that they were familiar with.

After observing the burial rites, they decided to depart on their return to the place of their origin. After some consideration, Mountain Thunder and Smiles A Lot made the decision to travel to the Palus band's village with their friends that were family as well. Cunning Fox assured them that he would send a message to the Wallowa with word of their decision.

Raven had come to admire and befriend another brave of the Upper Red Fish band over this stay. He was Son of Coyote. He was a brother to Young Old Man, having a different mother yet the same father, and had fought with them against the Paiute. He had taken care, along with Raven, to see that his brother's body was given all respect since retrieving him from where he had fallen. During this time around one another, they had begun to appreciate a growing friendship between them.

Coyote was away to Kamiah during the time that his brother and the party of vision quest seekers, along with Raven, had had their life-changing experiences. He was, however, well informed of the story of Cloud Shadow's part in it all. While they discussed their common interests, Coyote asked if he could return with them to the Palus band village.

"I would like to be able to meet your father and hope to speak with him concerning some matters," he stated.

"We would be glad for you to come with us when we leave. I remember you telling me that you have not yet taken a wife, so I encourage you to come and feel free to stay with us as long as you like. I am quite certain that my father would be honored to speak with you on any matter you would like," Raven replied with confidence.

Once the time had come to go, they had developed an even stronger bond with this band of their tribe through these latest shared experiences. Howling Wolf knew that as long as he lived, he would never forget the events of this visit.

After some time in their return travel, it began to reveal that Son of Coyote was a person of seriousness who was deep in thought a lot of the time, not unlike his recently deceased brother. Although that was a trait that was viewed with appreciation among the Nimipu.

Meanwhile, back at the Palus camp, Lovely Butterfly longed for the return of Vixen and Rainbow. She had so enjoyed having Rainbow to interact with each lighttime, for her maternal interest was quite lively, and her niece catered to that strong feeling in her. She had not had any children of her own, being unusually particular when it came to a mate. She had never been certain why it was, but any suitors that she had somewhat entertained always disappointed her in some manner, and she would put them off to the prospects of any further consideration. It seemed to involve their lack of gravity in general. After all, she was the youngest daughter of Cloud Shadow, and she expected a lot.

Wild Wind and Songbird were enjoying their love for one another, as well as their little boy, Sweet Breeze.

Little Wing was beginning to show that she was with child, and Shadow was glad for the expectancy with a bit of pride as well.

The number of visitors to come asking for Cloud Shadow's medicine through the warm and hot time was unprecedented. His importance grew with each passing winter. There would never be a single chief over all the bands, but Shadow had become the most prominent individual among the Nimipu at that time.

As the returning party drew ever closer to their destination, another development was evolving. Unknown to everyone, up till this time, was a private objective for Smiles A Lot that had taken hold with her from the moment that she laid eyes on Howling Wolf. The joy that overcame her at seeing him return safely from the battle with the Paiutes was pure. Now it was beginning to become apparent to the others as she began to reveal to Wolf her affection for him. She knew that just being someone who was nearby was not going to be enough. He had not been oblivious to her presence either. He had always found her a pleasant distraction from everything else going on around him. She had a character that made her a standout, just being herself. So when she approached him away from the others and began to make known to him her desires, he took her in his arms, and their closeness began to generate the responses of becoming one in body and mind. They made love in the darkness at the edge of their campsite.

Now the order of travel had changed with everyone accepting this new development, with Howling Wolf and Smiles A Lot determined to stay close as they rode along beside one another. Wolf had previously experienced an overwhelming sense of loss with the death of Panther, and now he had an overwhelming sense of gain. He had to admit that it was a strange conflict of feelings in his young life. Yet he now was filled with affection for Smiles A Lot.

Mountain Thunder didn't feel slighted by the development now that his best friend had also become his brother.

Raven and Vixen were also glad for the relationship, having become very fond of Smiles A Lot, and Coyote was pleased for them as well, all seeming to be a pleasant time he was experiencing with the family of Cloud Shadow.

Eventually, they did make it back to the Palus band encampment to a mixed emotional reunion of extreme happiness at seeing them enter the village and then the extreme sadness to find that Panther had failed to come home. Little Wing took it, along with the death of Talon, as an end to another path she had traveled. It was a hardship that she would need to overcome.

There was elation, however, over the love between Howling Wolf and Smiles A Lot, along with having her brother staying among them, who it was apparent was a dynamic individual. Mutually, Thunder was impressed with the Palus band and felt at home there right away.

Then there was Son of Coyote. Butterfly wasn't sure why she was drawn to Coyote, but she was, in a way like nothing she had ever felt before. To the point where before she could only think about seeing Rainbow again to her not able to stop being absorbed with thoughts of this man, Coyote. She had been told by more than a few wise people that they believed the Life Giver had a special purpose for her since the time that she was pulled from the raging river and brought back from a near-death experience. Now she wondered about that too.

Raven introduced Coyote to Cloud Shadow, and then after all the news had been reviewed, he made it known that Coyote very much wanted to council with Shadow concerning a matter.

"I would hear you now if you would like," Shadow invited.

"Thank you. I am honored to be here to be heard by you," Coyote began.

CHAPTER 57

THE CONTINUING SHADOW

Coyote related the story of his vision quest to Cloud Shadow. Of how he had stayed beside the small lake in the Red Fish mountains, believing that it was the area that he should meet his spirit guide and would gain the vision he sought for himself and his people. He had tarried in this place for several lighttimes, praying and fasting and waiting with patience and determination. The area had an array of animal life teeming there.

As he mused over that which he had been taught and had experienced himself in this life, he took an interest in watching the osprey hawks diving down to the surface of the lake, snagging unsuspecting fish there. He observed that like all hawks, they were skilled at catching their prey. He felt compelled to keep a vigil over the surface of the water for a couple lighttimes now to observe each attempt that was made by any fishing hawks.

Then, doing so for a relatively lengthy period of focusing his attention on these stealthy fishers, darkness came over that place, and he slept. While he slept, he dreamed a vivid dream that he was watching over the lake's surface, not at all seeming like a dream. He watched with the expectation that he would see a hawk come into view soon, hunting for a target. As he scanned the sky, the hunter appeared, and the sun was high with a pale blue background, making it hard to get a good look at it as it circled overhead. While trying to see clearly, not at all certain with any distinction of this apparition, it dropped from the sky with diving speed. As he watched, he realized that this hawk was not dark on the back and white on the underside like all the others, but all white.

The white hawk pulled up in time to grasp a gleaming fish and lift off with it secured in a death grip within its talons. To Coyote, it was all so real. After he awoke, he told himself that it was no dream but a vision, and the white bird was his spirit guide.

Even after he left that place, he still wasn't certain what it all meant, but he had confidence that it would become clear as time went on. Then he said, "Can you reveal the meaning?"

Cloud Shadow remained silent for some time as if in a trance. Then he asked Coyote, "What do you know of the coming of the white men?"

"I have heard that they have been seen around the place they call the Big Water," he replied.

Shadow proceeded to tell Coyote what he knew on the subject in question. After giving him the insight, he told him, "I believe that you have received a vision of a white bird coming to the Nimipu people to help us to face the coming of the white men, and it will be given to you to decide what it is to be done concerning this knowledge."

Shadow had come to feel a strong appreciation for Son of Coyote in this short span of time they had been in each other's presence.

Coyote left the lodge deep in thought, feeling a responsibility for his people like never before.

Butterfly confided with Flower and Vixen in regard to her interest in Coyote. They assured her that they would do anything they could to help her come to a satisfactory resolution to her inquiries concerning if he was the one she was waiting for or if she should look for another.

Coyote was encouraged to stay with the people of the Palus for a while. He let it be known that he considered the invitation the best proposal he had had in a long while.

As sometime passed, they began to adjust to the new normal that had come to be. The cold time was beginning to show itself, and through much diligence once again, enough sustenance had been accumulated to get them by for this season. Soon they would be enclosed by it, but before that time came upon them, they celebrated a couple of weddings.

Howling Wolf and Smiles A Lot, along with Son of Coyote and Lovely Butterfly, were celebrated in marriage by the Palus band.

Coyote felt honored to be marrying the daughter of Cloud Shadow, as well as finding her to be all he could want in a woman.

Butterfly soon decided that Coyote was the man she had been waiting for all this time, and so they became enamored with one another, to everyone's delight. Even the other braves whom she had rejected felt that they were a good match. In its course, a warming trend came around, as the circle of life would have it, with more out of the lodge activities for the Nimipu people.

Mountain Thunder was mostly absorbed with the vast herds of fine ponies that the Palus band owned. He and Howling Wolf were enjoying the soft and warm fragrant breezes that were filling their lighttimes while among the ponies in particular.

Little Wing had emerged from a long dark period with the death of her son. Yet the situation with her pregnancy could not be ignored, especially when the time came to give birth. It came at darktime when her pains grew intense, and then her water burst. Both Rain and Running Wild assisted her. When the time came that the child should enter the world, it delayed doing so. When the delay went on so long, it prompted Running Wild to seek out Shadow. She did not have to go far, for he was nearby, also worried at the delay. They all had much faith in the medicine of Cloud Shadow. Running Wild asked him to come and pray over the birthing.

It wasn't something that was known as any common occurrence among the people that the father would be involved with the delivery of the child. However, Shadow readily agreed.

When Running Wild and Shadow arrived in the lodge where Little Wing lay with her difficulties getting the better of her, Cloud Shadow knelt beside her, placing his strong hand on the top of her head. He began to pray. He prayed to the Life Giver for intervention to help the mother and child to achieve that which was needed. He hoped that it was his will that they lived to continue in what he might have intended for them.

From the time that Shadow knelt down, he blocked the light off from the fire that shone over the area of the birth canal. He was casting a shadow, and from within that shadow came forth a son. The scenario was not lost on Running Wild and Rain, for they both made gestures acknowledging the obvious event.

Before her full term had come, Little Wing had requested that if the child was a boy, he be named Panther. Shadow had no intention of denying her that, but after the boy was cut free from his mother's cord and placed in her arms, all of Cloud Shadow's wives unanimously agreed that he would be called A Shadow Too.

Along with the joy that came with the passing of the cold time, there was also a joy from the presence of this fine boy child helping to continue the legacy of Cloud Shadow, carrying his name in part as well.

When the conditions allowed, Coyote made the announcement that Butterfly and himself were going to be leaving for the Upper Red Fish band's village soon.

Butterfly was grateful to have still been among the Palus band for the birth of her new little brother, having made sure to get some time to hold him and speak to him of her happiness at his coming.

Everyone understood their leaving, although it was not without regret not to have them near any longer.

Cloud Shadow had some parting words for Coyote. "I have greatly cared for you since our first encounter. I also have much interest in your path in life. I will look forward to coming events with you. I am proud to have you as my son and knowing that my daughter has you for her man. Go with strength and all our good hopes for you to remain in the will of the Great Spirit for the coming times of our people."

The following early time, they left to make a new beginning for themselves and those that would come after.

Flower was the most affected by Butterfly's leaving, having felt solely responsible for her since the day she was born. Although she knew that it had just been the way she felt, not really the way of it, with many looking after her all along.

CHAPTER 58

MANY ARROWS LIVES ON

Not long after the departing of Coyote and Butterfly, the Palus band had another occurrence that came in the form of a lone visitor. No one took much notice with the approach of a single rider. It wasn't until he began to come closer that some started to take notice of his appearance. His buckskin dress was of the bleached white quality that had only been seen among the Absaroke people, although his pony, being mostly black, had a dapple of white about its rear. It raised the question of Appaloosa blood flowing in its veins. A stallion it was, with deep pride in its gait, but it did not outshine the one who sat astride him.

While he still sat upon his mount, some began to gather around. The rider's presence was brought to Shadow's attention, so that he, too, came to look at this stranger in their midst. Shortly after seeing him, he knew that this young man was indeed Absaroke. It amazed him and also caused him to grin a wide grin, which was returned by the young man. When the stranger smiled that smile, Shadow felt he was looking at his old friend Many Arrows all over again.

Then it was made known to all that this was the son of Many Arrows, Eagle Eyes. He was that same one who had presented Cloud Shadow with his father's precious bow when he had returned the boy's father's body to his people.

When that story came out, it had an emotional effect on all who had come to know Many Arrows within the band. Shadow's sons were particularly taken by this Absaroke among them. There first reaction was to befriend him and spend their time getting better acquainted. Cloud Shadow had to refrain himself from getting in the middle of their activities, being so intrigued by his arrival.

The feeling was mutual, in that the man Cloud Shadow had a profound importance to Eagle Eyes ever since he was old enough to comprehend the stories that were told concerning the friendship and respect that was given to him and his family. They were retelling the tales of his grandfather's encounter with Black Eagle, which also included the remembrance of Big Cat, bringing Mountain Thunder's immediate family into the discussion. It seemed to be fate that Howling Wolf, Mountain Thunder, and Eagle Eyes were to become so close in friendship. Cloud Shadow felt that Many Arrows looked on in gladness at the occurrence.

The young trio of recent development sat mounted on their ponies, peering at the massive waterfall known to Palus band as the people's falls. The volume of water crashing to the great depths below created a perpetual mist that could give some appreciated relief from the intense heat that was common in the area during this time of the seasons. It was also a sight that never grew old to those who lived within its proximity and for those who did not live near to it, it being an amazing thing. The fact that it was located on the Palus river, not being near as substantial as the Winding or Mother River, it could be thought to seem out of place. Nonetheless, it certainly was a great falls to behold.

Wolf and Thunder and Eagle Eyes pondered the significance of their fine view, as well as an adventure in the near term. Hearing recent telling of other's adventures caused them to desire more of their own, particularly now with them having this alliance, which was an encouraging advantage they felt.

While they were about the area, they saw riders draw near to the Palus encampment. They decided to investigate this new development. They arrived back in the village at the same time that Red Dreamer and a small party of Waptailmin arrived there.

There was a general excitement over the coming of their friends and neighbors. Eagle Eyes recalled his father speaking of these excellent people after it had been conveyed to him by Wolf who the newcomers were. Thunder was also interested, having no personal contact with the Waptailmin himself.

After the greetings they were accustomed to and a personal welcome from Cloud Shadow to his close friend, along with an invitation to enter his lodge for conversation, the other Waptailmin braves intermingled, having become close in association with these Nimipu.

"It does my heart good to see you again here," Shadow began. "Have you come to congratulate me on the birth of my new son?" he added.

"I am surprised to hear that, being I was not aware of this matter and that you are still up for such things. Although now that I have heard this good news, I am very happy for you upon knowing it," Dreamer responded.

They continued speaking on various matters. Shadow told of his meeting Son of Coyote and of his vision, along with him becoming Butterfly's husband. It ended with them both going to live with the band of the Upper Red Fish river. The Waptailmin medicine man found it all a very interesting tale.

Then Dreamer timely interjected with gravity. "There has been another development that I think you will also find interesting." Having said that, he reached into a pouch he had with him and pulled out a round metallic object and slipped it over his hand. There it stayed, encircling his wrist. "A bracelet, it is called," he stated while they both looked on it. "The object that you have, I was told, is called a button."

"A bracelet?" Shadow questioned what he had just heard, holding out his hand, beckoning for his friend to hand him the object for further examination. "A bracelet and a button?"

"That's the words the white men use for them. They are trading them to the people who live along the Big Water," he explained. "Some who live along the Mother River had traded for them with the Big Water people. Then some Waptailmin were able to obtain some through trade with the Mother River people, and now you see this one I have brought to you, having been made by these white men whom seem to be a part of our lives now," he added with a look of exasperation.

"It is a strange thing to look upon this white man ornament. I thank you for bringing it to show me. It causes me even more wonder concerning these times. I am not able to say anything else about it for now. I will come to visit you soon, Red Dreamer. Possibly, we will have some more understanding of what we ought to think on the matter," Shadow stated, handing the object back to his friend. "Now come and meet my new son, A Shadow Too."

"A Shadow Too, I think I really should meet this one who is being honored in such away," he responded.

After finding Little Wing and giving Dreamer the opportunity to see his son, Shadow went on to tell of the circumstances that led to him being given that name.

"I believe that it was meant to be, my friend. The Life Giver has once again worked a work for you and your family," Dreamer pronounced.

"Thank you for your good words. I am happy to speak of this thing with you, my friend," Shadow replied as they walked along beside one another, just enjoying being able to spend time together at this period of their lives.

Shadow had mentioned to Dreamer that he planned to come to visit him also in the not-too-distant time. Some of the Waptailmin braves were prodding Wolf and his companions to come to the land of their narrow river to venture and hunt with them, and they would host them to a time of bounty for their effort, they assured them.

So their visit ended with the standing invitation to come to their lands for a while. With warm farewells, they left for their homeland.

Wolf related the experiences that he had had not so long before to Mountain Thunder and Eagle Eyes with these Waptailmin people.

On another occasion, Shadow spoke with them as well concerning the long-standing friendship he had come to know among the Waptailmin.

They, as a committed group, began to make their plans to leave for Dreamer's camp not long hence.

Shadow was fascinated with A Shadow Too, enjoying just observing him as he gained a grasp of the emerging world around him. Little Wing was very much absorbed with the boy child. He was a joy to all that spent time with him.

Beside his routines around the village, Shadow did pray and meditate on the matter of the metallic object that Dreamer had shown him. The very idea that white men were trading with the coastal tribes was an astonishing concept. For so much of his existence now, he had never heard of these white men. Here, late in his life, they had become an ever-present part of it. That thought presented a feeling of an ominous outcome. He hoped that it would not be so.

Shadow's disturbing thoughts were interrupted by children's laughter. Looking around him, he had the pleasure to watch little Rainbow and Sweet Breeze playing chase with one another. It brought a smile to his face, which he was glad for. He thanked the Life Giver for the many blessings in his life and then went to ask his wives for a meal. He had a hunger that had sprung up, which resulted from a lifting of a heaviness he had been under for too long now.

CHAPTER 59

A Swan Song

The time came for the small party to go to meet their Waptailmin hosts as they had conveyed to them, yet not being all so long since their arrangements together.

While in their travels, Shadow began to tell about the time when he and Spotted Feather and Many Arrows came on this same trek. How he had been telling them of the greatness of the Mother River and his telling them of the giant fish with its bones on the outside, who lived in the great river. That they wanted to believe him but were having their doubts. Yet while they were here, they were able to see both.

Eagle Eyes was very glad he had made the arduous trip to these lands of the Nimipu, for it proved to be all he hoped it would. It caused him to feel like he was being able to experience more of his father, who had been removed from his life to soon.

Shadow went on to tell of the excellent hunting in the vicinity of Tahoma. At the mention of Tahoma, the conversation took a turn toward the spiritual side. There were questions asked and plenty of time and attention given for the answers. Shadow began to speak of the spiritual realm as he felt he understood it. He began by saying, "As long as we are air-breathing creatures, we will never fully understand it all, but we are given to understand a certain degree about such things. What I do believe, I know I have already spoken of to Raven and Wild Wind, is that the Great Spirit, as with everything, controls the spirit realm. We have spirits within each of us that we are born with. There are many other spirits in life as well, some for good and some for bad. Bad spirits try not to be subject to their creator and would mislead us if we let them and seek control whenever they can. Pray therefore to the Great Spirit to keep you in his wisdom and good intentions, and he will do so. Also, spirit guides are given to help you to follow the way you should go."

The young men believed they grasped the concepts that Shadow had been teaching them. They gave special attention to Eagle Eyes, with him not being fluent in their language. Although being very intelligent and being around a father who had come to understand the language of the Nimipu fairly well, he was getting it more each passing lighttime, and they were all well versed in sign talk.

When they came to the Mother River, Eagle Eyes had to express his sense of appreciation for its expanse, like none he had encountered. Now they had to get to the other side, crossing where there was almost no noticeable current.

Not long after, they came to the Narrow River of the Waptailmin, and their excitement grew to be among those fine people again. To Shadow, it was beginning to feel like a home away from home.

When they arrived at their village, the young men there took Wolf and Thunder and Eagle Eyes into their circle of interests, as they all began to work themselves into the height of anticipation for an adventure, hunting the nearby mountains.

Shadow and Dreamer, along with some other elders, gathered in the communal lodge of their tribe. They proceeded with the usual formalities and honors given to their guests. He discussed how the journey had been for them, along with other common matters, eventually coming to the topic of their deepest concerns—white men. One thing they all agreed on was that the white men possessed some knowledge that they did not, such as how to build giant winged canoes and the metallic objects that they traded. Both they could only marvel at. While they continued their discussion on these things, one of the elders there produced a string of blue beads. They were so alien to those who looked upon them. They were of a color not seen in their surroundings that they could be reproduced by them. They, like the buttons and bracelets, were another trade item of the whites.

Swan Song was Red Dreamer's youngest daughter. Having had no sons of his own, he placed a lot of devotion toward his daughters. His oldest daughter had since married, leaving only his youngest yet still with him. She had a strong sense about the man she was waiting for in her life and was very excited to see him come to her home. Or rather, her father's home.

That someone was Mountain Thunder, and as it often happened, he took notice of her as she was peering at him. He was taken with a genuine interest in her during that exchange of looks between them. There was also another who took notice of those engaging looks they shared—the young Waptailmin brave Strong Bow, who was determined to win Swan Song by any means necessary.

While the young braves played and contested between themselves, they also would interrupt their games to plan their hunt. Eagle Eyes was very much looking forward to the exploring of that region, having heard his father speak of it in his early memories.

Mountain Thunder was able to be around the lodge of Red Dreamer on occasion, which also allowed him more encounters with Swan Song. Before long, it was becoming evident to all who were present that there was developing a closeness between them, which was not lost on Strong Bow.

Eventually, the hunt was planned out, and the preparations were completed. Their departure was designated that early time. They left for their extended hunt. Shadow and Dreamer remained behind, leaving the rigors of the hunt to the younger men.

Howling Wolf, Mountain Thunder, Eagle Eyes, and Strong Bow, along with a number of other Waptailmin braves, took to the trail seeking adventure, yet with the essential purpose of securing meat for the peoples of their tribes.

All who followed the trail into the regions of these mountains were taken with the wondrous atmosphere that enveloped them there. Although none more so than Eagle Eyes, who, finding himself in this place of his imaginings since childhood, was thoroughly enchanted, which roused feelings of happiness and joy as well. The fineries of the Creator was all around, within the abundance of the glory of Earth Mother.

The usual tactics of the Waptailmin hunters—using the meadows for their benefits of a gathering place for the hooved animals to graze—was again in their plans for this particular effort.

*****

Shadow continued with Dreamer with their contemplations of these worrisome unending appearances of the Whiteman. Shadow again, after another period of silence, spoke. "There must be white women too."

Dreamer looked startled. His brows narrowed with the suggestion. "That is a thought that never occurred to me. They say that it is common for the white men to have hairy faces. I suppose that the white women could also have the hairy face," he ended with a questioning look. Shadow shrugged his shoulders and shook his head at such a suggestion.

"What about the white bird coming down from the light?" Dreamer inquired.

"I believe there is some relationship between the coming of the white bird and the white man. But just what that is, I do not know," Shadow replied.

*****

The party of hunters found a good location to hold up for the approaching darkness. After getting settled in for the darktime, as was their way, they had a storytelling session. Eagle Eyes enjoyed it when unexpectedly, there began a series of requests for him to contribute a story. Not wanting to make too much of it, he began a tale.

Wolf helped with translation when he felt it was needed, and sign talk was being used too.

"I would like to tell of a hunt I took part in while accompanying my father many cold times ago." The party of hunters were glad for this voice from another place. He continued, "I was quite young, and my father was anxious to teach me many things. It had been snowing a lot, and it was very deep throughout the land, and there had been a sighting of a small group of buffalo not far from our winter camp. We had been making use of our snowshoes that allowed us movement, for we had no other way. The snow was too deep for the ponies to travel in, and my father wanted me to experience a form of hunting that I yet had not seen."

The party was becoming curious now that he had set the scene.

He continued, "My father told me to come, for they were going to depart, having already prepared. Certain ones brought bow and arrows while others had spears. Everyone carried a substantial length of corded hide as well, of which I wondered at. After some time, we came to the location of the stranded buffalo in snow up to their shoulders. When we drew near, they began to panic, using their last efforts to leave from that place without any success. I was allowed to cast arrows at a cow, attempting to contribute to the kill, which I managed to do, while others put their spears to use. Then there was the long grueling procedure of butchering in the deep snow. Then using their hides to load the meat onto, to be laboriously pulled along with aid from the lengths of cord, till finally making it back to the village."

The listeners gave their various gestures of appreciation, having never heard of such a hunt as that. Some had questions concerning the snowshoes Eagle Eyes had referred to.

CHAPTER 60

An Affection Caused Danger

Shadow said his farewells to Dreamer and his family, as well as other Waptailmin elders he had come to know through his time among them. He promised to keep them in his thoughts and prayers. They likewise gave their sincere parting gestures, with hopes for a reunion in the not-too-distant time. The well-wishes between Shadow and Dreamer did not portray the uneasiness they both felt over the continuing encroachment of the white men. He left for home without concern for Howling Wolf's well-being, feeling confident that he was able to make his way now as well as any could.

*****

The hunters continued up the trail the following early time, with the understanding that by the time the sun was high above them, they would be in the area where they would begin their hunting.

Strong Bow had been steadily thinking on this development concerning the woman whom he desired, and up until just recently, he believed it was a plausible outcome. Now this visiting Nimipu came into their village, and all his plans had been put in doubt. So much so that he was seriously considering doing things that were unheard of to his knowledge, such as maiming or murdering this guest of the tribe. He had put a lot of thought into this dilemma, but he never spoke of it to his peers. Even so, there was one who watched him closely concerning this matter, who understood fully what a disappointment Swan Song's new interest had been to Strong Bow.

This individual was a brave who had come to have a close relationship with Howling Wolf since their outing to Pahpo and the Haven of the Tribes. He was a cousin to Swan Song called Far Jumper. He revealed to Wolf to keep a watch on Strong Bow, who was very jealous of Mountain Thunder over Swan Song.

Wolf tried not to be overly concerned. After all, disappointment was just part of life, and they all had their share of it. He would try to keep the information in reserve to be further considered, if needed.

When they arrived at the determined place, the party stopped to make their base camp there. It was already deemed an excellent place to hunt from through past experiences. The men were anxious to begin, being an inherent trait with them, the pursuit of the wary prey.

*****

The people of the Palus band were glad for the return of their medicine man. Shadow's immediate family was even more pleased, always feeling more secure with his presence there, along with an appreciation for his caring ways. Likewise, Shadow was relieved to be home. His age was causing him to be more inclined toward a softer existence when it was to be had. The travel had wearied him, with the intense thoughts concerning the white people being a burdensome weight on his mind. He was thankful for the shelter of his band and family. It felt like a refuge for him when he arrived. Running Wild, Rain, and Little Wing greeted him so warmly. His sons Raven and Wild Wind grasped his shoulders, along with their smiles for him, and A Shadow-Too pulled at his leggings as if to give him his greetings as well. Yes, it was good to be home.

He stooped down, picking up A Shadow Too from his place much nearer to the ground. "My son, you are growing like the tall grass grows. You are a joy for my tired eyes, to see you doing so well."

Cloud Shadow felt content, surrounded by the people of his own blood. Having his young boy as a part of his life at this stage seemed to be a witness of a sort to his own mortality like nothing else had been before. Even so, he appreciated him coming into his life in a very positive and fulfilling way.

*****

That late time in the hunters' camp, the quietness was broken with the howls of wolves. They stoked the fires more brightly and kept them burning bright throughout the darktime.

The hunters had hoped to find a grazing herd in the nearby meadow the following early time, but it had not happened. Now, instead, they agreed to make a sweeping hunt through a designated area in the vicinity. They teamed up into small groups to scour the land for game.

Howling Wolf, Mountain Thunder, and Eagle Eyes went on their own as a consorted effort. Strong Bow watched them as they slipped out of view.

Far Jumper, along with some of the other braves, made their final preparations to depart. They called to Strong Bow to come along.

"You go on. I will follow soon," he answered.

Far Jumper was concerned at his reply. He consoled himself with the knowledge that he had spoken to Wolf over his concerns and tried to focus his attention on the hunt that lied ahead.

Strong Bow had the idea that if he could eliminate Thunder by an arranged what appeared to be an accident, it would take care of the problem that had developed for him in regard to his love interests. He contemplated the possibility of finding him in a vulnerable place below him in this mountainous terrain, so that a large stone could be dislodged to fall upon his perceived foe and accomplish his desired ending.

He sprang from his standing position toward the higher ground in the direction that he had seen Mountain Thunder moving toward as well. He moved swiftly and stealthily across the difficult landscape.

Eagle Eyes began to wax poetic on their glorious surroundings and expressed his thankfulness for the opportunity to even be there at this time with such good friends.

"Be quite now," Wolf spoke. "It is time we began to spread out to stalk for prey." With a glancing look at the others, they all took heed and began to apply themselves to the task at hand.

Strong Bow had spotted Mountain Thunder below and ahead of where he peered out from in his concealment. He planned to follow as closely as possible and plot the place to create the fatal incident.

The trio had managed to take down a couple of deer and were getting ready to begin a swing around on a wide loop that would bring them back to the base camp. There was a loud crashing sound, causing them to quickly look up the embankment with a start, just at the moment that allowed them to move away from a series of large stones. One in particular was even larger than the rest. Immediately, they felt that they had just avoided serious injury or possible death.

Then, still being overwhelmed with this near disaster, came a shrill cry for help directly above them. It was frantic and unending. The trio hurried to its source, and there in a desperate fix was Strong Bow, hanging onto the thin branches of a bush while the full weight of his body dangled over the edge of a clift, and there was a long drop below him.

Strong Bow's eyes locked onto theirs, still pleading for assistance. Thunder advanced toward him, while Wolf and Eagle Eyes made a link of support by holding onto a small tree. Between them, they were able to draw him up from his precarious situation.

Right away, they questioned this series of events in their thoughts, but not saying anything out loud.

"I slipped and almost went over the side!" Strong Bow exclaimed.

Wolf noticed a branch on the ground that had the appearance of having been used for prying.

"Well, it is good for you that we were nearby to help you in your trouble," Mountain Thunder declared.

"Yes, that is a very good thing," Strong Bow agreed. "I don't know what I would have done without you."

"You probably would have died. You look well enough though. Let us return to meet up with the others," Wolf stated.

CHAPTER 61

A Tragic Ending

Once they had returned to the camp, the trio refrained from bringing up the suspicious circumstances they had witnessed recently. Without any input from them, a questioning of Strong Bow began.

"Where did you go to, Strong Bow? We expected your participation in the hunt but never knew of your whereabouts until now," inquired Far Jumper.

"I had a thought to hunt elsewhere on my own, so that is what I did. I am not a child that I cannot go and do as I please," Strong Bow retorted.

"Well, if you wanted to hunt by yourself, why did you come with us?" Far Jumper further questioned.

"I do not have to answer anyone here concerning what I want to do. Do not ask me anymore about this thing," he concluded.

All agreed to leave that topic for the time, although Far Jumper's concerns and suspicions were still left in an unsatisfactory state. After he had concluded his speaking with Strong Bow, he looked over at the trio with a look of interest. They, in turn, gave him a wondering look. He felt that they had some relevant information that they were withholding for discretion's sake.

Strong Bow wandered over to where he had erected a lean-to structure for his sleeping area. He had already determined that he would be leaving the party.

Wolf, Thunder, and Eagle Eyes had decided to keep their troubling story to themselves for the time being. The following early time, as it had been previously planned, there was an organized effort to have a point man at a designated meadow at the right time with hopes of finding a grazing herd of elk there. The other hunters were readied to supply the needed onslaught at the appropriate moment. All except Strong Bow, who, to everyone's surprise, informed them that he was not staying any longer but was returning to the village. He left the party there. They wondered curiously about him as he rode off.

As the scout was able to observe the meadow with the first opportunity that the lighting would allow, it revealed the herd was present. He went to give the news. Then they moved in to encircle the meadow.

Wolf, Thunder, and Eagle Eyes moved up closer for a good line of sight, looking for a target, when someone cast an arrow at the herd prematurely. Now there was nothing else for it but to begin their attempt at taking down as many of the startled beasts as possible. A rain of arrows broke forth, along with a stray bowshot that brought an arrow shattering on a tree that was between Wolf and Thunder.

Strong Bow had a bad feeling in regard to the times ahead. He felt certain his arrow missed Mountain Thunder and felt that he really had run out of chances to kill his rival. Now he was heading down from the high country, back to where they had come. His mind was reeling and was altogether distracted while he was directing his pony toward a loose footing area. Just as his thoughts were at the least attentive, the pony slid, stumbled, and then had quite an obvious breaking of a foreleg, causing it to collapse. When the pony collapsed, it fell on top of Strong Bow, pinning his leg under the pony's weight.

After a long period of struggle, he found he could not get free from his predicament. He began to cry out for help. He continued to cry out for a considerable time, to no avail.

The hunt in the meadow, despite an awkward beginning, ended well. The hunters had taken down many elk and were busy butchering their kill.

After spending several more lighttimes at their base camp in preparation, with all the meat butchered and bundled, along with all their other provisions packed up, the party left for home. They felt good at their success, giving thanks to the Life Giver for providing for them once again as they proceeded along in contentment.

They had been traveling for a good part of the lighttime when a shout went out, capturing everyone's attention. The party came to a halt, and they began to dismount. Within a short while, they were all standing near a site of an astonishing occurrence. There before them were the scant remains of a pony and a man, who were obviously the source of food for the habitant carnivore and scavenger.

It wasn't at all clear of the details of what had taken place. If it wasn't for the objects of bow and arrows and flint knife, they wouldn't have even known that this was the remains of Strong Bow and his pony.

The lighttime that he had made his final attempt at ending Thunder's life and had his fateful fall, he lay helpless after slitting his ponies throat to stop its relentless wriggling. He was trapped beneath it, so far up his thigh that he had no hope of getting lose. As he lay helpless, the end began to draw near. Whether they had wandered there by chance or were drawn by the smell of blood, the wolves drew closer as they determined what they had found.

This party of hunters could only wonder at the details that brought about his death. They collected the personal items that laid on the ground and collected the few skeletal remains to give to his family.

Their homecoming was bittersweet, having secured an abundance of fresh meat yet having to bear the burden of Strong Bow's demise.

Dreamer, along with the other elders of the tribe, were drawn into an investigation of the circumstances surrounding his death. Each question asked led to further inquiry, until eventually it became apparent that he had been bent on payment of harm or death toward Mountain Thunder, brought on by extreme jealously. This behavior in turn came back to him in a just repayment, bringing about his death by the worst of circumstances. It was a scenario that was so rare with those who had come to know of it that none could recall anything even remotely similar.

Mountain Thunder was somewhat torn emotionally over the events that had transpired of late. He tried to not be totally absorbed with these developments. Yet Swan Song would not let him be aloof on the matter, prying as to all that took place between himself and Strong Bow. Thunder wasn't very forthcoming in the beginning, but he soon found himself under the spell of someone with a stronger will than himself.

Swan Song was saddened at the account, but mostly she was glad for Mountain Thunder's safe return. She embraced him, placing her head on his chest and holding him close. He likewise placed his face against her head, smelling the freshness of her hair, which typified her manner. He also held her tightly to himself.

The trio had remained with the Waptailmin for a while upon their return to the village, long enough for their share of the elk meat to have been smoke dried for transport, as well as the marriage of Mountain Thunder and Swan Song.

"I am honored to have a member of the Wallowa band of the Nimipu as my new son and am happy for my youngest daughter to have this fine young brave to be her man," expounded Red Dreamer after the ceremonial joining of the couple and just before the marriage celebration began.

There was a festive mood within the village among the people of the Narrow River, with the daughter of one of their most renown given in marriage to a member of a beloved neighboring tribe.

Thunder had let Swan Song know that he wanted to return with Howling Wolf to the Palus band. He told her his closest family member, his sister, was living there as the wife of Howling Wolf and that he wanted them to meet and also have her be part of the newlywed couples rejoicing. Swan Song thought it sounded like a wonderful plan and was looking forward to it.

The following early time, they left. All were anxious for the travel. Swan Song hadn't been on a journey to that distant place and was pleased to be doing so. At the time of their leaving, it came with much emotion, as they departed for the land of the Palus.

It was fine weather for their trip, and on their arrival at the village, with their ponies loaded with dried meat and hides, it was a joyous reunion. It was even made more so with the news of Thunder's wedding to Dreamer's youngest daughter.

The meeting of Smiles A Lot and Swan Song was one of true appreciation. They embraced one another fondly and remained near each other for an extended time, relishing the time together.

A Shadow Too was a competition for the center of attention, seemingly being in the middle of every occasion. It was obvious to all who were there how Cloud Shadow doted on his young son. It was also apparent to everyone the happiness that took place between them.

Once again, the people of the Palus band began to settle in with the approaching of the cold time, making their usual preparations with an urgent flurry of activity that in time brought about the desired results, being the stores that would see them through till they were able to move about freely in more accommodating conditions.

CHAPTER 62

Kamiah, Sought After

Near dusk time, when Cloud Shadow was surrounded by his male family members, he spoke of a plan he had. "I would like to make a journey to the place of our origin and to stand before the heart of the monster once again. Raven and Wild Wind have been there in their time, but Howling Wolf and little A Shadow Too had not. I myself have been too long from the refreshing that comes from spending time there."

"I am glad to hear that from you at this time and look forward to making that trip to the place of such importance with you, Father," Wolf added with all sincerity.

At a later time, as Wolf and Thunder and Eagle Eyes were conversing, Thunder stated, "I am very interested in having the experience of that sacred place of our people and could enjoy going with you there."

Eagle Eyes interjected, saying, "I, too, will come with you and after will be leaving to return to my homeland. It is time to be going back to my family and country."

His statement took Wolf by surprise, although it made perfect sense. "I might want to make the trip to your country with you, my friend. I will pray and ponder such a thing while the time for our leaving draws closer."

"I also am liking the idea of such an adventure. It sounds like a fine time of seeing places and things that I have not yet had the opportunity to," Mountain Thunder expounded with the look of genuine intrigue on his face.

It was just the type of thing that young men sought after, and they were of no exception. The seed had been planted, and their interests were growing, surely to continue growing more as the time went by.

A Shadow Too had learned to talk as the cold time passed over the land, and talk he did. Now that he had been taught to walk and talk, there were times when some wished he would stay still and be quiet. Although, he was very much loved and so happily tolerated by all.

He had come to understand that he and his father, along with a group of other close companions, were to be leaving their camp there on the rivers of the Palus and Winding, to go away to visit a very special place. He was so excited, he could hardly contain himself, which caused him to be even more anxious than usual, which was becoming very anxious. Although he wasn't alone with that excitement, it was beginning to take hold of all the involved party.

The trio agreed on a plan to go to the homelands of Eagle Eyes and his tribe of the Absaroke. It had blossomed over the time of its conception to become a point of constant thought and anticipation. They were filled with the possibilities of so much to look forward to.

Even Shadow was getting caught up in the anxious anticipation, beginning to have similar feelings with the coming pilgrimage to Kamiah and those sacred surroundings. He was very much looking forward to sharing that experience with his sons, whom had not yet been there.

The time came that they were able to leave for their destinations. The wives and mothers had their concerns but kept them to themselves, knowing that this was the way of it for them. Not that they were disappointed with their lives. They felt that their lives were full and enjoyed. They appreciated them, more often than not.

Being mounted and packed, A Shadow Too started out riding double with his brother Wolf, prepared to move from rider to rider when the need arose.

"I'm ready. It's time for us to be going," A Shadow Too declared.

Cloud Shadow, along with Raven and Wind, had spent time with Howling Wolf and Mountain Thunder, speaking at length on the perils of the buffalo country.

Shadow concluded by saying, "I would never try to tell you not to go to that place. There are too many reasons that you should. Just don't forget that there are many enemies there. Keep in prayer for guidance, for you will need it."

Howling Wolf took to heart the instructions he received, as in all things he had been taught by his much-respected elders. Even though he had been plainly told of the dangers that inhabited that place, he still very much looked forward to experiencing it for himself, as did Mountain Thunder.

Everyone in the party was elated at the prospects of their travels.

A Shadow Too was having the time of his life, being on this trip with these men of such fascination who seemed to him must be the bravest and wisest of all.

Cloud Shadow talked to A Shadow Too often of these wonderful lands that the Great Spirit had provided the Nimipu with. That it was the best land for his favorite people and should be fully appreciated by them for all time.

He was easily able to believe what his father told him just by taking observation of his surroundings. It certainly seemed to his young mind that its greatness was understood at every turn in the trail or vista they came to.

Once they reached the Kooskia River, they began to follow the trail that hugged the canyon walls that were prevalent along this course.

They stayed over during the dark times where they pleased, enjoying their journey as a close-knit group, with all things in common. Also, with the knowledge of Eagle Eyes leaving the lands of the Nimipu, possibly never to come this way again. He had become part of the family from the beginning of his arrival among them, only to be reinforced with each passing lighttime. Now his parting was drawing near, along with the uncertainty of the outcome of Wolf and Thunder's venture into the lands of which Talon had lost his life, as well as Little Bear, Many Arrows, and many others who Cloud Shadow was deeply attached.

"Father, after we go to the place of our origin, I want to go with Eagle Eyes also to see his country. I think that would be best, so I would know that everything went well with them," A Shadow Too announced.

"That would be something that a young brave would want to do. I understand your thinking, my son, for I also have those same feelings. Although you will have to wait your turn. I, being your father, know that this is not the time for you to make that journey," Shadow responded.

"Well, you know best, my father. I trust in your wisdom. I will wait to hear of their tale on their return," A Shadow Too replied with all gravity. The others exchanged glances at one another, being impressed with the little one's audacity.

In their time, they came into the vicinity of Kamiah, the sacred place they sought. Cloud Shadow planned on staying with the Kooskia band while they were there, but he intended to go to the sacred grounds first of all.

When they approached the location of the petrified heart of the monster, as always, for Cloud Shadow, he felt a surge of power within himself, amounting to a renewing of sorts for him. Wolf and Thunder, who had not yet spent time at this, their place of beginnings, were moved inwardly with a swelling of pride and importance. A Shadow Too, who harbored strong anxiousness for this experience, being yet so young, also received a gift of exhilaration at his coming into the sphere of power and influence. So much so that the others in the party could not but help notice that there was a profound change of countenance come over the boy as he stood in the presence of the large heart stone.

No one spoke for an extended period, captured by the eventful encounter with their past and present, all except Eagle Eyes, who was staying at some distance, waiting on his friends.

After a while, the party reunited to continue to the Kooskia band's village for a visit there.

Although Yellow Jacket no longer lived, Cloud Shadow and company were warmly welcomed and honored among their fellow tribe members who had come to revere Cloud Shadow for his wisdom and medicine, as did all the Nimipu within their lands.

When the time came that the trio was to depart on their trip to the lands of the Salish, Siksika, and Absaroke, as well as many other tribes, Cloud Shadow earnestly beseeched them to go by and visit his friend Spotted Feather, knowing it would be out of their way.

Eagle Eyes assured him himself that he would be honored to visit this venerable friend on behalf of Cloud Shadow as well as Many Arrows.

Again, the emotional parting, and then they were off on their venture to those places of many prospects.

Chapter 63

The Trio Becomes a Foursome

Wolf was thinking back to what his father had requested of them before they departed from the Kooskia band. Now that he and Thunder and Eagle Eyes had come into the buffalo country, they would go to pay a visit to Spotted Feather, to bring word from Cloud Shadow and pay their respects.

Their trip thus far had certainly been memorable. The journey up the old buffalo hunt pass was inspiring, filling him with awe for its beauty and an even deeper appreciation of Earth Mother. It was an arduous trek but at the same time exhilarating. He reflected also to their joint experience at the sacred place, which was uplifting to him. All things considered, he was in good spirits concerning the events of their venture and was looking forward to what lay ahead.

He had heard many stories about this place and had imagined it many ways, but in his own eyes, it was different yet.

"This area where we are headed my father spoke of often, but I have not gone there myself," Eagle Eyes made mention. "It is where mine and your father killed the bear that attacked and killed your father's childhood friend, Little Bear. It also is where they first met Spotted Feather, whom I have never had the privilege to meet. It is good that we have come here together, my friends, to hopefully be able to meet this good man."

"I am glad also that we are able to come here together. It seems that it is right that we are to meet these friends of our fathers," Wolf replied with an air of satisfaction.

They came into the lands of the Salish people, of whom Spotted Feather was a prominent figure of much esteem. They also were well acquainted with the legend of Cloud Shadow and had a respect for the memory of Many Arrows. The trio soon found themselves being escorted toward the village. The Appaloosa ponies they rode immediately gave them passage without reservations.

They were pleased to find that Spotted Feather still lived. Shadow had told the story of the grievous wound his friend had received in the battle with the Kenistenoag. Although Shadow had visited with him on their return from recovering Wild Wind, he was still concerned at the toll it might have taken on his longevity.

Spotted Feather, having received an account of the approaching visitors, made himself available to greet them. Beside Spotted Feather stood his son, whom had been born to him at a time when he had come to believe that he would have no more children.

Tall Calm One was younger than Wolf but was mature for his number of winters.

When the visiting party presented themselves before Spotted Feather and his son, they were invited to dismount and enter his lodge for refreshment and rest.

Spotted Feather was not given to any foolishness at this time in his life but could not help being taken with a silly glee since his first good look at Howling Wolf and Eagle Eyes. It seemed as though he was looking at Cloud Shadow and Many Arrows from their youth.

They all spent a pleasant time going over many things. Spotted Feather was happy to hear Shadow was well and had a new son. Also that he had sent a special greeting along with Howling Wolf.

Tall Calm One was very much enjoying this unexpected company of young adventurers that were connected to his family and tribe through past relationships.

The trio remained at the Salish village for several lighttimes. While they visited, they made their plans for their departing and spoke of it on occasion. Tall Calm One stayed close with the visitors, creating a fast friendship as well.

"I would very much like to continue with you on your travel to see the lands of the Absaroke and spend more time with you," he made known while they sat together in his father's lodge.

It came as somewhat of a surprise to Spotted Feather initially, but he soon recovered from it when he put himself in his son's place. It was exactly what he would have wanted to do.

*****

In the meantime, Cloud Shadow and his young son had spent a number of lighttimes among the Kooskia band, also spending additional time at the site of the battle between Coyote and the monster, where the monster's heart still stood as the reminder of Coyote's victory there.

A Shadow Too was ecstatic with their trek to the place of their origin and coming to know some of their tribe members from another band other than their own. Since their return home, he began to feel as an experienced traveler now, with knowledge of importance to his credits.

He immediately began to act on his new source of confidence, being emboldened to increase his field of exploration. No one was surprised at that, for it was common with his family. His wanderings kept him away more from the village with each passing lighttime.

With this change in his behavior, he also grew in physical stature. So much so that Cloud Shadow went out to his herd and picked him out a placid gelding. After bringing it back into camp, he located A Shadow Too to present it to him.

"Now that you are an experienced traveler, it is time you had a pony to take you to all the places you will need to go," his father told him.

"Thank you, Father. You are right about it being time for me to have a pony. I have need of one right away," A Shadow Too responded.

"Well then, we shouldn't spend any more time. I will give you some instruction so that you can be on your way," his father let him know.

Cloud Shadow helped his son onto the pony's back, and they rode about the camp area for some time.

From that time forward, A Shadow Too mounted the gelding on his own by pulling and climbing his way up.

He was soon seen riding about with some other boys, enjoying this newly found freedom.

*****

Spotted Feather spoke to his guests before their departing. "It has been a pleasant honor to have you here, and also seeming good and right that you have come. Give our sincere hopes for peace and happiness to your families from our people. I will pray for a fine trip on your journey," he ended with a parting hug and pat on the shoulder for his dear son on his leaving from him.

As it always was for venturers, it was good to be back on the trail. It was the same with these young men as they left for the Absaroka territory.

It was a fine time to be traveling with the weather being as nice as any could hope for. There had been a splendid sunrise, which seemed a greeting from the trail, beckoning them on.

Tall Calm One was elated at the prospects that lay before them. They had already talked of going to the land of smoking water, which had long been a tale of their rearing since they could recall. Although Eagle Eyes knew of the place by personal experience and had invited them to see it for themselves.

Along their travels, they came across a small herd of buffalo. It was the first buffalo Wolf and Thunder had ever seen. They had been around their hides and robes all their lives, but on the hoof, this was their only encounter thus far.

"We must spend some time for Thunder and I to take down some buffalo. We have never had the chance in our young lives to do so before now," Howling Wolf spoke as he studied the herd in the foreground.

"My father told of the Nimipu having no buffalo in their land. It was hard to understand that it could be so, but hearing what you say, it is as we were told," Tall Calm One responded to Wolf's request.

"If you kill several buffalo, we must butcher them all and take as much as we can carry with us. I think you should take one each only," Eagle Eyes plainly explained.

It made good sense that they should not kill more than they could use, so they agreed to the terms their host suggested.

They were both experienced hunters, but this was definitely different for them. They had never approached such large dangerous animals on horseback and run with one while looking for an opportunity to cast an arrow into a spot that would bring it down.

Eagle Eyes and Tall Calm One traded ponies with them with the understanding that their ponies were trained to react to the dodging and darting of the fleeing buffalo as they were being pursued.

"I hope the best for you, my friends. It is a skill that improves with each attempt, but you have a good chance of success, being excellent horseman and archers," Eagle Eyes encouraged them with praise of a truth he well knew.

CHAPTER 64

CLOUD SHADOW'S MUSINGS

Howling Wolf felt confident that he and his close companion, who had become like a brother to him, would succeed. Mountain Thunder also exuded an air of competency as they set out on this test of abilities. They were not only confident but also happy to be given this opportunity. Since childhood, this was considered a defining event to achieving the complete hunter's status.

Now here they were, at that place and time where they could achieve that status for their lives.

They separated, while coming nearer to the grazing animals before their pursuit began, hoping and trying not to spook them to soon, as well as giving one another plenty of space to operate.

The ponies began to show signs of anxiousness, for they well understood what was about to take place.

Thunder's mount broke toward the herd as he had given it free rein to do so,

When Wolf saw the action begin, he gave his mount a prodding heel, bursting forth into the commotion that instantly ensued.

That stimulating fun Wolf felt come over him to a point where he began to holler, "Ai-ye, ai-ye!" over and over. He knew that once he unleashed his arrows, it would soon come to an end, so he tried to enjoy the chase as it unfolded.

Thunder thought he could hear Wolf hollering with joy and also let loose with his own shouts of glee, feeling that same thrilling sensation.

Not long after, they chose themselves a target, which the ponies readily gave them access to. Howling Wolf cast an arrow, and the cow fell with the one lethal missile. Mountain Thunder's young bull took several, but it was to his credit that he stayed with it and was able to place all of his arrows into the same animal, bringing it down in its final attempt of defiance.

After the rest of the herd had scattered and there was only Wolf and Thunder mounted on the ponies, with their prey lying there dead, Eagle Eyes and Tall Calm One approached with the pack animals.

"I felt like I was watching a lesson being given on how to take down a fleeing buffalo as I looked on at your hunting efforts!" Eagle Eyes exclaimed.

"I have never seen it done better," Tall Calm One reinforced the statement as they drew closer.

"It was a fine experience!" Wolf exclaimed in return to his friend's kind words.

"This was a very good time," Thunder responded with a contagious look of excitement.

Howling Wolf gave an audible thanks to the Life Giver for providing these buffalo. In unison, the others gave their thanks as well.

*****

A Shadow Too sat on his pony, staring into the Palus River falls pouring down its precipice. It made for a mesmerizing sight. His friend Weasel shouted at him through the roar, "Come on, Stalking Shadow! Let's go see what our mothers have cooked up at home."

The name Stalking Shadow had been attached to him by his friends, and he had excepted it.

When he arrived back at the village, he found Raven, Leaping Buck, Wind, and Cloud Shadow conversing on various things, one being the subject of Wolf and Mountain Thunder and as to how things might be progressing for them.

Stalking Shadow never wondered how his brother was doing. He felt he knew that he was in control of his environment, whatever it was. He did, however, envy him, being on such an adventure. Also, he was determined that he would have such experiences of his own when it was the right time.

*****

Eagle Eyes led them right to the Absaroke encampment. Even though there were several locations where they might have been, his initial guess turned out to be correct.

As usual, the encampment made for an impressive sight, with the stark white hides covering their tipis, presenting themselves with eloquence. Their large horse herds spread out along the lush green grasslands, beside a beautiful meandering creek that was shrouded with fine leafy trees.

The Absaroke braves gathered to meet the approaching riders, being curious as to just who they consisted of. They recognized Eagle Eyes right away, yet with inquiring minds, they wanted to know the particulars concerning his companions.

Eagle Eyes stated with authority, "These are my close friends whose families have been friends of this village since the times of our grandfathers. We should treat them honorably, with all respect."

These words were repeated throughout the tribe and accepted as good reason to be hospitable to the visitors.

As they were shown the location of Eagle Eyes's family's lodges, they dismounted there to be well received by his brothers and sisters and their children. All were very happy at his return, as well as some young women who had been pining for him in his absence.

This leg of their travels had come to a conclusion. They were able to enjoy the benefits of the Absaroke village. It included Eagle Eyes's sisters being practiced at the arts of accommodations toward the men of their favor, these recent visitors being among them.

They went to much effort to see to their comforts, lounging on an array of fine pelts and feasting on a variety of meats prepared in imaginative ways.

One of his younger sisters took an amorous interest in Tall Calm One, providing him with some experiences that he had not yet known before this time.

Sunshine, she was called, did not have much experience in these things either but had been taught by others that they were skills she needed to possess as an Absaroke woman. Tall Calm One found he was in full agreement.

Not long after their arrival there, it was brought to their attention that there had been a trespass on their village amounting to the theft of a number of their ponies. Shortly thereafter, a group of braves gathered to pursue the perpetrators. At hearing of these things, Eagle Eyes and his companions chose to join in.

It was found within a short time that the thieves had left in the direction of the smoking waters, being the direction that had been considered by the venturers as their next destination before the theft had occurred.

They moved at a rapid pace in their efforts to overtake them. The Absaroke themselves had done the same to other tribes, but they still were not willing to concede the loss without an attempt to regain these ponies.

Tall Calm One, Howling Wolf, and Mountain Thunder were enjoying the chase. It was exhilarating, rushing headlong into a new and wonderful landscape.

*****

Cloud Shadow looked out over the Palus encampment from where he stood, reminiscing over his life as he also watched his young son run off with some other boys for a time together of activities that the location offered them. He could place himself and Little Bear in that same scenario all so many winters ago. From that thought, he began to trace all the other evens of his life, stemming from his childhood. He didn't stop to focus on any particular time and was able to summarize it up to the present, now being known among his people as a respected medicine man. He spoke out audibly to no visible entity, "I thank you, Great Spirit, for your goodness to me and my family."

He then thought to himself, not for the first time, surely no white man could change this life that we have lived for so long. It always seemed to catch him off guard that he even had such a thought to ponder and how it could distract him from that which appeared to be the obvious. The familiar livelihood that he looked upon before him.

*****

After some time in pursuit, they came upon what apparently was a past campsite of those who had stolen from them. They held up there for a short while, surveying the evidence that could be found.

Eagle Eyes conferred there with some of his peers. When he broke from the discerning party, he spoke to his visiting friends. "Utes, it is the sign we see here where they stayed. They will continue in this direction, as they seek to return to their country that borders the land of the thorn plants," he explained.

They again left in pursuit. As they continued watching their tracks, they felt that they were gaining on the distance that lay between them.

When they arrived at a place where they believed they would be able to overtake them, they held up with the coming darkness.

Chapter 65

Ominous News

"When the lighttime comes to us again, we will soon be in the land of smoking water. You will see and smell a land like none you have ever known," Eagle Eyes assured his friends.

"We are very much wanting to come into those lands, having been told of such a place since our childhood," Wolf spoke while peering off in the direction they were headed to.

Mountain Thunder and Tall Calm One gave agreeing gestures with tones of awe inspired imaginings.

At first light, they continued their chase of these bold invaders. As they had surmised previously, before long, they came on a view of their ponies being driven by the Utes who had stolen them.

They planned to stay back far enough to maintain an advantage for surprise.

The Absaroke braves didn't pay any special attention to this strange landscape they were passing through, but for the visitors, they were seeing sights that were altogether unique to them.

As they went on, they looked as the smoke rose from the bubbling multicolored rings of mud and water. They also could not help but notice the pungent stench coming off the pools, like nothing they ever witnessed before now.

*****

Raven entered Cloud Shadow's lodge with a sense of urgency. "Father," he blurted out. "I have just arrived from meeting up with members of the Kooskia band on the Winding River and they had a strange tale: that white men traveling with a Shoshone woman and a black man have come to their village by way of the land of the rising sun and are staying there at their village. They say they are on their way to the Big Water. That they were starving when they arrived and are trying to become strong again and to make dugout canoes to travel the rivers with. They say that they may pass through this area along the Winding River sometime soon."

"Tell me again what they said," Shadow responded, not believing what his ears had just heard. Raven went on to repeat this news of shocking content.

Cloud Shadow asked that Wind be brought to his lodge so that they could further discuss this matter within the family. When he arrived, they talked at length concerning the possibility of such a thing, it being so hard to accept as fact. After some time of back-and-forth uncertainties, Shadow finally, with a look of utmost seriousness, spoke to his oldest sons. "I want you to keep a close watch for these mysterious travelers, that you might see them if they come this way."

They promised him they would.

*****

Through their covert observations, the Absaroke were able to determine that it was a rather small group driving their stolen ponies. They purposed to get in a position where they would be able to swoop in among them and take control over the ponies and get them heading back to the grassy hills of Absaroka. They plotted the place to make their bold move.

*****

Stalking Shadow began to develop a curiosity concerning this talk of white men that was heard about more and more during these times.

"Father, I would like to know more of these white men that are being spoke of," he inquired of Cloud Shadow.

"Yes, my son, it is time that you should be told this story that you ask of me," Shadow began.

After hearing his father tell of all that he knew of the matter, he responded with, "It is a strange thing to hear, not seeming at all to be part of our lives in these lands we inherited from our ancestors."

"We all feel the same when we think on this matter of such unfamiliar beginnings," Cloud Shadow replied, staring into deep thought.

"I will also watch for their coming, Father. I am very interested to see such ones as these," he concluded.

The Palus band had been camped next to the Winding River when the news of these approaching white men came to them. After hearing this, they moved the encampment farther up the Palus River. They were uncomfortable with the thought of them possibly entering their village.

*****

The Absaroke were in position as the stolen ponies and their captors approached the chosen location for surprise and interception. The Ute braves were not being cautious, feeling that they had gotten clear of being overtaken.

Eagle Eyes and the others broke from their concealment, hollering and waving to turn the small herd. When the Utes caught sight of them, they fled and were able to get away from any quick retribution.

It was at that moment that Howling Wolf caught his first glimpse of the Knife Edge mountains. It so distracted him that he almost lost his ability to help to turn the ponies at the necessary time. He told himself that he would return sometime to be able to experience those mountains more intimately.

Some of the braves wanted to continue after the Utes, but it was decided to push for home, having been gone too long on such an abrupt departure.

The Utes, however, had a different feeling about this undoing of their efforts. They wanted someone to pay a price for their trouble. They decided to follow the Absaroke, seeking to spill some blood.

There was an air of accomplishment among the Absaroke and their guests. They were in a celebratory mood, making them a bit off guard.

Howling Wolf was in thought of their venture, home, and his family when he began to feel a strong longing to be back among his own people and lands again and he was missing his woman as well.

He had just, at that point, decided to make preparations to return very soon. It was just before he felt a terrible pain at the base of his neck, and then all was black and silent for him.

*****

Raven, Wild Wind, and Stalking Shadow were on a high plateau overlooking the Winding River. There was a strong breeze blowing, which was typical there, as they peered over the stretch of river below them. At first, they couldn't tell what it was that had gotten their attention, but something different had appeared on the river, that much was obvious to them.

"I think we are seeing canoes. Let us get closer, my brothers," Raven spoke, with all of their eyes fixed on the development before them.

They made their way to get near the river. They managed to be in position to have a clear view of the procession of dugouts as they passed by. One of the white men, having red hair, raised an arm in salutation to them as they went by.

The sons of Cloud Shadow could only watch transfixed, too stunned to respond in any manner. This parade eventually traveled out of their sight.

For the first time since Wolf's departure, Cloud Shadow believed that he had a premonition that his venturing son was in some type of trouble. Feeling at a loss as to what he could do about it, he began to pray.

He gave himself over to an extended time in some of the most heartfelt beseeching on behalf of his son that he even knew that he was capable of. He then felt a sense of relief and gratification sweep over him, quite convinced of an intervening by the Life Giver.

*****

Howling Wolf could hear a woman weeping in his dream. He also became aware of an annoying bright light. Then he opened his eyes, staring up from a travois, seeing the face of a sister of Eagle Eyes standing near to him with tears in her eyes.

*****

Cloud Shadow stepped from his lodge at the sound of running ponies to see his sons galloping up then coming to a short stop in front of where he stood.

"Father," Raven spoke in a loud voice. "The white men, we saw them."

This was another hard thing to bear for Cloud Shadow. Ever since he had first heard it spoken of, he had had a difficult time accepting it. Now, here once again, his mind stumbled over these words as well.

"You saw white men? Come closer and speak to me clearly of this sighting, my son," he asked of Raven with a troubled look on his face.

"Wind and A Shadow Too saw them also, Father," he blurted out as he motioned to his brothers to come and reinforce his words.

They sat conversing for quite a while on what they had witnessed and what they felt it would mean for the coming time. After they concluded with that session of the discussion, their father stated,

"I will seek out more information on this movement of these white men through our lands from the Kooskia band."

*****

Wolf began to have some recollection of the previous events leading up to his fall. "Were we attacked?" he inquired of Eagle Eyes, who sat near to him as he lay unmoving on the ground inside the tipi lodge.

"Yes, my friend. They trailed us, waiting for an opportunity to retaliate. You were struck by a glancing blow from an arrow that caused you much harm. We chased after the Utes and managed to kill one. The others got away," Eagle Eyes informed him.

*****

Cloud Shadow, accompanied by Stalking Shadow, left for Waptailmin village to counsel with their friend Red Dreamer and to ask if his people had also seen the mysterious travelers.

*****

Several lighttimes had passed, and Wolf still could not move his head or limbs. "I would like for you to take me to the place where I could bathe in the smoking water that smells," he said to his friends that were nearby.

CHAPTER 66

WOLF ON THE MEND

Mountain Thunder replied, "That sounds like a strange thing that you ask. Is there a reason you would want to do that?"

"Yes. Each time I seek guidance for my healing, I receive memories of those smoking waters. I've come to believe that it is the sign that I need to follow after, if you will help me to do so," Wolf explained.

"Well, I for one am not wanting to doubt what you say is so, and I have no ideas of my own. I will help you get to the place where you can bathe in that water," Eagle Eyes stated.

"We all will help. We very much want you to recover. It's worth trying, so just say when you want to go," Tall Calm One added, having a look of grave concern behind his words.

The others nodded in agreement, causing Howling Wolf to say, "I would like to leave out at the next sunrise, my good friends. Thank you for being so willing to do this for me."

*****

When Cloud Shadow and Stalking Shadow arrived at the Waptailmin village, they were welcomed warmly. Red Dreamer showed them into his lodge to converse, which they had done so many times before, being considered a high honor between them.

They began with their usual polite casual discussions, all leading up to an opening for Cloud Shadow to state, "I recently received word of a disturbing occurrence coming to me by way of the Kooskia band."

Dreamer shifted his body somewhat, as if in preparation for what he was about to hear.

Shadow continued by telling of white men arriving at the encampment of the Kooskia band and what all they knew of taking place there. Then he told of his sons' encounter with that party on the Winding River. He then asked, "Have you heard of this mysterious group being spotted on the Mother River?"

"Yes, my good friend. I felt certain that you had come to speak of this thing. My people did have sightings of these white men. They are in our country, we know now. The time has come of which we have been waiting to know. It is here. What are your ideas on what we should do that might be a help to our people concerning this matter?" Dreamer calmly reacted.

Cloud Shadow picked up his friend's sentiments, understanding that they are here, with fears being realized, it being another situation to face up to.

"You know me well, my friend. I have also come to ask you to come with me to visit with our tribe members, the Kooskia band, that we might obtain more understanding of these white men who stayed there among them," Cloud Shadow confided to his friend, who he considered to be his solid ally in this matter.

"I am glad that you have come for me to go with you, to hear it told by your tribe members. Let us go and receive this story from those who have sat with these strangers," Dreamer responded to his friend's invitation.

*****

In the lands of the Absaroke, the small group of friends left for the place of the smoking water that smells. They all began to share in the belief that bathing in those waters could help Howling Wolf recover.

*****

Stalking Shadow had asked to be included in the visit to the Kooskia band. So he was with them when they arrived there and were greeted by the elders.

Red Dreamer was no stranger to them, and they had met A Shadow Too the last time Cloud Shadow came to visit.

*****

They lowered Howling Wolf into the smoking water while he was still upon the travois he had been on since his injury. The place they had come to had many such pools. They then went about meticulously checking them for suitability in regard to access and temperature. Many were obviously not usable. Finally, they narrowed it down to one that best met their need, and there he was placed for a time.

After spending awhile in the water, feeling that he had had enough, he asked that they bring him out for a time to adjust. He couldn't tell that he felt any different from before he had spent the session in the hot sulfurous bath. He would continue with it for a while yet before he would concede to his paralysis.

*****

When the formalities had been covered, Cloud Shadow put the subject that they most wanted to discuss to the forefront. "We very much desire to hear you tell the story of the party of white men coming to your village."

Chief Twisted Hair sat among them and began to speak of their encounter. "I could hardly believe my eyes when I first saw them," he stated. "There was a man like us who they had speak sign talk to us. There also was a Shoshone woman with a small child who was skilled at sign talk. That is how we communicated. We talk about white men, and yes, there were a number of them. There were a couple who made their decisions for the party. Lewis and Clark, they were called. Also, there was a huge black man. He was maybe the most startling of them all."

After these words, Shadow and Dreamer shook their heads in near disbelief.

"For all the surprise and initial mistrust that their appearing caused, they were mostly good and polite, and we agreed to care for their ponies for them to use again on their return," Twisted Hair concluded.

"Their coming back here?" Cloud Shadow blurted out with his voice full of bewilderment.

"Yes, that is their plan. It was made clear by them," the chief answered in response.

*****

Howling Wolf surprised his friends when, after a few sessions in the hot springs, he sat up and moved his arms, and then his hands and fingers. Then he moved his head side to side.

"Look!" exclaimed Mountain Thunder. "It is working."

It wasn't long after that Wolf was on his feet and walking about and thanking the Great Spirit for his healing.

"It is time I returned home. I will be leaving very soon. Let us be on our way. I have kept all of you from tending to your own affairs for too long now."

Everyone was elated to see Howling Wolf and Mountain Thunder come riding back into the Palus encampment on that memorable lighttime, having just made it through the pass before it was closed in by heavy snows.

Not long after Wolf's return, the cold time began to set in. Cloud Shadow's family had a pleasant distraction to keep their attention actively engaged, with the tales that Wolf and Thunder had to share with them.

They told of their visitations with Spotted Feather. Their time spent with his son, Tall Calm One, and visiting in the Absaroke village. Venturing into the land of the smoking waters and the perils that they encountered there.

On occasion, Wolf would reflect to his farewells to his friends Tall Calm One and Eagle Eyes, it being emotional then as it still was even now.

He would visualize seeing Tall Calm One standing with his arm around Eagle Eyes's sister, Sunshine, looking like he had no intention of letting her go. It brought a smile to his face. As did looking at his wife, Smiles A Lot, looking like she would give birth to a baby at any time. It was good to be back home.

When the warming came once more to the Palus, Cloud Shadow caught the attention of A Shadow Too as he was passing by with his friend Weasel. "Come and speak with me, my son. I have a request of you."

Stalking Shadow immediately came over to where his father stood. "Yes, Father?" he inquired.

"I would have you go to the Upper Red Fish band's encampment to speak with Coyote and your sister to find how it is with them," he stated.

"Yes, Father. I would very much like to do that for you, as well as for myself," he responded.

"Good. Find yourself a companion to share your experiences," Cloud Shadow suggested, seeing Weasel standing nearby with a curious aura radiating from him.

It was not long from the time that his father had made the request of him that Stalking Shadow and Weasel left on their venture. Both were riding fine ponies that were gifted to them by Cloud Shadow as a gesture of appreciation for their undertaking, along with pack ponies to meet the need for additional provisions.

CHAPTER 67

A White Bird for the Time

Stalking Shadow and Weasel were thrilled to be on the trail together, with so much possibility before them. It was their time now to go with the wind, to travel the lands all about them.

"I am so glad that your father had this idea for us," Weasel proclaimed.

"Yes, I feel that it is very good to be able to do this at this time for us. I needed to get outside of the Palus territory again. I feel it is what I am about, to go and see new things and places. This is just what I wanted, and it was given to me. It is a fine feeling to be able to move about such a beautiful land that we are in. I have never been to the place we are going, but I was given good direction to get us there, so let us enjoy every moment of this adventure," Stalking Shadow responded to his friend's disclosure of his feelings.

With that, they proceeded to take in all they could as open individuals to all that was before them.

The trip was not without its difficulties, but through determination, they overcame them, and eventually, they came within proximity of the village they sought.

As they drew closer, they were met by braves on horseback making certain of who it was that approached their camp.

When it was determined that friends had come to visit, they were given the hospitality of a peaceful people toward guests.

After Stalking Shadow made it known whom he was related to and that he hoped to find his sister here and well, they directed him to where Son of Coyote and Lovely Butterfly had their tipi lodge. There the duo found Butterfly with a young girl working at tanning hides.

She had not seen her brother since he was a toddler but could not fail to recognize a son of Cloud Shadow. "My brother, A Shadow Too, is that you that I see?" she inquired.

"Yes, my sister. It is I and my friend Weasel here to visit with you and your husband. Our father sends his love and prayers with us and desires to know how it is with you," Stalking Shadow replied.

Coyote had gone to Kamiah. He had uttered something about a return of the monster, although he did not seem to be clear on his own understanding of what he was speaking of.

It was at this time that the white men had returned to the Kooskia band's encampment, only to once again disappear into the mountains from where they had come.

"Come and meet my family," Butterfly beckoned to her brother. "This is Moonlight. At the time of her birth, even though it was at night, it was so bright out because of the large full moon. It was almost like lighttime." The young girl there before him seemed to be not much younger than himself.

He greeted her, introducing himself as her uncle. She acted pleased at making his acquaintance yet being too shy to respond.

Butterfly left him standing there as she went inside the lodge, saying, "There is someone else I want you to meet." When she came back out, she held a small infant boy in her arms. "This is your nephew, White Bird. White Bird, meet your uncle, A Shadow Too," she announced with a big smile, handing the baby to Stalking Shadow. "Coyote says the name is big medicine," she added.

Stalking Shadow walked around the area for a while with the boy in his arms. "Well, my nephew, we will be looking to you in the coming time to lead us in this age of the encroaching white men. Great Spirit, I pray for my nephew to receive the mind of a wise leader. That he will stand as a testimony of our people. We are

Nimipu, and we will not be forgotten in the fight for our place in this life."

The child seemed to understand the significance of those words that were spoken by his uncle as he smiled with a look of liveliness and intellect.

"This one will be one to be looked up to for all our time, I am certain," Stalking Shadow stated as he handed the child back to his mother.

Cunning Fox came to meet Stalking Shadow while he was there, having heard of him but yet not having met him. They stayed together and visited for a while.

After a number of sleeps, Stalking Shadow told that they would be departing. "We go to visit the Wallowa band. I hope to see all of you not all so long from this time. Take care of my nephew for all our sakes, my sister." Not fully understanding why he made his last statement, he ended his discourse. Not long after, they left for the lands of Wallowa.

A Shadow Too had a personal reason for going to the Wallowa lands. As they proceeded on their journey, he spoke to Weasel of his interests there. "I want to go and meet the people of the Wallowa band. Also after some time with them, I have a need for you to help me with another matter," Stalking Shadow explained.

"I, too, want to go there to see that place and meet our tribe members whom we have not known. As for another thing that you have decided to do, I am ready to be part of the plan. I came along to share in the experiences of our venture, so lead on, my friend," Weasel replied with that eagerness that he was known for.

Once they had gotten across the Winding River, it would not be much longer to arrive at the encampment of the Wallowa band.

Back at the Palus village, the family of Cloud Shadow was fretting over a recent development, being that of sudden failing of the health of their medicine man.

Weasel and Stalking Shadow spent time among the Wallowa band, establishing a relationship between them, as was their intention. After a time among these tribe members, they bid them farewell.

Mountain Thunder and Swan Song were the last to say farewell, encouraging them in all future actions to be undertaken.

It wasn't until they had left from among the Wallowa band that Stalking Shadow began to confide in Weasel concerning his idea on their next endeavor.

Ever since he could remember, he had always loved to hear Cloud Shadow's tale of his spirit guide vision quest into the Wallowa mountains. Now he intended to have one of his own.

"I am going to need you to keep a watch over the ponies for some time while I go on foot into these mountains to seek a vision for my life," he asked of Weasel.

"I will be waiting for you on your return, my friend," Weasel responded with all sincerity.

A Shadow Too had been preparing for this in his heart and mind, with prayer, as he climbed into the mountains of this wondrous place. He felt some confidence that he had entered the mountains at the place his father had told of.

After some time of ascending the way before him, he came to a place where he had to hold up, not being able to climb any farther. There he waited and prayed, fasting and meditating as well.

He was there for a while, having lost his awareness of how long he had been there with any certainty. At some point during the light-time, he heard the sound of falling rocks. Looking up, he was faced with the coal black eyes of a large male mountain goat. A Shadow Too was delighted, being completely entranced by his visitor. He then knew that this spirit guide was communicating with him through his own thoughts, being told, "When you return home, you will find that your father has passed from this life to the next. Be not troubled. He awaits you there. Look to your time in this life, for many trials await you and your people here yet. I will be your guide for these times. Know that I am there watching and leading the way." At that, the goat bounded away, traversing impossible ground.

Shadow was stunned with the news of his father. He had an empty feeling deep inside yet was also in awe of his experience in this place of wonder and beauty.

He lingered there, not wanting to leave that location of solace.

Back at the Palus camp, there was a burial underway. They had gathered to bury their medicine man, Cloud Shadow. He had gone quickly, being content and fulfilled, leaving all things of which he had no power of influence over behind with no reservations. He put his last efforts into making his family to understand these things. The sadness was deep and grave, but there also was a sense of satisfaction of having him being part of their lives.

A Shadow Too finally gathered himself and left that lofty habitation to descend to where the rest of his life awaited him.

The empty feeling that Shadow felt concerning his father held him in its grip until it was replaced with a strong recalling of holding his nephew, White Bird, in his arms, and an inclination to see the unfolding of the times to come.

He continued down to see what the Life Giver had planned for his life while peering into the horizon, to where the lands of his people would never fail to draw at their hearts and minds until the end of days.

ABOUT THE AUTHOR

David Gordon Alderton was born in Tacoma, Washington. His father was in the Air Force and traveled a lot as a child. He did a tour in Germany as a member of the United States Army. He always enjoyed the great outdoors, travel, adventure, exploration, and history. He enjoyed reading from a young age, along with an interest in Native American culture. He was always trying to be grounded in truth, as he understood it. David has a faith in that truth that kept him going in this life, and he trusts in the next as well. Living in this world has been his education, having the interest to learn, which includes the mistakes of mankind. As the saying goes, if we don't learn from them, we are doomed to repeat them. He is always hoping for the best, not only for himself but also for mankind, believing we all come from the same origin. Stories being an important part of our existence. David genuinely subscribes to a standard of communication that promotes the common good.

CPSIA information can be obtained
at www.ICGtesting.com
Printed in the USA
LVHW030707170522
718962LV00001B/21